THE
GLOBETROTTER
DIARIES

THIS BOOK IS DEDICATED TO TOM, FELLOW GLOBETROTTER

First published in 2013 by

Glitterati
INCORPORATED

New York | London

Glitterati Incorporated
New York | London

New York Office:
322 East 57th Street #19T
New York, NY 10019
Telephone: 212 362 9119

London Office:
1 Rona Road
London NW3 2HY
Tel/Fax: +44 (0) 207 267 8339

www.GlitteratiIncorporated.com
media@GlitteratiIncorporated.com for inquiries

First edition, 2013

Library of Congress Cataloging-in-Publication
data is available from the publisher.

Hardcover edition ISBN: 978-0-9851696-6-4
Design: Sarah Morgan Karp/smk-design.com

Printed and bound in China

10 9 8 7 6 5 4 3 2 1

TALES, TIPS AND TACTICS FOR TRAVELING THE 7 CONTINENTS

THE GLOBETROTTER DIARIES

MICHAEL CLINTON

FOREWORD BY PETER GREENBERG

Glitterati
INCORPORATED

New York | London

Atacama, Chile

Sedona, Arizona

CONTENTS

TWA Constellation

FOREWORD

PETER GREENBERG

I first traveled at the age of six months. My mother carried me, wrapped in a warm, woolen blanket, on her lap on an American Airlines DC-6, flying west across the country, from New York to Los Angeles. I don't remember the flight, of course, but I am reminded often of the journey. When the plane landed, my mother was presented with a certificate—now framed and signed by the pilot and all three stewardesses. inducting me as the first member of American Airlines Sky Cradle Club.

And I've been flying ever since. More than 400,000 miles a year. I've been to more than 151 countries and my passports (I've kept all the old ones) have stamps from countries that no longer exist. The passports are not just a physical history of my travels, they're artwork. They also represent a passion for travel that has never subsided...only increased.

I guess that makes me a globetrotter, but it also begs a definition of terms.

Because being a globetrotter is not just about stamps in passports, or some official acknowledgment or report card of the number of places you've landed. Being a globetrotter is not about a race to go everywhere—or any-where—or to accrue the most number of frequent flyer miles. Being a glo-betrotter is not about an addiction to airports and the smell of jet fuel. It is not about airline food and hostile border guards. Or having bragging rights at cocktail parties about the latest over the top hotel suites or how many upgrades you landed on your last five trips.

It is so much more than that. Michael Clinton knows that being a real globetrotter is about embracing the passionate pursuit of travel that ex-ists at the threshold of history, arriving at the crossroads of understanding and compassion, and finding yourself at the beginning of the road to true discovery. Being a globetrotter is one of life's greatest and profound thera-peutic opportunities. And if we're lucky, being a globetrotter allows us to benefit from a constant change of scenery that almost instantly readies our mind for creativity.

12

Being a globetrotter is not about checking off a bucket list. In fact, it's not about any list whatsoever. People are always asking me--because they know they always will get an answer—about where I've just traveled. And I am always amused—and then often concerned—by their reaction when I tell them about my most recent travel experience. "Oh, I don't want to go there..." they will say, "it's not on my list."

List? Who publishes this list? And what's on it? It seems that one of the reasons why Americans always pick France as their number one foreign travel destination is that we are a nation of failed art history majors who feel that since they studied the painting in college that they should at least visit the artwork. How sadly one-dimensional.

Yes, Clinton takes us to Paris, because, like me, he has had a long standing love affair with the city. But he then goes way beyond the city of light, because, when it comes to travel, about the only list you should have are all the places you've never been, all the experiences around the world you've never had.

And then, part of the definition of being a globetrotter also includes a few non-negotiable rules. And the first rule is abandoning some bad and dangerous five letter words:

Later.

True Globetrotters despise this word. It's a word that needs to leave your vocabulary immediately. Why? Whether it's about travel—or anything else to do with your life—every time you use the word "later" in a sentence, you either don't do it as well, or worse, you don't do it at all. Even the use of "later" in common phrases is usually a bad idea. When saying goodbye to a friend, I never say, "See you later." That means never. I always say, "See you soon."

Plans.

True globetrotters know this is word that strikes at the heart of genuine and authentic travel experiences. Globetrotters laugh at "plans." Because right at the heart of being a globetrotter is the acknowledgement that the best travel experiences happen when no plans are involved, or more likely, when the original plans don't work. That's when you turn right instead of left, go up instead of down, leave at 3 am instead of noon, and are pleasantly

confronted with some of your life's most memorable moments, characters   **13**
and ultimately lifelong friends, that you then meet on the road at the most
unlikely times and places.

Michael Clinton is a true globetrotter who celebrates the travel life, with
a portfolio of special experiences that are not a result of or aided by guidebooks or led by brochures. He is, thankfully, a reluctant tourist but a driven
traveler, who is not only in the pursuit of finding new cultures, but is committed to identifying with them. He is an astute observer on his travels, but
Michael is not looking at destinations as single entities as much as he is a
student of the human condition, not to mention the essential components of
the process of travel.

As any globetrotter knows, if you want to enjoy the experience, it also
helps to master the journey itself; and Michael Clinton is one of the masters.
In the process of divulging his travel tactics, including why he likes certain
airports (like terminal 5 at London's Heathrow) and what really constitutes
(or expands) a business trip. With every chapter, ranging from his Christmas in the driest desert in the world to the brave new world of Shanghai,
Michael the globetrotter takes us on a magical mystery tour. His obser-
vations and his photos capture the essence of not just the where, but the
why of travel.

And, of course, the finesse of travel.

Perhaps the best definition of travel is that at the end of the day, it is an
experience meant to be shared. And I thank Michael for sharing these experiences with us. Here's to globetrotting!

Antarctic Peninsula

INTRODUCTION:

ON BECOMING A GLOBETROTTER

It all started with my first overseas trip to Ireland and England when I was twelve years old, and I've been roaming the world ever since. That first trip evolved from a family reunion, and it led me to a lifetime of passion for travel and its lingering images, which in turn led me along my own personal road to self-discovery.

As a child growing up in a working-class family in Pennsylvania, the idea of visiting another country seemed about as viable as a plan to visit another planet. And as I was the oldest of six children, going to the lake an hour away was about as far as the family budget would stretch.

So when my father's brother and his wife, Janet, who lived in their native New York City, took a trip to visit the birthplace of my grandfather in County Monaghan, Ireland, it stirred a curiosity in my eleven-year-old self. Their subsequent visit to our family, and the description of the Irish countryside, along with the stories of my grandfather's youth before he set out for America, set my young mind in motion.

That night, as my mother tucked me in, I asked her if I too could go to Ireland to visit our relatives.

"Someday," she said, "someday when you are older."

"How about next summer?" I asked.

"We'll talk about it tomorrow," she said, in her best stern motherly voice, kissing me goodnight.

At breakfast the next morning, it was my first question of the day, this time posed to my father.

"Well," he said, to my mother's concerned look, "why not? If you can save the money on your own, then you can go!" In my mind, the deal was done.

So began the winter of my destiny. I shoveled snow, delivered newspapers, and worked as many odd jobs in the neighborhood as I could. And much to my parents' chagrin, I presented them with my bulging savings book in early spring, complete with my plan to set off for Ireland during the next summer.

To their credit, they agreed; "Well, a deal's a deal," and within weeks, phone calls had been made to my cousins in Ireland (County Monaghan), plans finalized and flights booked. In July I took my first flight to New York, where I was met by my aunt and uncle, who then put me on a gleaming TWA Boeing 707 destined for Shannon. In my red and white TWA flight bag was an extra ticket to London to visit my grandmother's family, courtesy of my parents, who had dipped into their savings to reward my youthful determination and resourcefulness with "bonus miles." These would be the first of many I'd earn in my life of travel. To me, that gift was better than any new bicycle or stereo. And of course my first camera, a Kodak Brownie, was tucked safely into that same TWA flight bag.

My Irish cousins welcomed me with open arms and treated me royally during my month-long visit, driving me from one end of the country to the other. I learned about peat bogs and Irish football, glimpsed the haunting coastline of Galway, and lined up to kiss the famous Blarney stone. They taught me about their Irish way of life, from milking the family's cows to enjoying a hearty tea in the afternoon, complete with conversations about the happenings in the local town, Silverstream. Perhaps my most vivid memory is of sleeping in the bed that my grandfather was born in before he set off for America. His picture hung above the bed, and somehow I felt that he was watching over me, especially since he was no longer alive when I made that trip.

When my flight from Dublin to London descended through the clouds and we snaked along the Thames to Heathrow, I was rewarded with my first look at Big Ben. That landing approach over London was to become symbolic of the excitement of visiting so many cities for the first time, seeing them from the air and getting a sense of what was in store.

In London I visited Chelsea, the neighborhood where my grandmother lived as a young girl, and had my first taste of tourism—a ride on a double-decker bus to Madame Tussaud's and to Buckingham Palace for the changing of the guard. I chronicled all of it in pictures and words for my family back home so that they too could "meet" our relatives through my photographs and "see the sights" through my experiences.

That summer changed everything for me. It was the beginning of my love affair with exploring the world, my excitement in meeting its people and learning its customs. But it was also the metaphor for my young life: By setting my goal and then realizing it, I learned that if one has a dream, it can be realized through hard work and determination, regardless of what advantages one has or hasn't in life. My twelve-year-old self set a lifetime goal to travel around the world, and that summer put me on a course to believing that I would achieve it. The question of course was exactly how and when. Not until I was eighteen, the year after my freshman year of college at the University of Pittsburgh, was I able to continue the journey.

While most teenagers saved for their first car, I spent those intervening years saving for two funds: my travel fund and my college fund. And as I daydreamed about the places I would go and studied the pictures from my first trip, more money would find itself in my travel fund than in my college fund. Finally, like thousands of teenage baby boomers, I headed to Europe in the early 1970s, complete with backpack, Eurail pass, youth hostel card and my father's beloved Argus camera in hand. My goal was to photograph my three-month trip and keep a diary, aptly titled, "The Journal of a Wandering Student."

I started with three weeks in France to practice my four years' worth of high-school French, and from there I managed to travel to twenty-one other countries, from Sweden to Italy, from Spain to the Soviet Union.

In Barcelona I discovered the genius of Gaudi; as I explored the Sagrada Familia Cathedral, walking the connectors across its steeples high above the city, I learned how one architect could have a profound impact on a cityscape. On a cool summer evening in Warsaw, not far from the rebuilt old city, I savored the romance of a Chopin concert; I thought about the cataclysmic impact World War II had on the city, and spent hours in the Rijkmuseum studying Vermeer and Rembrandt.

I tasted my first espresso in Florence and wondered how one sip could satisfy anyone—in America we drank mugs of coffee. I ate my first wiener schnitzel in a small restaurant in the Schwabing neighborhood of Munich, followed by a long walk through the Englischer gardens, an oasis in that Bavarian city.

Years later, as the Publisher of *GQ* magazine, riding in limousines to the men's shows, staying at the Ritz, and dining at Lucas Carton, I would sometimes slip away to a sandwich stand in the Tuileries. There I would order a cheese baguette and reminisce about how that first summer trip had so enriched and inspired my young life.

Every day of those three months were simply dazzling, as if life was beginning anew each day. I would try to capture each moment with my father's camera, each shot its own unique jewel in my mind. Today I look back at some of those photographs, like the one of St. Basil's in Moscow, and remember the day that I sat in Red Square debating democracy and communism with a Russian student named Irina. Or I ponder the shot of the Matterhorn, where I experienced my first hike in the majesty of the Swiss Alps and where I met Julie, who would travel with me for the next several weeks.

I did return home, fulfilled for the moment, to finish college and then graduate school. But my mind was always on my life's goal, and I worked up itineraries and fantasized about photographic expeditions to Africa and other exotic locales. I was determined that my boyhood dream would become my lifetime reality.

Today, more than thirty years later, I've been to 121 countries and seven continents, crisscrossing the Atlantic and Pacific countless times. My wanderlust has taken me to remote villages in the Himalayas, the Perito Moreno glacier in Patagonia and the rainforests of Tasmania, always with cameras in tow. Somehow I've managed to marry my two great loves—travel and photography—with a thriving magazine publishing career, family responsibilities, service on a number of professional and non-profit boards and hobbies like flying and skiing. It's not because I'm super-human, but because I keep going back to that early lesson—that ultimately we are all responsible for fulfilling our own dreams, mine being to see as much of the world as possible, to learn what I might about myself and about people in general.

While my friends tease that I collect countries like other people collect cars or art, my life has been a collection of memories and photographs of the many nuances that experiencing even one country can bring. In Italy, for example, I learned the differences between Tuscany and Sicily and the country's many tastes from Ribollita to Bolognese; I savored the mesmerizing light in St. Mark's in Venice and took in the breathtaking views of Ravello. Each of these vignettes lives in my mind along with hundreds of others that I've tried to capture in photographs as a way to appreciate the world's incredible diversity.

Travel can open you up in ways that you never thought possible. It allows you to explore the core of your inner soul, to challenge your own beliefs, relationships, and spirituality. To celebrate my fortieth birthday, I bonded with friends while climbing to the top of Mt. Kilimanjaro. From the beginning of the hike in Arusha, Tanzania, up to the highest point of Uhuru, we shared in the excitement of one of the world's great experiences, embracing when we reached the peak as the sun began to rise over Africa. That trip led me to a new dimension in my travel experience—to be more adventurous and to seek out even more unusual places. I promised myself that I would mix more adventure into my visits to major cities and sights around the world. Perhaps one of the most memorable was a trek in the Himalayas through the Villages of Western Nepal, stopping at schools to watch the children in class and at homes to learn about the simple life in a Nepalese village, where meals are prepared with homegrown fruits and vegetables.

Another great moment was taking one of the first boats from Chau Doc in Vietnam to Phnom Penh via the Mekong Delta. When our boat was not allowed to proceed at the border, my travel companions and I hired a local Cambodian who took us up the river for the three-hour journey in his small motorboat. Whether in Cambodia, Myanmar, or the Fijian Islands, local people were always there to lend a helping hand to a foreign traveler who was interested enough to visit their country and to try and understand their way of life.

Travel brings out emotions and behaviors in expected and unexpected ways. I've wept at the sheer beauty of the late afternoon light descending on the Serengeti, the silence only interrupted by an occasional hyena or cheetah, and laughed with merchants in the Bazaars of Istanbul and Marrakech as we haggled with each other for the price; more often than not, I found myself buying more. Like the time I agreed to buy four Turkish rugs from one merchant who convinced me that I was making a great investment and could sell them for double in New York. Well, like my photographs, the four rugs are proudly displayed in my New York home, along with thangka boxes from Tibet, wooden figurines from Djakarta and ceremonial masks from Tanzania. Each of these items has a story that conjures up a memory and, like the photographs, transports me back to that particular moment.

For me, traveling is a symphony of sounds and sights, smells and touch. This plays out in the souks of Marrakech, as merchants summon visitors into their shops to touch their brightly colored fabrics, the smell of cooking tagine hanging in the air, the call of the muezzin in the distance.

20

Some people travel for the culture, or the architecture, or the landscapes. I travel to experience it all, and most places offer it all. For the traveler, there is nothing more exciting than a complete bombardment of all of this happening at once, as it does in culturally rich destinations.

On the island of Nukubati in Fiji, a group of us attended a Sunday church service several months after 9/11. The pastor and his congregation prayed for their visiting American friends and asked one of us to speak about how everyone was healing in New York. That experience in a small clapboard church that held maybe fifty parishioners led to a bidding to spend the morning in the village, complete with invitations into local homes to share kava and food and to hear local music and watch local welcoming dance ceremonies. Those few hours convinced me that while everyday life may be different in many places, there is indeed a family of man who share in our pain, our happiness and our well-being. If I can capture some of these moments in my photography, then I will have succeeded in bringing this message home to family, friends and strangers.

The American West may have the majestic Rockies, but the Namibian sand dunes are equally awe-inspiring, as are the wide-open spaces of Patagonia. God seems to have been fair with the spread of natural beauty in the world. And man seems to have caught on to that inspiration too. Whether at the Taj Mahal, the Shwedagon Palace in Rangoon, or Macchu Pichu, for centuries, man has challenged himself to create sights of grandeur, beauty and exquisite design for his own pleasure and sense of accomplishment.

I've attempted to capture some of this too, teaching me to respect and understand our differences, yet celebrate our similarities. I hope that as you turn these pages, you too will unleash your own wanderlust to help you discover your own truths. You may find yourself dreaming of distant lands as I did, those many years ago.

Travel and photography have become my own personal answer to a life-long search for knowledge and understanding, and it has been my key to the inner calm and happiness we all search for in our lives. Hopefully, these essays will show you how I've been able to satisfy my own life's quest, and allow you to think about your own, contemplating ideas that you tucked away many years ago, have just rediscovered, or are just now developing. Whatever those dreams, find the globetrotter in you and go in search of them—you might be surprised at the satisfaction that it will bring to you. Hurry, your world awaits!

TIPS

FROM WORLD-CLASS GLOBETROTTERS

We are kindred spirits, we globetrotters. We take great pride in knowing the best aircraft to fly and the airlines that are most on their game. We can tell you where the best airport lounges in the world are, the name of a great out-of-the-way restaurant in a Buenos Aires neighborhood or about a small guesthouse along the Mekong.

You will see world-class globetrotters at airports and in major cities. They seem to glide through it all, knowing the tricks of the trade. How to travel light, how to move through customs and security effortlessly, how to manage all of the complexities of twenty-first century travel with great aplomb.

While writing this book, I called on some of my friends, whom I admire. Those who have traveled the world and know the ins and outs. They gave me some tips to share with all of you. Use them and you'll earn your globetrotter status too.

Author's Diaries

SALAD DAYS

Ninety-four days of backpacking around twenty-two countries is how I spent the summer after my freshman year of college. It was to be my own Grand Tour, my own personal adventure, and I believed that it would probably be my first and last time in Europe. After all, taking this kind of trip was a luxury in my family, and very few of my relatives had ever left the United States. Little did I know that I'd cross the Atlantic well over a hundred times in the years to come.

I'd been dreaming about this trip since my early teens, saving money for it and even dipping into my student loans to make it happen. I'd imagined that it would change my life in ways that I didn't yet understand. And indeed it did. With openness to the world, I left with a backpack and sleeping bag, a round-trip airplane ticket, a pre-arranged "mini-trek" into the Soviet Union, Poland, and Czechoslovakia, a two-month student Eurail Pass and my diary. Aptly called "The Journal of a Wandering Student," it's been tucked away on my bookshelf for years, and in preparation for this book, I realized that it was time to take it down and read it again.

Ahhhh, to be eighteen years old and to view the wonders of the world through those eyes. At times I didn't recognize myself as I read the journal, but at other times I remembered the exact moments in the entry. How I felt the first time I saw Paris, the eerie feeling of standing in Red Square looking at Lenin's tomb, the view of the Matterhorn in Zermatt; all of these moments rushed back to me. These were just a few of the events of that trip that made me realize how much I didn't know and how the trip would influence the way I would live my life from that point on.

Like many students in those days, I began my trip by flying to Amsterdam, a town that was teeming with students from all over the world, students who filled the hostels, shared meals at the Leidseplein and hung out together at the Dam. Shortly after arriving, I met up with the seven other students from the U.K., Ireland, and Australia, who would join the overland trip to the Soviet Union. We would all travel together for twenty-one days, from Amsterdam to Hamburg, Copenhagen, Stockholm, Helsinki, Leningrad, Novogrod, Moscow, Smolensk, Minsk, Warsaw, Prague and then to Bruges, where the trip would end.

Our transportation was a large SUV style van with all of our gear on the roof, including tents and camping gear. We would spend most nights at campsites along the way. We all bonded instantly, and before we knew it, we were sharing great times in Tivoli and at Drottningholm Palace in Stockholm, and then sharing a beer on the waterfront in Helsinki. My diary is filled with notes of Scandinavian history and the foods we all tried for the first time (think lots of unique fish dishes) and the discovery of the distinct culture of each country. But through all of it, we were most excited about visiting the USSR. And for a young American like me, the only American on the trip, this excursion delivered its own special form of apprehension.

As a student, I'd fallen in love with all things Russian: its tragic, yet poetic history, its ambiguity about being a part of the West or not, the romantic and sweeping literature of the nineteenth-century writers from Tolstoy and Dostoevsky to the late twentieth-century work of Yevtushenko and Solzhenitsyn. I'd read all of it, and my interest in going there was to retrace history, to follow the footsteps of Father Gapon on Bloody Sunday in St. Petersburg at the time of the Revolution, and to get a first-hand look at the current political and economic system. America and the Soviet Union were at odds on all fronts, and with a student's curiosity, I needed to understand why.

"Being sucked into a vacuum," is what I wrote in my diary as we entered the country via the drab town of Vyborg, near the Finnish border. It was dark and gloomy, and an excruciating two-hour customs inspection greeted us, as every inch of the car was searched along with our bags. We had to claim all of our money with the idea being that when we left we had to claim what we spent. At the time, I didn't realize how hungry the black market was for anything Western. The border guards were unfriendly and the people along the road seemed tired and exhausted. The minute we got out of the van we were accosted by locals who were looking to buy jeans, western music, anything they couldn't get there. Intrigued by the idea of it, we all sold whatever we could. Knowing that we couldn't take rubles out of the country, we'd have to spend what we collected while we were there. Imagine how a bunch of students felt about that, as we planned our fine dining, vodka-filled nights, visits to the Bolshoi and more.

Our first impression upon arriving was that it Russia seemed like a broken down place filled with sadness and despair. We walked the streets of

Leningrad, along Nevsky Prospekt to Peter and Paul Fortress, the Winter Palace, and St. Isaac's. The buildings were rundown with chunks missing and graffiti everywhere. The St. Petersburg that I'd dreamed about was in need of a major overhaul. Unfortunately, I've not been back since then, but I know that today, the city of St. Petersburg and all of its historic sights sparkle, as major restorations have taken place in recent years. At the time of my visit, people shared water in common glasses at the Boaa machines. Today, Russia has as many different brands and products as any major European city. Even Evian and Pellegrino are on Russian shelves.

Since the collapse of the Soviet Union, with the acknowledgement that the free market system is the way to build economic progress, the transformation has been stunning. But during the harsh realities of the Soviet Union, one could see huge iconic photographs of Lenin along the roads and signs that read "Long Live Communism" amid the primitive housing and overall drabness.

Our memorable moments included the intricacy of the Faberge eggs and the splendor of the Hermitage, the awe of the Kremlin, the architectural delight of St. Basil's and the two-hour experience to visit the displayed sarcophagus of Lenin himself. We dined on Stroganoff and Georgian Red Wine at the National Hotel, saw *Don Quixote* at the Palace of Congresses and bought rounds of vodka—all with our black market money. But perhaps our best time was with the Russians themselves. Our Intourist guides were fellow students with whom we got into vigorous debates with about politics and war, and we tried to convince them that a Russian didn't invent the radio and television. We stayed up late with our fellow campers at the Intourist campsites, trying to communicate with them in our broken Russian. And what we learned is that regardless of the political system, most people want the same things: prosperity, health and a good future for their children. Deep into the night, our Russian friends sang us folk songs and camp songs and we returned the favor with American ballads and our folk songs. Here we were, just people, having a good time, wondering why our countries were such enemies. It was the first of many such experiences that I would have in my life, as I traveled to the Middle East and Myanmar and other places where there were political tensions. Usually, the people wanted peace and harmony. I realized that my love for Russia was for its past, but my appreciation for its present came from my conversations with its people.

I know that I have to go back there, as it has become as Western as any major country with Gucci and Armani in the malls and Mercedes and BMW on the streets. Many Russian people are prosperous and happy, and I know that I would not recognize much—only the monuments and the buildings are reminders of the past.

As we left the USSR and entered Poland, there seemed to be a palpable lift in the mood and the prosperity. The Poles seemed happy and the city of Warsaw was bustling. The Germans had demolished it during World War II, and what we saw was a rebuilt city that was modern and efficient. The Old Town was re-constructed, and the Jewish ghetto, which was so brutally walled-in and systematically demolished, was now memorialized by a small park that gave some emotional refuge for the atrocities committed there.

The Poles were welcoming, as we strolled through Lazienki Park and took in the local flavor. We all commented on how different our Poland experience was from our Soviet experience. And of course today Poland, Russia and the other Eastern bloc countries have transformed into vibrant, dynamic places that have joined the West in creating prosperity for their people.

As our group drove to Prague, then through Germany to Belgium, we knew that we had experienced a remarkable time together and on our last night, we talked about what we had learned, what our dreams would be, and how we would stay in touch with each other for years to come. Of course, it was with all the intensity that young people have and what travelers promise each other when they meet in places far and wide. We said our goodbyes through teary eyes and with memories seared in our minds, but in reality we never did stay in touch. I have all seven of their names and addresses written down in my diary, but a Facebook search turned up nothing. Yet we all live together in a tapestry of memories and learning about the world and ourselves during that summer of discovery. And that is often how it should work. Throughout my diary, I've listed meeting up with Rich from Florida, or Susan from Minneapolis. It's filled with first names and some of the things that we shared as fellow travelers. Only one of them, Lydia Petrowsky, whom I met in Vienna and who lived in Toronto, was someone I stayed in touch with, as we dated cross-border when we returned. But that is rare. We meet people when we travel and have an intensity and intimacy with them in ways that we wouldn't even have with certain friends and family. I've come to the conclusion that this is part of the magic and mystery of traveling. It's almost a catharsis that you share with others, as you talk about life philosophy and share in the unique experiences that you're having together. But these are passing moments that shouldn't carry on into the future.

One of the great things about keeping a travel journal is that it captures your impressions at a moment in time and not only records your experiences, but also what you choose to remember. I've kept travel journals my whole life, and when I read them, they give me instant recall on a trip that I may have forgotten. I probably go a bit overboard on writing too much down, but "more is more" in my mind. In my student diary, I kept a tally of how many days I spent in each country. France won with nineteen days, followed by Spain with twelve days. My journal sketched out a typical day and how a student should go about navigating a new city. (I was already assembling travel tips at the age of eighteen). Here are a few suggested tips that I passed on to many fellow students.

● Always take an overnight train. You may miss out on some scenery, but you'll save on a hotel bill.

● When you arrive early in the morning, find the nearest locker and stow your gear (a bit more challenging in a post 9/11 world).

● Exchange money into local currency (this was in a pre-euro world).

● Go to the tourist office for maps and brochures, buy a coffee, figure out what train you'll take to depart the city; if it's a popular run, make a reservation before you leave the station.

● Once you determine what part of town you want to stay in, figure out if there is a hostel nearby or go to the hotel service at the train station and look for other students; find someone who looks normal and see if they want to share a room. More often than not, this was a great way to meet people and to save money.

My diary outlined how you could get by on spending less than $10 a day for food and what restaurants had cheap but plentiful meals. It identified towns and cities that were student friendly and easy routes to travel, and it was filled with pages of tips that I got from fellow travelers.

● Don't go to Ibiza, where it is too expensive and could be dangerous, but instead go to the small island of Formentera that was nearby.

28 This was a tip that I followed up on, taking a boat from Barcelona to Ibiza, then transferring to smaller boat to Formentera. There, for four days, a group of us slept in our sleeping bags on the beach of Bluebar. We had breakfast at the Maria Jesus cafe every morning, mingling with students and hippies and watching the waves of the Mediterranean. We bicycled into small Spanish villages like San Francisco Javier and San Fernandos and ate dinners at La Tortuga, feasting on roasted Formentera pig baked with apples. It was a lazy few days of soaking up the sun and it was a tip that I passed on to many other travelers who were looking for an out-of-the-way experience.

Another tip given to me was to visit certain smaller cities. Rome and Florence were important stops, but could be a bit daunting, while a trip to Perugia in Umbria could be a rich experience. Or while Zurich and Geneva may be on your list, how about Berne or Basel? Through my travels, I've had amazing experiences in these smaller towns and found myself going out of my way to get there. I learned this during that summer in Europe.

After discovering Paris (more on that in another story in this book), I set off to visit some smaller places and to this day, those experiences are what resonate in unique ways. My French trip would take me to Chartres, then Tours, Poitiers, Bordeaux, Toulouse, on a side trip to Albi to visit the Toulouse-Lautrec Museum and then to Carcassonne. Many of these places wouldn't be on the list of a first-time trip to France, but in my mind, I thought that it would show me the real France and give me an opportunity to practice my French, since the Parisians could be a bit unforgiving on that subject.

So, off I went, first to Chartres to step foot into the Cathedral built before 1200, a massive Gothic style building made of enormous blocks of stone, incredible stained glass windows and a concrete screen depicting the life of Christ. While there I met a fellow student, listed only as "Bonnie" in my journal, an American from Boston. We decided to do some hitchhiking or become what the locals called an "auto-stopper." In hindsight, hitchhiking for the fun of it may not have been a smart idea, but in reality, we met some great French people. One of our "drivers" was a farmer named Jean, who was returning from a holiday in Normandy, driving an old Citroen. Not only did we have a great conversation with him (in French), but also he invited us to join him for a roadside lunch, where he proceeded to set up a gingham tablecloth, laying out cheese, sandwiches, beer and homemade apple cider. To Bonnie and me, this was the perfect way to meet the locals.

Jean was the one who told us that we had to visit Chenonceau in the

Loire region, and he decided that he would drop us off there before he headed south. I have to admit that at the time, I'd never even heard of Che-nonceau, even though it is said that it is the second most visited castle after Versailles. And in a word, it is spectacular and should be on everyone's list of must-sees in France. A mix of Gothic and early Renaissance architecture, the structure was first started in the 1430s and has a rich and interesting his-tory. For the uninitiated, it is the white French castle that is built over a river with arches that give it such a unique dimension. A photograph of it is often shown as an example of the French Chateau country.

Some of its provenance includes it being the home of Francis I of France, then passed on to Henry II, who gave it to his mistress, Diane de Poitiers, who lived there in the mid 1550s until Henry's death, when his widow, Catherine de Medici, expelled her from the place. The first fireworks in France happened there, during the ascension to the throne of Francis II in 1560, and during the French Revolution the structure was saved by the en-terprising owner, Madame Louise Dupin, who convinced the revolutionar-ies that it had to remain in her hands, and as it was the only bridge for miles and miles, she would assure that they could use it for those purposes. During World War II, the castle was used as an escape route from the Nazi occupied zone on one side of the River Cher to the free Vichy Zone, and in the last two hundred years, it has been owned by a Scotsman and a Cuban, and is now back in the hands of a French family.

Had it not been for our benefactor, Jean, we would not have discovered this incredible French landmark. We ended up spending eight hours there, absorbed in its history, its many elaborate rooms, and the stunning gardens that surround it. Even now, that day at Chenonceau stands out as a great travel discovery.

We moved on to Poitiers, driven by a professor from Paris who recom-mended this ancient city that belonged to the Duchy of Aquitaine, built on the ancient Roman road from Bordeaux to Paris. Then it was on to An-gouleme, recommended by a driver from Rouen. Our drivers gave us the three or five sights that we should see in each place. And while I wouldn't recommend hitchhiking to any student, what we learned from our French drivers was a lot more than any book could tell us.

One place that I knew I wanted to visit was the small museum dedicated to Toulouse-Lautrec in the small town of Albi. Part of the Albi Cathedral, the museum did not disappoint. There I saw his many masterpieces from the

30 "The English Gentleman at the Moulin Rouge" to many of his paintings of Jane Avril to his colorful portrait of Aristide Bruant. Filled with posters and lithographs and his writings, it was a museum that any Lautrec fan would enjoy for hours. And it was only one example from that summer of an art history discovery that would stay with me for my whole life. It was on that trip that I learned about the Dutch School and the works of Vermeer and Rembrandt. It was in the Louvre that I saw Gericault's "Raft of the Medusa" and learned about Delacroix and Ingres. As a student of economics and political science, I fell short on art appreciation, but that summer made me richer in my understanding of art. Mona Lisa was "La Joconde," Van Gogh painted more than sunflowers and the Impressionists, the group that redefined art in the nineteenth century, became my new interest; I followed up by reading about all of them. But an art of summer like this was only the beginning. It spilled into architecture and urban design and literature. What a delight to discover Gaudi in Barcelona, for example, an architect that I had never heard of until I visited the bizarre but inspirational Sagrada Familia Cathedral in that city.

Indeed, like many others before me, I was humbled by what I didn't know and that summer made me realize that I had to make every day work for me, to learn about all aspects of European countries and their influences on the world. For that reason, I tell every high school and college student that I meet to give themselves the greatest gift possible: Take a backpack and go roam Europe. What you learn in a book cannot duplicate the experience of standing in Giverny or in the Roman Forum or below the Eiffel Tower. It will change you in ways that you can only understand once you've done it.

My final stop on my tour of "the other France" (since I'd decided against Lyons and Marseilles and the Riviera) would be Carcassonne, a fortified French town that was founded by the Visigoths in the Golden Age. Like so many places throughout Europe, it has its own story to tell, one rich in the role that it played in the Crusades and how it was saved from being demolished in the mid-1800s but became a masterpiece of restoration of towers and turrets and drawbridges that make it a place that could almost be in a fairy tale. Walking through its cobble-stoned streets and looking up at its floodlit walls in the evening made me nominate Carcassonne as another of the must-sees of Europe's smaller towns and cities.

Throughout that summer, I visited Salzburg, birthplace of Mozart, as well as places like Lausanne, where we changed trains for Brig, and Visp, as we headed to Zermatt and the Matterhorn. It was here that we experienced a small Swiss town in the Alps, where no cars were allowed, and we settled in what must have been the cleanest and nicest hostel that I'd ever seen. During our first day (this was with Chris and Julie—first names only!), we headed up to Schwarzsee, a four-hour hike up the mountain to above the timberline, where we saw glaciers, frozen rivers, and clouds below us. We chilled some wine in a cold mountain stream and had a feast as we took in the magnificent view. This first-time experience led me to my lifelong love affair with hiking in mountainous regions from the Himalayas to Patagonia to the American West.

One day in a summer ignited an interest that became one of my life's loves. Maybe it was because I was only eighteen, but I do believe that one could have the same experience at age fifty and still be excited about a new course of adventure. What is your Matterhorn? I know people who've had profound experiences when they traveled. A friend went to Bali and moved there, and has now been there for ten years. A husband and wife visited Santa Fe, New Mexico, and she refused to leave. Her husband had to go back to New York to sell their apartment and their weekend house. It can happen.

So indeed, that summer did change my life in many ways. I turned nineteen in Amsterdam, a week before I left to return home. I didn't want to go home. That whole week I thought about my options. Should I join the group of students whom I'd just met who would be traveling overland to South Africa? Should I stay in Europe and enroll in school there? I'd been seduced by ninety-four days of an experience that made me a young man of knowledge in so many subjects.

In my diary I wrote, "Going home leaves me with a sad and empty feeling that I've never felt before. In a way, I feel like I don't belong there anymore." At the time I couldn't have appreciated that I'd just gone through one of the most intense growth experiences that anyone could have in their life. I didn't belong where I'd come from anymore. That summer had changed me. It had taught me to move forward, to learn, and to realize that I would spend my life traveling the world for knowledge and new experiences.

On an early September morning, I boarded a KLM flight home to the states to begin my sophomore year at college. My mind was filled with Chopin and Mozart, Degas and Botticelli, Hesse and Flaubert. And as we flew over the Dutch countryside heading across the Atlantic, I knew that my life had just begun.

Easthampton, New York Airport

TRAVEL TACTICS FOR THE FLYING CLASS

Here's my goal: I will always find the best flying experience in today's complex world of airline schedules, delays, security issues and crowds. The flying experience is like one big jigsaw puzzle, and I'm a junkie with this type of thing. You'll often find me scouring websites, searching for the best fares, connections and upgrades. Some people spend time cruising sports sites, or they surf for fashion, or home décor, or even gaming sites. My game of choice is travel. Yup, I'm addicted to travel websites. There it is—I'm a travelaholic.

This has been a lifelong addiction for me, going back to the days when my family would take a Sunday drive to our local airport. As a ten-year-old boy I would collect airline timetables and map out imaginary trips. When I was a teenager, there was a local airline called Mohawk Airlines that offered a weekend pass, and somehow a friend and I convinced our parents to let us go flying all over the Northeast. We mapped out seven or eight flights, arriving home to Pittsburgh late Sunday night, fat and happy with flying experiences. I started to fine-tune my airline skills at an early age, and this is a story of what I've learned along the way.

I've logged millions of air miles. I never get bored, nor am I ever surprised by what airline executives come up with to try and get my attention. Recently, there was a series of full-page ads from one European carrier that promised many miles and free tickets if you signed up for their new credit card. At first glance, it seemed like a deal that was too good to be true. And it was, once you read through the restrictions, surcharges, and extra fees involved. First lesson: Read the fine print.

There has been a lot of press regarding passengers' rights and who could blame those who get involved? Making passengers sit on a runway for eight hours is inexcusable. I don't care if there are no gates, or no personnel, there's a way to figure it out and get those people out of that plane.

In the era of Facebook, Twitter, and other social media, my first suggestion if you are ever stuck on a plane is to get everyone to communicate with the outside world. Call the airline, call the airline president's office, call the mayor's office, call the local television station. Raise some hell.

One of my favorite games is the announcement while you are sitting on the plane at the gate that goes something like this: "Ladies and Gentlemen, we are having some mechanical issues and we'll get back to you shortly." The moment I hear that I spring into action, developing a Plan B, because my experience is that fifty percent of the time the flight is cancelled. I start by calling the airline to find out my options and to have them hold me a seat on the next available flight, long before the deluge hits to re-route everyone else. My favorite call is always to the helpline of the American Express Platinum desk—even if I didn't book that particular flight with them, they will get me out of a jam. It has been proven time and time again.

Once while waiting to board a flight from Atlanta to New York, the gate agent announced that the flight was being cancelled, and pandemonium broke out among the passengers as they all rushed to the desk. Here's the best approach: Get on the phone with the airline, explain the situation and get yourself re-booked. In this case, I was able to arrange for three of us to get re-routed to Washington, then on to New York. We quietly slipped away to the gate for the Washington flight, as our fellow passengers on the original flight were in a state of disarray.

In the complex, electronic, computerized world of airline scheduling and capacity, you're not on your way until your flight leaves a gate. And as we know, airports can be chaotic, especially when weather affects the system. It's particularly challenging at major transfer airports, like Chicago's O'Hare. A colleague and I once found ourselves in this dilemma in Chicago, and we hit the phones to learn that every flight out of Chicago to New York that particular night was booked. And since our flight had just been cancelled, we started working other airports. Instead of New York, we would fly to Philadelphia, Washington, or Boston. Nothing. While I worked the airline phones, he worked the hotels in case we had to spend the night. Due to the weather and major conventions in town, we were coming up with nothing within thirty miles of the airport. It sure looked like we'd be spending the night sleeping on the floor at our gate. But, here's the trick: Don't give up. Keep calling the airline back and keep inquiring about seats. On the fourth call to the same airline, two seats miraculously appeared on a flight to JFK. It was the last flight out of Chicago, and I have no idea how they opened up, but they did, and we grabbed them.

A good place to work your way out of a flight jam is the airline's lounge. The personnel there are skilled and fast at trying to sort things out. Because it's usually the airline's best customers who frequent their lounge, the staff goes out of their way, regardless of what you paid for your ticket. And by the way, if you can't afford to join an airline's travel club, this is another benefit of the American Express Platinum Card—it gets you access to a lot of clubs at no extra cost. Full disclosure: I have no association with American Express, except for being a cardholder for thirty-plus years, and the Platinum Card is one of the best travel investments that you can make.

Can you imagine being an airline employee dealing with the public today? It takes a special breed. Here's another suggestion: Always be nice to these agents. It's not their fault that a major storm has rolled in, or that the plane is late or has a mechanical problem. Don't take it out on them. If you're nice, they'll go the extra mile and you'll find yourself with convenient reschedules, upgrades, even bonuses. Once when I found myself stuck in Memphis for six hours, the airline personnel at the lounge not only gave us food vouchers, but after hearing my story they threw in a $250 travel voucher for my inconvenience. It sure helped to make me feel good about the situation.

When you're planning your trip, always have a Plan B in mind. But first be smart about your Plan A. Early morning flights experience fewer delays. I'm always happy to get the 6:00 a.m. flight because it flies and I get to my connection on time. Security lines are usually better then too. Always check in online and print your boarding passes beforehand. And pick your seats on line too—there's nothing worse than a middle seat in the back of the plane.

A lot of people look at me like I'm crazy when I ask what type of aircraft they'll be flying. I'm telling you that it makes all the difference, and this is an easy thing to find out as you look at your alternatives. Flying a 737 across the country or an MD80 on a four-hour flight is not my idea of airline fun. I always prefer the Airbus or a 757 or 767. They are roomier and the experience is more comfortable, especially if you're in coach. And if you can get on a 777 or the new A380, grab it.

If you're lucky enough to decide between first and business class, my opinion is that most business class cabins are as good as first class today. Unless you are a rock star or you just won an Oscar and need total privacy from your public, first class can be, well, a bit isolating. And sometimes just a bit precious. Try business class on any long haul carrier and you will have the pampering that you crave: flatbeds, good food, good service and space to spread out. Trust me on this.

What's the best way to maximize your flying experience? Well, it goes back to the idea of loyalty. Airline loyalty, a concept that was developed in the early 1980s, is alive and well today. Earning status on your airline of choice opens up a lot of opportunity that will make your flying experience easier. First of all, you get preferential treatment through security lines, you get better seat choices, you get to board your flight earlier (and bring your non-status flying companion with you). Loyalty can lead to unexpected upgrades, an extra bonus on long-haul flights. And when you collect all of those frequent flyer miles, you can have a lot of fun figuring out the best way to use them (more on that in a moment). So (airline) monogamy has its privileges. I say work it, get that super-duper status that makes you feel a bit like minor royalty as you work your way through the airport.

The byproduct of all of that travel and airline credit card use is, of course, to amass as many frequent flyer miles as possible. And there is nothing better than scoring two business-class tickets to Rome and feeling like you've just won the lottery. I mean *free tickets*. Of course we spent a lot of money to earn those miles, but let's just enjoy the fantasy.

There's no question that planning to use earned miles has become one big obstacle course, but this is a game I love to play. Like navigating any obstacle course, you need to have quick reflexes and stamina, and you need to focus on the end goal. With the restrictions in the frequent flyer mile system today, a playbook for maneuvering the system would help. There are lots of websites and apps that can tell you what you want to know, but I find that airline personnel, meaning a live person on the other end of a phone line, have a lot of knowledge that can get you to your goal.

Some of you may know that airlines often open up their frequent flyer seats, 327 days, or 340 days, or 330 days prior to the flight—this is a moving target. And if you call at 12:01 a.m. on that designated day, you're supposed to get your first choice of seats. I remember once getting through to an airline at 12:10 a.m. to find that the business-class seats available on miles from New York to South Africa were gone. How could that be? I had visions of obsessed mileage owners sitting at their desks, waiting for the big mileage race! What I was able to learn was that the airline only designated two seats for this particular flight and yes; the first one to reach the airline got them!

Now that was exasperating, for sure. But forty minutes later I'd booked a flight through Paris to Johannesburg, and while it would take longer than the non-stop, they were still *free tickets*.

Here are my favorite tricks for scoring frequent flyer seats.

WORK THE PARTNER AIRLINE. Flying LanChile to Santiago on American Airlines miles is like a dream, and it seems that flights are always available. Many partner airlines are as good if not better than your main airline of choice. (Think Emirates and Singapore to name two).

WHETHER YOU'RE FLYING domestic or international, always ask, "What is the cheapest coach ticket that I can buy in order to use upgrades to business class?" Often times it's better to buy a ticket and upgrade (with fewer miles by the way) than to use all of the miles for business-class seats.

IT MAY BE A LITTLE INCONVENIENT, but travel through stopover cities. I once flew from New York City to Amsterdam to get to Edinburgh. A few hours at the Schiphol airport can be a lot of fun and I was happy because I was traveling on *free tickets*.

THINK ABOUT FLYING TO INTERNATIONAL DESTINATIONS on American holidays. Most people stay in the U.S. for Thanksgiving, Christmas, or the Fourth of July. Generally, these are the best times to get the flights that you want. The same with off-season destinations. I had some friends who took themselves and their two kids to St. Bart's in August, all on frequent flyer miles. And St. Petersburg in Russia can be magical in February.

I'm always amused when someone complains that they called in January for spring break flights to the Caribbean and couldn't use their frequent flyer miles. Duh? I call them the amateurs. Working in advance with some of these tips will get you a success rate of 90 percent or more. It's been my secret sauce for years. And while my friends and family make fun of the fact that I have flights booked nearly a year in advance, I'm the one having the last laugh. One of those friends paid $1,500 for a round-trip flight to Europe and I sat next to him on my *free ticket*. I'm just sayin'.

38   Yes, there are many valid complaints about airlines and flying, and it's true that the glory days of flying are behind us. In those days, people dressed up, manners were part of the experience, the food was free and you read a book instead of working your emails at 35,000 feet (10,668 meters). Those were special days for sure. But that's not what it's all about today.

To me, flying still has a bit of romance. I once had breakfast in Paris, flew to London for lunch and a few meetings, and then took the Concorde home and had dinner in New York. Flying from New York to Dubai transports you to a place that is so different from what we know. And in the future, we'll probably fly from New York to Beijing in four hours, as aircraft design and engineering improves.

The challenges will still be there: cancelled flights, maintenance issues, lost luggage, obstacles that may seem insurmountable. But for me, it's all worth it. I'll be figuring out alternatives and best prices and ways to use my frequent flyer miles to get to the experiences that I crave. There's no better feeling than lifting off the runway to a destination that you've dreamed about or are returning to that brings you joy and fulfillment.

Settling back into my business-class seat with *free tickets* taking me to my next adventure makes me realize that I'm still that ten-year-old with dreams. And I hope my dreams will always be with me and with you too.

TIPS

LAUREEN ONG

President, *The Travel Channel*

● On long-haul flights, take the one that leaves at midnight.
  Go to the airport showered and ready to sleep.

● Start adjusting your body to the new time zone a couple of days before
  you leave. Eat light the day before and try to avoid eating on the flight.
  Drink lots of water.

● Change some money into local currency before you leave so you don't
  have to do it at the airport. Bring local cash in small denominations.

● Negotiate, negotiate, negotiate. Especially in Asia.

● For longer trips, bring clothing that you're prepared to leave behind—
  you will buy things and will have limited space in your suitcase.

Icelandic Landscape

LONG ICELAND DAYS

Country number 121. And yes, I went to the volcano—call her Eyjafjal-lajokull—but more on that later. Why is Iceland the perfect place to go to? Well, if you love the outdoors, if you love adventure and if you love magnificent scenery, then put this place on your list.

Six of us left JFK for a four-day weekend, and here is what makes it a perfect long weekend destination (although I now realize that I could easily do ten days here with side trips to Greenland and the Faroe Islands). The flight is four hours and fifty minutes. You land at 6:30 a.m., so you have a full day. And the flight home leaves at 5:00 p.m., so you get four full days.

Reykjavik is a modern, clean, friendly city, and although they had a meltdown during the financial crisis, everyone is pretty upbeat about the future. But before you learn more about this city, there are a few things that you need to know about Iceland. Here is my favorite factoid: This country, which got its independence from Denmark in 1944, is actually located on two continents: the North American plate and the Eurasian plate. These two massive tectonic plates create a fault line across the center of the island. In fact, you can go visit the fissures and step on two different continents within minutes.

By the way, Eyjafjallajokull has put Iceland on the map around the world, and the famous volcano (which stranded millions of people in Europe, myself included) is about 75 miles (121 kilometers) due east of Reykjavik. But more about that in a moment.

Here is the headline on Iceland: It is *spectacularly* beautiful. Get this—volcanoes, glaciers, geysers, thermal pools, lava fields. Hiking, fishing, glacier walks, kayaking, rafting, great boating. We almost capsized on our way back from checking out the world famous puffins that live on islands nearby. Stay tuned for that story!

Iceland has the biggest waterfall in all of Europe. I've seen Iguacu and I've seen Victoria Falls, and Gullfoss holds its own; very impressive. And while the geyser fields may not be as big as those in places like the Atacama Desert in Chile, here's your great piece of trivia: Geysir, the destination, is the geyser that all other geysers around the world are named after. Yup, it was all established here.

On our first morning, we checked out the city. Sophisticated, stylish, with great cafes, restaurants, museums and galleries, all with lots of Scandinavian influences. All day, we were asking about our friend Eyjafjallajokull. Was she still spewing? How did it affect the city? (They'd had a dusting of ash about a week before, although most of it goes east.) As we met the locals, we asked about her. "Is she in a good mood? Should we go visit her?" By mid-afternoon of our first day, the plan was set in motion for the next day. I mean how cranky could she be? Well, she could blow a gasket any minute, but that is always the risk, isn't it?

While we made our plan, we decided to charter a boat to go out to see the puffins since 60 percent of these strange birds with penguin-like features breed in Iceland. So off we went into the sea to see the wacky birds in action, swimming, flying and setting up shop for their next four months on land to breed with the same mate. Yep, this creature is monogamous, the same mate for life (I'll let you all make your own judgment). Anyway, we were in this rickety trawler, and as we were heading back, the boat tilted forty-five degrees and everything went haywire. We thought we were about to capsize and we started preparing to hit the water. Then we were righted and bobbing around a bit, and soon we were moving again. The first officer kind of shrugged and said "earthquake," although it wasn't, and we never really got a good explanation. I chalked it up to the Icelandic beer on board that the crew was drinking!

On Day Two we head to Eyjafjallajokull—a little apprehensive, a little anxious. The drive down is beautiful. We passed some amazing waterfalls, lush green mountains, and black sand hills. We got to the town of Hvolsvollur where we were told to go, no farther, and it all looks pretty calm. We drove farther south, basically to the base of the volcano, in search of the famous plume and *bang,* the mountain was covered with a huge cloud, an ominous cloud, a rainstorm cloud, and we figure, "Well that ain't *the* cloud." All around us there was calm village life, farmers going about their business, serene sheep and the Icelandic ponies. It was bucolic and tranquil. And then,

all of a sudden, *boom!* We realized that there is no big drama here, that this   **43**
mighty mountain purrs like a kitten, and, well, for the moment, everything
seemed just fine. So, we decided to go have lunch.

Back in Reykjavik, we realized that we expected to see volcanic devastation, Pompeii revisited, massive destruction. And while this volcano has
created havoc all over Europe and has reminded us that Mother Nature will
behave any way that she wants, for now, on her home turf, it's pretty calm.
But it could all change in an instant, not just with her, but also with any of
the other twenty-two volcanoes on this island country.

I know, you're feeling a little let down. You wanted mayhem and volcanic ash spewing all over us. Well, it's pretty certain that if you come to
Iceland that won't be happening. But you will have instant hot water due to
the geothermal activity that Iceland is harnessing for clean power, and you'll
be able to drive to the western peninsula to visit Snaefellsnes, which we did
on our third day.

You'll stop in a town called Stykkishólmur, and you'll realize that you've
just taken one of the most magnificent drives that you'll ever take in your
life, and you'll eat some of the freshest seafood and drink some of the cleanest water and breathe some of the best air on the planet. And you'll forget
about Björk and that duck dress. You'll see that the Icelandic people are
proud of how their Viking ancestors established the first democratic parliament here in AD 930, and you can go to Thingvellir Park, a UNESCO
World Heritage site situated on a sweeping, haunting and stunningly beautiful plain, to see where it all happened.

And if you don't want to experience any of that, then you can go to the
101 for a dining experience that rivals those of New York City, London or
Tokyo, or visit one of the small jazz clubs or pubs. And since it doesn't get
dark until 1:00 a.m. in the summer, yes, that is 1:00 in the morning, you
have a long day in which to try it all.

So, readers, I have to say, I'll be back to visit Vatnajokull, the world's
third largest icecap (after Antarctica and Greenland), and the Askja Caldera
and, well, a long list of places.

Iceland. Put it in your future. You won't be disappointed, I promise!

Elgin, Scotland

SCOTLAND DISCOVERY

In a lifetime of travel, somehow a trip to Scotland had eluded me. It seemed like such a gap in my travels that when people heard that I hadn't been there, they told me that I had to make it a priority, and finally I did.

My British colleague Duncan Edwards told me about his hike up Ben Nevis, the tallest point on the British Isles, and that really got me focused on finding the time to take the trip. But I knew there was more to it than that. Here was a country that could trace its history back more than six thousand years. And over the years I'd been mesmerized by Mary, Queen of Scots, along with Macbeth, Heathcliff and even the talents of Ewan McGregor!

I rounded up a few people from my travel group and we booked a trip for late August. Not being golfers, but rather history buffs and outdoorsy types, we mapped out what we thought would be the ideal ten-day trip. We'd start in Edinburgh, then head to Ben Nevis, drive along the Loch to Inverness and Nairn, then head west through the Highlands to the Isle of Skye, not just for what we were told was its haunting beauty, but also to go to the end of the peninsula to dine at what was one of the most famous restaurants in Scotland, if not all of Britain, Three Chimneys. And finally, we'd end up in Glasgow, to have a comparative experience to Edinburgh, its famous rival city.

It seemed like the ideal itinerary for a first visit and it was also a short jaunt from New York, with a non-stop flight right into Edinburgh. Of course, I couldn't take the non-stop because I had decided to use frequent flyer miles and that would entail a flight to Amsterdam with a connection to Edinburgh. Sometimes that kind of layover is worth it, especially when a free ticket is involved.

One of the great travel tips is that you should learn how to schedule flights to maximize your time. On this particular flight, we landed at Schiphol Airport at 6:00 a.m., and with a four-hour layover that would still get us to Edinburgh before noon. Schiphol has a very convenient place called Yotel, one of the great inventions for travelers. Here you can rent a room for a few hours and take a nap in a noise-free, plush room all decked out in white comforters, television, WiFi and a bathroom like one you'd find on a great yacht. Checking in is all done via an automated kiosk and an attendant hands you your key. For three hours we napped, showered and had a quick breakfast, and then we boarded our connecting flight, arriving in Edinburgh rested and ready to hit the streets.

Before we left for Scotland, we were told to expect some rain because it rained a lot there. And it did. Every day. But it didn't really matter because there was so much to take in that we almost didn't notice. Well, at least until we got to the Highlands and couldn't see two feet in front of us. But now I understand why the Scots dress the way they do in such stylish raingear.

We landed in Edinburgh on a sunny and warm August morning, flying over incredibly lush green fields and farms as we made our descent into this expansive city of half a million people on the Firth of Forth. I instantly fell in love with the city. Not just because we arrived during the famous Fringe Festival that is now one of the largest arts festivals in the world with street theater and every space brimming with singers, dancers and performers, but it is because in Edinburgh you have an instant feeling of history, architecture, politics and culture all rolled into one walkable city that is what one would call "very civilized."

Edinburgh is the seat of the Scottish Parliament, established in 1997, and its most magical monument to government is the Edinburgh Castle, which sits high above the city, and has overlooked its populace for centuries. The castle is home to St. Margaret's Chapel, the twelfth-century Norman chapel dedicated to Queen Margaret and the Stone of Destiny, Scotland's historic coronation seat. You can also stroll around Old Town and New Town, constantly looking up at the architectural splendor. The Royal Mile, a stroll from the Castle to the Palace of Holyroodhouse, is a walk that deserves at least half a day.

But what made me really love Edinburgh are the seven hills that surround the city, particularly the highest, Arthur's Seat, at 823 feet (250 meters). And where there is a hill to climb, I itch to get there as soon as I can. We decided to spend a few hours exploring, and it was worth every single minute of it. Getting to the top is a moderate hike, but there are plenty of trails for the more casual walker to stroll without having to go to the very top. At the top you will be rewarded with a spectacular view of the city and miles and miles of Scottish scenery.

Throughout the city, there are so many great diversions to choose from that it's a traveler's delight. Think the Museum of Childhood, The Edinburgh Dungeon and the Edinburgh Butterfly and Insect World. It's also a shopper's paradise with Jenner's, considered the oldest department store in the world, and Hector Russell, where you can pick up some tailor-made kilts. And there are so many restaurants, pubs and cafes in Edinburgh that your biggest challenge will be to decide which ones to focus on. But definitely put The Witchery by the Castle on your list.

After three days in Edinburgh (we could have easily spent five), we rented a car and started our drive to Fort William, the jump-off point for Ben Nevis, located in the center of Scotland. According to the guidebooks, any Scottish summit over three thousand feet (914 meters) is considered a Munro, named after Sir Henry Munro. There are nearly three hundred Munroes in Scotland, and hikers there try to collect as many of them as possible. Ben Nevis is the granddaddy of them all at 4,406 feet (1,343 meters).

Now here's the thing about this day hike to the top of Ben Nevis. While it may be sunny at the base, the top can be rainy and snowy and covered with mist. I was told to check in with the hiking center at the base of the mountain to confirm that the conditions on that day would be "climber friendly." The good luck for all of us was that we were good to go, although we had to be prepared for conditions that could change during the day, causing us to turn around and return to the base.

The starting point of the hike is right out of your fantasy of what a hike in Scotland should be You begin by walking past pastoral settings of small farms, babbling brooks and along well-worn paths that meander along the base of the mountain. Three of our group decided to attempt the summit that day, leaving at around 8:00 a.m. with our backpacks filled with raingear, energy bars, water, cell phones and a change of socks should we need them.

The hike started with ideal weather conditions, as we took in the views of the glorious Scottish countryside below us. And as we hiked higher, the vistas opened up, as did our trails, but they became steeper as we got above 1,500 feet (457 meters). Along the trail, our fellow hikers seemed to be enjoying the day as much as we were and there was a general camaraderie, as we all set out to conquer the top of the mountain. Several hours into the hike, we looked up to see what would be a very long and steep ascent alongside the mountain, one that we estimated would take us at least an hour to ascend. It was then that my two friends let me know that the three hours so far was enough for them and that they would rather go back down.

"Really?" I thought. We'd gotten this far and were almost halfway there, but they'd made up their minds. So I had to make a decision. Go back with them, or continue on by myself. It took me about thirty seconds to make up my mind that I would continue on.

It's always a bit of a risk to go it alone on a hike or a climb, as there is potential danger. But I'd come this far and I was not going to pass on the opportunity to stand on the top of Ben. Sometimes we just have to keep moving forward and figure out how we will handle it as we go. My solution was simple. I approached a couple who were hiking slightly behind us, asking them if I could become a part of their hike, just so that I could have some support if I needed it. I said so long to my friends and off I went with my new Scottish friends, who had come from Glasgow on their third attempt to get to the top (on all of the other efforts, they had to turn around due to weather). I hoped that I would be their lucky charm.

What is remarkable about hiking a mountain is how quickly conditions can change, and that is exactly what happened that day. First the terrain changed, becoming steeper, rockier and a bit more treacherous. What had started out as a fairly easy hike had turned into one that required some good skills with footing and balance and minimizing the chance to slip and fall. In addition to those issues, it started to rain and the fog rolled in and before we knew it, we were completely socked in by the weather.

"Damn!" my Scottish friend Ian said. "This is what happened to us the last time!" And at that point, they said, "We want to stop for a while and decide if we are going to continue." Hikers coming down the hill told us that it was pretty bad, but they'd been to the top and said we probably had another forty-five minutes in front of us.

It was decision time again, and as I pulled out my raingear and tugged it over my hiking shorts and shirt, I vowed to continue on with or without my new friends. After a few minutes without convincing them to join me, I did go on, assuming that I would get there within an hour.

It got windier and foggier, and I have to say I'd never experienced these conditions on any of my mountain hikes in Patagonia or the Himalayas. As the rain pelted down, I continued heading up the mountain, occasionally slipping on some moss and also meeting hikers on their way down. At one point, I literally had to take one step at a time, focusing on the trail so that I didn't leave it. "This might be a stupid idea," I thought, but there I was in the middle of it, so to speak, and so I persevered.

There were occasional openings in the fog that allowed me to see five feet in front of me, and I met with the occasional hikers who said it wasn't much worse at the top, which encouraged me to keep going. And as I climbed, I didn't run into anyone else on their way up, just those on their way down, so I knew this was going to be a solo act.

About forty-five minutes later I still wasn't at the top, but I knew it was somewhere up there and calculated that maybe it was fifteen minutes or so away. All of a sudden, there were no hikers returning down, which seemed a bit eerie, reinforcing my thought that I might have done something pretty stupid. Trudging forward, I just focused on where I was going and suddenly in front of me were a group of five people standing together, not moving.

"How much farther to the top?" I asked.

"You're at the top!" one of them said.

"This is it?" I thought. It seemed like a pretty ordinary spot until one of the people in the group told me to walk a few feet away and I would come to a grouping of stones that symbolized the top, along with some old abandoned structures that marked the peak.

Well, there it is. I made it. I pulled out my phone to text my friends below and to text my colleague Duncan in London to tell him that I was standing at the top of Ben Nevis, and that the weather had permitted that day. In the rain and the wind and the fog, it was hard to imagine that it was August, but then again, that's the micro-weather on the top of this and many other mountains. I felt a great accomplishment that I'd made it. To me, this was worth the trip to Scotland. And it was more than just adding another notch on my travel belt.

Only a fellow Globetrotter will understand the satisfaction of going to a new place, or reaching a new milestone. To feel the fulfillment of standing there only reminded me that this is what makes me me. We all try to figure out what it is that's core to who we are, and if we're lucky enough to pursue it, then we become more of ourselves. Someone once asked me, "What makes you you?" I had my answer right away: A burning desire to have as many experiences around the world as I possibly can. This day had given me more of myself.

As I started the trip down (with my new friends that were the small group I'd met at the top), I ran into Ian and his wife and encouraged them on. They too would make it that day, heading back to Glasgow feeling accomplished. Somehow, going down is always easier, even though the physical trip down can be dangerous at times. It's really because the adrenaline and the anticipation has settled down to a regular beat. Halfway down the mountain, I said goodbye to my small group, and finally I was at the base of the mountain, again enjoying a lovely Scottish late afternoon. My friends met me with hot tea, and we drove back to the Inverlochy Castle, where we were staying. That night, after a great dinner in front of the fireplace, I had a great night's sleep and wondered if I'd be able to bag any more Munroes on this trip.

While this may have been one of my highlights, there was still so much to do and see on our visit. We headed north along the Glen Mor to Loch Ness, Inverness and the town of Nairn. Along the way we stopped at Urquhart Castle, beautifully situated on the edge of the Loch Ness and well worth a visit. Of course we looked for Nessie, the famous Loch Ness monster, but I'd be lying if I said that we even thought maybe we'd seen her.

The Highlands where all of this is located symbolizes the romance of Scotland in its sparseness and its tragic history. Nowhere is this more apparent than on the Culloden Battlefield, a place that I had never heard of until I got there. It was here, in 1796, that the last major battle took place on British soil. The Jacobites were defeated here in one of the bloodiest battles in Britain's history. The place has a lot of emotional experience attached to it, and as you walk the battlefield and visit the superb visitor center, you begin to understand what happened there. I tell everyone that this is a must-see on a trip to Scotland. It gets a mention in the guidebooks, but needs to get the attention of more travelers so that they can appreciate the tragedy that the Scots have had in their long history.

Our ongoing journey took us through the Northwest Highlands, with some of the most magnificent scenery in all of Scotland. But, alas, the rain prevented us from seeing it in its full splendor as we made our way to the famed Isle of Skye.

Of all of the Scottish islands, this is the one that I dreamed about the most and I promise you, it over-delivers on many fronts. Sometimes referred to as the Misty Isle, it is a microcosm of everything that Scotland has to offer, including majestic scenery of rugged mountains and coastlines, the Cuillins, a range that stands out on it's own, the Dunvegan Castle, the Aros Center in Portree, a fantastic local art center, the Talisker Distillery, home of the well-known Talisker Scotch and, of course, Three Chimneys, one of the best restaurants in the country.

My first action upon arrival on the Isle of Skye was to breathe. It just seemed like the kind of place that had the purest air on earth. As we drove past farms (known as crofts) and along the waterfalls and the wide-open spaces, it all seemed deserving of its name. A few days there should be on anyone's agenda, but a trip there just to visit Three Chimneys is worth it. It's hard to believe when you approach the small town of Colbost on the shore of Loch Dunvegan that you will experience one of the best meals you've ever had. And while there are accommodations here, it's the restaurant that draws people from around the world to sample the haddock and the pot roast crown of Scottish grouse or Mallaig skate, all to be followed by the hot marmalade pudding with Drambuie custard. The 120-year-old former farmhouse is as charming as the dining room's decor and staff. Be sure and visit the Talisker Distillery, the only single malt scotch distillery on Skye and one of the few scotches to be mentioned by name in a poem, "The Scotsman's Return from Abroad," by Robert Louis Stevenson. Not only will you learn how scotch is made, you'll also have some great taste sensations to enhance your visit.

Our eight days in Scotland had been a huge feast, and we felt stuffed with all that we'd experienced as we pulled into Glasgow, our last stop on our ten-day visit. The competition between Glasgow and Edinburgh is well known, but I was committed to keeping an open mind after my instant love of Edinburgh. So I roamed the streets, visited the Gallery of Modern Art, the stunning City Chambers on George Square and the Botanic Gardens. And they were all, well, lovely. The Glasgow Cathedral and Glasgow Necropolis were exceptional in every way. But my heart was due east, so in the debate of Glasgow versus Edinburgh, I fall in the latter's camp.

But here is what I learned about Scotland. The country has so much richness in its culture, history, food and sights that it's almost overwhelming to take it all in. My own impression is that it was more interesting than England and Ireland put together, and that statement is going to cause me a lot of problems with my family and friends. But there you have it.

I now find myself paying attention to all things Scottish. And when I read about Andrew Carnegie or Walter Scott or the explorer David Livingstone, I learned that they are Scots. Go to Scotland to learn all about it. Play some golf. Do some fishing and hiking. Enjoy the festivals and the food and the scotch and the moors. Let the wind blow through your hair and breathe. Breathe in all that Scotland offers. And don't exhale.

Swakopmund, Namibia

WHY I LOVE TERMINAL 5 AT HEATHROW

There aren't too many people who use "love" and the name of an airport in the same sentence. Maybe there are a handful of airports that could fit that bill, mostly newer ones in Asia. Think Dubai, Beijing, Hong Kong. Personally, I'm happy in a lot of airports, but then again, that's me.

Airports are one thing, but there are certain terminals that seem to float above all of the chaos that the modern-day airport can create. Think of Jet Blue at JFK, now in the gorgeous Saarinen structure that once housed TWA. I also tend to be partial to Terminal 7 at JFK—it's manageable at a more human scale. (It houses British Airways, United, and Icelandair.)

But Terminal 5, or T5, the home of British Airways at London's Heathrow, stands out as one of my favorite terminals anywhere. As some of you may know, it took nearly fifteen years from conception to completion before T5 was opened. Eighty archeologists were involved in what was the largest-ever single site excavation in Britain's history, discovering that there was human life on this ground 8,500 years ago. There were administrative and political setbacks, but in March 2008, T5 opened to disastrous reviews. There were baggage-handling issues and technological snafus. But many opening days present problems to work out, and British Airways figured all of it out quickly, and today the terminal soars with efficiency.

Yes, life at airports and terminals sometimes runs amok, but it is usually Mother Nature wreaking havoc with flight departures and arrivals. Trust me, you want to be at T5 when this happens. During the course of a year I might be in London once or twice, but I also find myself transferring at T5 for other global destinations: Budapest, Zurich or Cape Town. Recently, I decided to take the 10:00 p.m. flight to London with a two-hour layover at T5 to connect to Milan. The British Airways flight to London is perfect because you can eat dinner at the Club World Lounge, board the plane, and be fast asleep in a Club World Class sleeper for a good solid five hours of sleep on the six-hour-plus trip to Heathrow. The two-hour layover for the one-and-one-half-hour flight to Milan was a treat, and it made me think of the ten reasons why I love T5, so here goes:

REASON #10 The terminal is open, airy and light. The architectural design with the waveform roof that is 128 feet (thirty-nine meters) high is a nod to the romance of flying, perhaps that of a bygone era, but it is a wink to that time. From the ground to the rooftop is a gigantic window that allows you to watch every conceivable airline and aircraft take off and land to and from destinations all over the world. The interior of T5 is spacious and the terminal has stacked vertical floors, creating less of a walk for flyers. Think about American Airlines Terminal 8 at JFK—you'd better be in great cardio shape to get from the start to the finish!

REASON #9 It has open seating areas that are lounge-like, where there are big departures/arrivals boards everywhere, lots of WiFi areas and big screen televisions for catching up on the news. You never have the sense that you're crammed into a waiting area, even with all of the crowds.

REASON #8 Ditto on the British Airways lounges—civilized, open, lots of different foods, reading and viewing options, and comfortable seating.

REASON #7 T5 is a shopper's paradise. Forgot a shirt? Pink is there along with Ted Baker and Harrods. Need a little luxury? The Gucci, Vuitton and Tiffany shops are as well designed and merchandised as any that you'd find on Rodeo Drive. T5 has all kinds of shops, including one of the most in-genious London/U.K. souvenir shops anywhere! One of my favorite stops at T5 is Dixon's, which sells every conceivable travel gadget that you may want or need. Think iPads, iPods, chargers, laptop covers and just about any type of travel accessory imaginable. I could spend my whole downtime in that store alone!

REASON #6 Hungry? There is every type of food for any type of taste. Wagamama, the Japanese restaurant, has amazing food and the best views for watching airplanes take off and land. Gordon Ramsey has a place called Plane Food. There are pubs and bagel shops, gourmet takeaway and, of course, Starbucks.

REASON #5 The very cool circular Vodka Bar with every type of vodka in the world available for your tasting.

REASON #4 There are lots of service desks for information, currency exchange, and British Airways customer service. Even the sometimes-nightmarish ordeal of getting through customs to connect to another international flight, which requires another security check, seems painless. I know, I can't believe I'm saying that either.

REASON #3 That soft female voice with the lovely British accent that announces the departure of flights. "British Airways announces the departure of flight 000 to Shanghai." It makes me feel like I'm in a James Bond movie, listening to her announce flights to Rome, Athens, Stockholm, Delhi. It takes me on an imaginary trip to faraway places.

REASON #2 People watching. With the exception of the Dubai airport, there is no better crossroads of humanity. Try figuring out who is from where and where they're going. It's a fun sport, for sure.

AND, FINALLY, REASON #1 is British Airways itself. Maybe I'm naïve, but boarding a BA flight just seems, well, comfy. The impeccable manners of the attendants, the assuring voice of the captain, the cabin service, the whole civilized vibe. Compare that to Continental at Newark. And I'm not even an Anglophile! Somehow, I feel safer and more pampered on British Airways.

So if you haven't been to T5, put it on your destination and your international connections list. Is being happy at an airport a contradiction? Not at Heathrow's T5; it makes traveling a pleasure. Have a lovely flight!

Paris, France

FOR THE LOVE OF PARIS

Consider this question: "Let's say that you only have three months to live and you can only pick one place to go for a final visit, where would you go?" For me, the answer is Paris. Even though I've given myself over to Italy and all things Italian, France and Paris are still in my blood, and I would have to return there to have one last reunion. Paris is like a first love, and therefore it's always with me. I haven't really been able to escape its charms and the emotions that it conjures up inside of me. And I hope to be there again and again before it's my time to exit stage left into the afterworld.

It all started in high school, when I chose French for my language requirement. Growing up in Pittsburgh, Pennsylvania, was about as far away from all things Parisian as one could get. Even though we had great museums and cultural institutions, my town was pretty much a meat and potatoes kind of place. So you can imagine how truly foreign it all seemed to me as I began to learn the language and to learn what the French and France was all about.

I fell hard. Marie Antoinette. Victor Hugo. Notre Dame. Madame Bovary. Albert Camus. Catherine DeNeuve. Ile de la Cité. Truffaut. I was swept into all of it. Even though I wasn't a smoker, Gauloise almost pulled me in too. All of it was brought to life for me by my French teacher, who had a passion for the language and the culture. She was *incroyable*. I told my friends how I could *tutoyer* them, and I would yell, *Zut Alors!* when I was angry.

Somehow, I got fixated on the sentence *Je suis mouillé jusqu'aux os* (I'm soaked to the bone) and would say it every time it rained. And if someone did something bad, I would just shout out *On y soit qui mal y pense!* (Evil be to he who thinks evil.) Now that really got them!

But it wasn't until I finished my freshman year of college, armed with my four years of high school French, that I actually stepped on French soil. *Zut Alors!* It was even better than I'd thought.

Today, I've been to Paris more than fifty times. Mostly for work, but even when going for work, there's always a sense of romance and style and *je ne sais quoi*. Once as my boss, Jack, and I walked down the long corridor at the Ritz, all decked out in black tie, he turned to me to tell me that I was getting the promotion that I'd hoped for. And then we went to our work event at a tented dinner on the Champ de Mars, complete with fireworks that went off above the Eiffel Tower to the music of "An American in Paris." Now that's the way to get promoted!

On a business flight from New York to Paris we developed engine trouble and had to return to JFK. I decided to cancel the trip, and left my boss (the same Jack) a message that I wouldn't be joining him. He phoned back and told me to take the Concorde the next day (it was the 1980s when life was a bit lush). So there I was, sipping champagne at mach speed, en route to the City of Light. You're not in Pittsburgh anymore, Michael.

Business dinners in Paris were at great restaurants like Lucas Carton, or Hotel Costes, or also in out-of-the-way places on the Left Bank like Le Cafetière, or at late nightclubs, like Bains Douches. And we'd stay at the Ritz, or the Crillon with the ghosts of Gary Cooper and Audrey Hepburn along with fashion and music royalty, Arab Sheiks and mysterious European women dripping in diamonds. And it was in Paris, I think at the Ritz, that I developed a taste for Château Pétrus, one of the great fine wines (thanks again, Jack). There were late-night parties at Karl Lagerfeld's house and after parties with Madonna.

Business has been good to me in Paris. Not just the trappings, but also the business of business. Here I got to learn about the luxury brands of Louis Vuitton, Hermes, Cartier and Dior. Here I got to appreciate the provenance of these names and what it meant to build a business that was precise and perfectly positioned, never moving from quality and taste. Doing business with all of these companies taught me perfection at its best.

As the Publishing Director of the American editions of *ELLE* and *Marie Claire,* I also learned how an elegant and keen creative French eye made all of the difference. It's no wonder both of those magazines have become the leaders around the world, bringing their vision to women from China to Argentina.

No matter how many times I'm in Paris, I'm seduced. And here are the things that I've learned about that seduction. First of all, you should go there with someone that you love. And I don't mean your mother. This is a city that deserves your romantic life at full tilt. In fact, it's probably the best place on Earth to go when you're in your highest state of love and lust, when you're a little gaga over the person who you want to take long walks with or have a lingering coffee with at dusk in some cafe on the Left Bank. But even if you're on the other side of lust and you're still in love, this is a good bet. Go to Paris with that person first. Then go again and again. And then go with your mother and your kids and your best friends, or even by yourself.

But I promise you, that when you're there, the whisper of romance will still be that voice inside of you. How is it that this city has managed to maintain its sense of romance for so long? Well, this is now turning into a story about Paris and romance. So, proceed at your own risk—it may make you melancholy and sad for lost loves. You decide.

Let's start with the weather. A sunny hot June day, a drizzly April morning, or a crisp cold January Sunday. I've been there at all of those times, and it makes no difference. Romance is romance year round in Paris.

Try one of the small hotels, tucked away on the Left Bank somewhere, or even in Le Marais or off the Champs Elysees. There are plenty of places to choose from that will give you your own Private Paris. My personal favorite is L'Hotel, a place that I discovered on my twenty-ninth birthday on one of my own romantic sojourns. Originally part of La Reine Margot, this charming and circular building with stunning design and decor was created as the *Pavillon d'Amour* or Pavilion of Love (need I say more?) in the early nineteenth century. From the quintessential French lobby, you can look straight up to the roof through the open atrium in the center hall. This has been a secret hideaway for nearly two centuries, hosting everyone from Princess Grace to Elizabeth Taylor and Richard Burton. During one of my own stays there I bumped into one of the most famous Hollywood actresses with her handsome male friend in tow. No questions please. You could spend the entire weekend holed up in the sumptuous rooms here or at the bar and restaurant, which might be one of the most romantic spots in the world; but then again, you do need to go out and get some fresh Parisian air.

My five favorite romantic experiences in the City of Light are easy to rattle off, so here we go in no particular order.

● Enter the Tuileries and walk west from the glass pyramid that is the entrance to the Louvre. A stroll through any part of this park is intoxicating, and it's great people watching, especially for those who sit around the ponds and fountains. Make sure that you stop and look at the many beautiful statues in the park, and if you slip to the side walkways as opposed to the main walkway, you'll feel a sense of privacy right in the middle of the city. There are several food and coffee stands there that require a stop just to take it all in. By the time you reach the other end, you'll already feel intoxicated. And then you'll reach Place de la Concorde, the culmination of your stroll, where you'll see all of Paris before you: the Eiffel Tower in the distance, the Arc de Triomphe, and the famous Hotel Crillon. What better spot to say, "Bonjour, Paris!"

60

● One of the unique spots here is the walkway along the Seine. For those of you who have been there, you know that the river runs below street level and that the walkways are on the river level. There are so many places where you can enter one of the walkways that you can't go wrong in your selection. But try it during the late afternoon, or just as the sun is setting. Here you'll experience the city in a way that will require you to make a late dinner reservation that night because I guarantee you that you and yours will want to spend some extra time at your hotel.

● On Ile de la Cité, enter Place Dauphine right off of the Pont Neuf. Now just stop and take this all in. Sit on one of the benches and have that long conversation that you've wanted to have about your relationship, or life, or maybe about the works of Jean Paul Sartre and the meaning of existentialism. Take a moment. From there, stroll over to the Pont des Arts to see the "locks of love" placed on the bridge by others in love, and then continue on to Ile St. Louis to get lost in the earliest days of the city. A stop at Notre Dame with a stroll over to Quai de la Tournelle will have you particularly warmed up. But be careful, you may blurt out your undying love, or better yet, a proposal after this walk.

● The area around Saint-Sulpice, the second largest church in the city, is located in the Luxembourg Quarter on the Left Bank. Built in 1646, this church and neighborhood got newfound fame in Dan Brown's *The DaVinci Code* as a spot that has lots of history to it, including the spot where, in the book, the Priory of Sion was established. The gnomon is a particularly interesting spot to visit there, a place that can identify the time of the equinoxes. Spend some time in the church, have a coffee in the neighborhood and then take a walk over to Les Jardins du Luxembourg, one of the most beautiful parks in the world. Established in the 1600s, this is the second largest park in the city, filled with more than one hundred statues, monuments and fountains, as well as intricate gardens. Here you'll find families and lovers strolling amidst these gorgeous grounds that serve as a garden for the French Senate. Work your way over to the Medici Fountain. That's the place. Tell the person you're with how you feel about her or him. This too, is the perfect place for a proposal. Or at least a kiss. Sit in the park and talk about your future together. Or your present.

● Walk just about any side street in the 6th or 7th arrondissement. Get lost **61**
in the streets of these neighborhoods that blend into each other. Find the
perfect place for lunch or dinner, stop at one of the boutiques for some shopping, sample some homemade cheeses or pastries. Forget time and where
you have to be later that day. Just get lost in the place and in the two of you.

This list could go on and so I thought I'd ask some friends about their favorite
romantic spots in Paris and here are some more ideas from the well traveled:
Place des Vosges in Le Marais, the Picasso and Rodin museums, La Mad-
eleine, Place Vendôme, Sacré Coeur, the Bois de Boulogne. Have tea at the
Ritz, a night at L'Opera and of course visit the Eiffel Tower, particularly at
night, looking down at the twinkling lights below.

For those of us who have the good fortune of going to Paris on business
on a regular basis, romance may not be our primary motivation when we get
there, but that's okay because this city can take care of other parts of your
life as well. In my free time during a business trip there, it's a treat to go for
a run through the streets, particularly along the Seine. There's always a new
show at the Musée des Beaux Arts or the Pompidou, or a chance to get reacquainted with the masters in the Louvre.

I can always tell by looking in my colleagues' eyes that while we all enjoy each other's company, there's something else tugging at our hearts. We
pass young couples strolling along the street, arm and arm, or watch what
is always unabashed public kissing in this city, and our brains start to churn.
We know that we have seven meetings the next day and that we have a lot of
business problems to solve. But, in the back of our minds, it's always there.

I often wonder when I can come back here for a purely romantic weekend.
No suits and ties, no briefcases, no business terms. And it's usually then that
I go to my calendar and begin to dream. And I remember that this doesn't
happen just to me. From kings and queens to struggling students, this is the
city where we dream about love. About who makes our heart beat just a little
stronger. About the importance of that quiet time of intimacy and together-
ness and just being the two of you. That's Paris, my friend. Go there with that
special someone. Again and again. Look into each other's eyes and then look
around you. It will be the memory that you should have when it's your time
to drift into the afterworld. And if we're lucky, in fact, heaven will be Paris.
Think about it.

Tuscan Sunflowers

VIVA ITALIA!

Because I've been fortunate enough to visit over 120 countries in the world, I will often times hear from friends, family, friends of friends, strangers, and well just about anyone who wants to know where they should go on vacation. It's always a tough question to answer because there are so many choices. The conversations always come down to "Well, then what are your five favorite destinations, Michael?"

Limiting the answer to five is like asking, "What are your favorite five books or five movies?" How can you pick only five? That said, there is one place for sure that's always on the list of my top favorites: Italy!

Why Italy? Let's start with the idea that it is one of the most beautiful countries on earth. Then mix in the history, the art, the food, the wine, the culture, the overall way of life, and you have one of the most perfect places on earth. I've been to Italy around seventy-five times, so this love affair has withstood the test of time. I even once left France for Italy, but that's another story.

My first trip there was as a student, and I made the usual stops in Rome, Florence and Venice (Rome was and continues to be my favorite), but it has been my work in the magazine publishing business that has taken me there more than sixty times over the past thirty years. During those trips I went to Milan to visit the major fashion designers, as well as to places outside of town that produce Armani, Zegna and Gucci, to name a few. Yet even with all of that business travel, I still return time and time again to enjoy *la dolce vita!*

I guess this is where I should admit that my secret wish is that I was born Italian. The natural sense of style, the natural appreciation of food, the beautiful complexions and skin tones, the language—all of it makes me want to be a part of it. My favorite people are Italian and even the closest people in my life are Italian. *E anche, studio Italiano ogni lunedi per due ore per due anni!*

Italy has a long, rich and colorful history that at times can become overwhelming. While the unification of all of the Italian states didn't take place until 1861 and the Italian Republic wasn't established until 1946, this is a land that has been thriving since the ninth century BC. It is here that the Etruscan civilization prevailed for more than seven hundred years. The Villa Giulia in the Borghese Gardens in Rome is one of the best museums in the country to visit to get a sense of the Etruscans. It's one of those oft-overlooked gems in a city of jewels.

What most of us know about the early days of Italy is the dominance of Rome that started around 350 BC and went on for another seven hundred years or more. We envision Cleopatra and Caesar and the enormous influence that Rome had on the rest of the world. I couldn't even begin to give you the history of this grand country, but there have been thousands of books written on the subject; pick your favorite and get into it!

What I can tell you about is where you might go for an amazing Italian experience. But where to begin? The Lake District in the North? Portofino or Positano? The hills of Tuscany or Umbria? The Amalfi Coast? Sardinia? Sicily? Then there's Bologna, Ancona, and the Puglia region. I've been able to spend time in all of those places, and I get into the same dilemma again and again with regards to which are my favorites. For those who have already done the major cities, there are two trips that I recommend.

One of the best ways to soak up the Italian life is to get a group of family or friends together and rent a house in Tuscany or Umbria. Leasing a villa or a farmhouse may seem a bit daunting, but it's actually a more affordable way to spend time in Italy and the choices are plentiful. There are many websites that have been vetted by the travel industry, so it's easier than you may think to find your own private Italy. Having done this several times, I can attest to the fact that you won't feel like a tourist, but more like a local.

As I write this story, I'm sitting in a five-bedroom stone farmhouse near Todi, Umbria looking out over the Umbrian countryside. We've just finished a breakfast of figs, pears, and grapes, all picked from the property, along with eggs and bread that were bought at the local market. This particular house sits on three acres of olive groves and has more than fifty varieties of antique roses, a gracious pergola for outdoor dining, and a swimming pool with breathtaking views of the neighboring countryside.

While it is a little remote, it gives us the sense of what living in the Italian countryside is all about. We are able to cook our own meals or have a cook come in to make us dinner, although what we love best is to drive to local towns and villages and sample the local recipes and drink the local wine.

On this particular trip, our daytrips have been to the towns of Perugia, Assisi, and Orvieto, all distinctive Umbrian towns with centuries of history behind them. Each of these towns has its own story and its own reason for being and it's easy to get lost in the sides streets for hours on end, discovering Renaissance buildings, tiny museums that celebrate the local history, and of course, food.

Let me interrupt this story by spending some time talking about Italian food and the discoveries that await you at every meal. There is nothing better than fresh mozzarella, or zucchini flowers, or the taste of prosciutto and melon. And in certain regions of this part of the world, you can partake of rabbit, wild boar, or fresh fish from the Mediterranean. But what continues to astonish me is the inventive ways to serve pasta. Imagine this: spaghetti noodles with lemon and butter and crushed pistachio nut sauce. My mouth waters just thinking about it. Or pappardelle noodles with pumpkin and ginger. Or tagliatelle with baby shrimp and zucchini pesto sauce. There is nothing better than discovering a local restaurant where the owner or chef has created his own unique flavors, all washed down with a wine that has been grown in their family vineyard for hundreds of years.

And then there's the antipasti and crostini and fresh vegetables to add to the feast. And don't forget that there are desserts of tiramisu or panna cotta to be tasted too. My favorite dessert ritual is to meander down one of the side streets to find a gelateria and have a fresh scoop of noccialo, and then take a post lunch or dinner walk through the streets. Italy is about bringing the five senses to life in ways that we forget about at home. Every meal is a joy there, even if it is a quick panino while you're on the run.

Umbria and Tuscany are both situated between Rome and Florence, and regardless of where you stay, there are countless places to visit. Some visits should be planned and some should be spontaneous. When in Tuscany you'll undoubtedly visit Florence or Pisa, but the places you shouldn't miss are places like the fortress town of Lucca that is more than two thousand years old, and the small coastal town of Forte dei Marmi, which is a short drive away and a great place to spend the day on the beach and enjoy great people watching. The Chianti region should also be high on your list of places to visit, particularly the towns of Greve in Chianti and Castellina in Chianti. It is in this area that we discovered the small town of Montespertoli, where we rented a house one summer. The local restaurants and vineyards more than welcoming—at times a local chef prepared different meals just for us, once he saw how much we appreciated his talents.

Whether you're in Tuscany or Umbria, most places that you'll want to visit are within two hours of each other. Our usual routine is to plan a day excursion, usually with a lunch and/or dinner stop. Some days we just drive the countryside or just stay at home to lounge around the pool. However you spend your day, you will get a sense of how the Italians appreciate life in its simplest forms. I'm not big on collecting lists of restaurants in an area beforehand; to me, it's always better to roam the streets, ask the locals, or just pick a place based on how it looks or smells. Finding a spot with outside dining overlooking the hills can only add to the pleasure of the local foods.

If the idea of a villa or house are not your style and you'd prefer to be pampered at a luxury hotel, my second suggestion is to head to the Amalfi coast, to the towns of Positano and Ravello and to the island of Capri. Here you'll be able to stay at some of the finest hotels and resorts in all of Italy, soaking up *la dolce vita* in one of the most stylish spots on earth. Many people prefer Capri, but I'm partial to the town of Ravello, high on the mountains above the coast with splendid views. But you can't go wrong wherever you stay; just make sure that you hire a boat to take you out on the water, take a side trip to Pompeii, and dine along the water in the town of Positano. Things to discover in small towns and villages are not as plentiful as in Tuscany or Umbria, but then again, this is a completely different experience.

And that is the magic of Italy! Once you determine the kind of experience you want, Italy has it to offer. A more rustic experience? Try Sicily. A chic resort? Try the Costa Smeralda on the northern coast of Sardinia. Want a more contemplative time? Go to the Lake District. Committed foodies can go anywhere, but I say go to Bologna, one of my favorite spots in Italy. And for the urban experience, I say Rome, period. Yes, I know, there is no other place like Venice and the art in Florence is unchallenged and Milan is a shopper's paradise and a no-nonsense business city, but for me it's all about Rome.

And that's why it deserves its own story and its own place in this book, as you'll soon discover. During all of the years that I've traveled to Italy, one thing has remained constant, and that is the hospitality of the Italian people. Whether you're at a local ceramic shop or at a meeting with the CEO of a global luxury company, there's something in the Italian spirit that is gracious and welcoming and considerate. At a business meeting, the conversation is always first about where you spent your holiday, or what great food you experienced, or what new Italian town you've discovered before the business gets underway. And the Italian people are thrilled when you attempt to speak their language, helping you along the way. And speaking of helping you along the way, it's not unheard of for an Italian to walk you to where you are trying to go, or having you follow them in their car to find the entrance to the autostrada. For all of these reasons and more, I know that I'll return to Italy time and time again, to sharpen my senses, to remind me that this is a place that for thousands of years has faced good times and bad but continues to prevail. It's one of those places that make me feel calm and satisfied. I may not be Italian, but I can still dream and pretend that I am. And that alone is worth the visit. *Viva Italia!*

Tuscany, Italy

THE ART OF THE BUSINESS SIDE TRIP

Like many people in their early twenties, I didn't have a lot of spare cash when I first arrived in New York to begin my publishing career. Those days were about making enough money to feed myself, find an apartment, and to try to take advantage of the nightlife in the city. So there was a real dry spell in my travel aspirations, as I couldn't afford to go anywhere. Well, the truth is, there was an early dry spell in getting my career off the ground, too. Like many before me, I arrived with no contacts and no real knowledge of what I was getting into by moving to the Big City. It's true that I'd been there multiple times to visit family, but that's a whole different experience. A newly minted college degree, some experience as the publisher of my college newspaper, and around $60 is what I had to begin with. Fortunately, I could stay with an aunt and uncle for a couple of months until I got situated, but I had a sense of urgency to find a paying job so that I could stay in Manhattan.

As I made my way to the various publishing houses, it became apparent that the prospects were pretty bleak, as were the possible salary levels. In the second week, someone connected me to NBC News, and while I could have become a page (a great way to start in those days), it was working in the news division conducting news polls that caught my interest. And so I started making random calls to Americans to query them on politics and social issues and their opinions on the topics of the day. Yes, I was one of those people who would call you just as you were sitting down to eat dinner! What NBC paid wasn't going to let me get established, since I only worked from 6:00 to 9:00 p.m. every night. But I had a job in New York, a foothold to get me started.

A friend's father suggested that he could get me into an executive training program at a major New York department store, and while I knew nothing about retail, it sounded pretty good—executive training. And so there I was: four weeks in New York and I had two jobs. My day job and my night job. Three weeks later I had an apartment with some roommates, coming in just shy of the eight-week limit at my aunt and uncle's place. I was now a New Yorker!

There was only one problem. I really hated that executive training job. So I spent all of my lunch hours trying to make contacts in the publishing business and fifteen months later, I landed my first full-time publishing job as a business reporter covering, of all things, retail! But this is not a story about building a career, it's a story about bosses and the influence that they can have on your life, particularly in the Art of the Business Side Trip.

Fortunately for me, I've had many bosses who have taught me a lot, but it was my first publishing boss who gave me the gift of business travel, or more importantly, the side benefits that it can bring. I'm one of those people who loves business travel. Getting out to see clients and talking to them about their business is fun for me, whether I was writing about them in those early days, or doing business with them in my growing publishing career. In that first job, I had to do a lot of travel around the country, interviewing CEOs of retail stores as well as companies that did business with retailers. Seeing Seattle, Dallas, and Chicago for the first time was exciting to me. To be twenty-three and have a job that paid me to fly around the country, stay at hotels, and order room service—I thought I'd died and gone to heaven! It fed my travel addiction, even though it was work. And as I ultimately traveled to conferences and conventions in the U.S. and Europe, it all just compounded. In those days, the frequent flyer programs were being born, so I was getting a double bonus for all the business travel that I was doing. Cha-ching!

My first boss, Steve, believed in taking advantage of a place you were traveling to. "The Fine Art of the Business Side Trip," as he called it, can enrich your life. Here's how it worked. If you had to be somewhere on business on a Monday, why not fly out on Friday and spend the weekend there, or at a nearby place? Steve wasn't suggesting that the company should pay for the hotel for Friday and Saturday night, but you were going anyway, so your airfare was covered, as was your trip to the airport. So all you needed was a friend or family member to share a hotel room to control costs. At the time, it seemed too good to be true. Little did I know that this was one of the great benefits of any business career.

Steve was an expert at the craft. We found ourselves skiing for the week-end before we started a conference, or taking a side trip to La Jolla before we needed to be in Los Angeles. This was really how I got to see America. Puget Sound, Santa Barbara, Tucson, Aspen, Nashville, New Orleans, Key Largo, and Cape Cod all became my playground before I started a business trip. And the same thing in Europe. If we needed to be in Milan or Munich or Paris, we would inevitably side-trip it to the Lake District, cross-country ski on the Konigsee, or explore the Loire Valley.

Maybe it's the kind of people who are attracted to the publishing busi-ness, but all of my bosses seemed to have a curiosity about the world, and they had as much fun taking side trips as I did. Over the years, I ended up in places such as Berlin, Cairo, Budapest, Kyoto, and the Great Barrier Reef, as side trips to business trips for the magazine industry. While on one Euro-pean trip, we actually had three days to kill between two conferences, and a group of us decided to go to Berlin. The wall had just come down and as our timing had it, we got there the week that the famous Checkpoint Charley was closed. There we were with rented hammers, chipping out pieces of the wall that still sit on my den shelf. And we got to travel into East Berlin to see the Mies van de Rohe architecture, as well as to see the Pergamon Museum and to witness the early days of the remaking of Berlin.

On my own I flew from London to Budapest on a Friday night to spend the weekend before flying to Milan on Sunday night to start a week of busi-ness there. What better way to immerse myself in this amazing European city than on a business side trip? I got to roam the streets of both Buda and Pest, camera in tow. Some of these trips have been real bonuses, like the time a group of us were traveling with our boss, who invited us all to join him and his family on Lizard Island off of the Australian Coast after our business was over in Sydney and Melbourne. Hey, if the boss was inviting us, who were we to say no?? After all, we didn't want to jeopardize our careers in any way, so there we went to hike, kayak, sunbathe, and enjoy great food. Business travel can be gruesome, right?

Perfecting the art of the business side trip has a few rules to it and here is what I have learned over the years. First, you have to make sure that your boss and your company have no issues with it. Fortunately, none of mine have; on the contrary they have encouraged it. I hear from friends who have ridiculous travel restrictions, like you have to leave on the 6:00 a.m. flight on the day of business and return on the next available flight after business; and by the way, you have to give the frequent flyer miles to the corporate travel department. That would be a deal breaker for me!

Next, it's all about mindset. If you like to travel and explore the world, this is not such a hurdle. I once worked with a woman who loved Paris but could never get herself organized to spend at least one free day there, let alone a few hours to catch an exhibit or shop on the Faubourg Saint-Honoré. She would go to Paris two or three times a year, but could never figure out how to enjoy her non-business hours there. When I suggested that she fly out on a Friday night, pay for her hotel on Saturday night and enjoy the city for the weekend, she looked at me like it was the most foreign concept to her. "Well, it's still a business trip. My head wouldn't be into it!" In her mind, a vacation was a vacation and a business trip was well, always a business trip. Certainly never my problem.

I acknowledge that logistics are a big issue, as we all navigate family commitments, like your cousin's thirty-eighth birthday and your aunt and uncle's anniversary. Seriously? You've gone to that anniversary dinner every year for twenty years—isn't it time to treat yourself to that weekend in Sonoma? There are family obligations that are must-dos, but if you're a true globetrotter, then everyone will understand that you are feeding your passion.

As you plan that business trip, plan the weekend side trip or extended stay, or tack on your vacation. Once when I was headed for a few days of business on the West Coast, I finished and then flew to Asia for vacation. And by the way, it's not just about the side trip. How about taking advantage of the city that you're visiting? I always check out what is happening in the museums or what sporting events are scheduled. There are always those few hours into which you can squeeze a quick visit to The Metropolitan Museum or an auction house that may be presenting something that fits your passion. I had a night to kill in London once and called a friend who suggested that we go see a new play that was just starting called *The Phantom of the Opera*. It was the first week that it was open, and I had what turned out to be a once-in-a-lifetime experience.

When you're traveling for business, clients appreciate this too. Instead of the requisite lunch date, find out what interests them and have your business meeting in that setting. I once closed a big deal at the International Center of Photography talking to our client while we looked at the work of the photographer Walker Evans. It sure beat sitting in a windowless office.

This is not a new idea. Taking clients to the Super Bowl or to a hockey game has always been a form of client entertainment. I'm suggesting that you take it to a new level. Find the client side trip that is unique. A friend of mine was performing a lead role on Broadway and I took the CEO of one of the companies that we do business with to the performance and then a private backstage visit. Priceless.

Regardless of our business, we all work hard. There are setbacks and reams of budget sheets and "clients from hell," and even though I work in a "glamorous business," there are lots of unglamorous days. So perfect the art of the business side trip. Yes, take advantage of the small ways you can include clients, but do it for you. You deserve it. For every place that you have to travel to, there's something interesting to see. Certainly within fifty miles (eighty kilometers) of where you need to be for business you can find something that will delight you. And on some of those trips, take your spouse, your partner, your best friend, or your kid.

You'll be surprised at the years and years of memories that you'll accumulate by perfecting the art of the business side trip. Those grueling budget sessions will be forgotten, as will those painful presentations that you have had to sit through. Instead, you'll remember that whitewater-rafting trip or that romantic walk along the Santa Monica beach. It will make all of your hard work worth it. And it will make you a more interesting person, too.

Paris, France

10 STRANDED, PART ONE

My boss and I flew out on a Monday night on the 11:30 p.m. flight to Paris on an Air France 777 with flatbeds. What could be wrong about being in Paris in April? Paris was in full spring bloom. The city was stunning, and I got a couple of great runs in along the Seine, even though we hit the ground running with appointments with some key clients.

Our primary reason for being there was for the *Marie Claire* magazine board meeting, but it so happened that Ralph Lauren was opening his amazing new store that week, so we were invited to a swanky black tie dinner. Ralph and his family hosted the dinner in St. Germain, in the new 1670 building that houses the store. It's pretty amazing—check it out when you go to Paris. At the dinner, we got to hobnob with Kevin Spacey, Gérard Depardieu, Anouk Aimée, Karl Lagerfeld, and lots of well-known Parisians!

Anyway, the next morning (early), we caught the Eurostar to London to attend the board meeting of our British company. When we got to the office, it was the first time that we heard about "The Volcano." We had an all-day meeting and then a great dinner at the Ivy, with the plan to finish up on Friday when some of my colleagues would fly home to New York, and I'd go on to Italy. *Not.*

It was odd to watch the news roll out over all of London and ultimately the U.K., and then all of Europe. And of course, we all thought it would only be a day or so and then we'd continue on with our travels. My assistant, Fran Crane, was working our corporate travel team, booking me first on a British Airways flight to Rome. The reopening of the airspace was pushed to Saturday night, so we booked a British Midland International flight that night. When that was pushed back, I went into seasoned traveler mode.

Figuring that there would be no planes flying, Fran started working the rails, and we managed to get a train back to Paris on Sunday morning, and then one to Lausanne, but we couldn't get a reservation from there to Milan, where I needed to be on Sunday night. So, my original idea of a side trip to Rome was history and Milan was the new destination.

On Saturday morning I headed over to St. Pancras station in London, and it was sheer pandemonium, as everyone was trying to get a train out of the U.K. It was then that I learned that Rail Europe was not taking any reservations and that the online site was suspended and, well, it was kind of take what you can get! There was complete paralysis as the news got out that British Airways had cancelled all flights and that Lufthansa had also cancelled all flights, globally. The situation continued to worsen, as every couple of hours it was announced that the skies would be empty, maybe until Monday. Or Tuesday. Or Wednesday.

So what do you do? London was having a beautiful, hot, sunny day, so it was back to the hotel and a great eight-mile run into Hyde Park, then a visit to the Van Gogh exhibit at the Royal Academy, and then to nab some theatre tickets. Sunday morning, I decided to venture to the Continent with my two reservations. Eurostar ran smoothly and right on time, and then the *merde* hit the fan!

Upon arriving at Gare du Nord, I learned that the train to Lausanne leaves from Gare de Lyons on the opposite end of Paris, and I had forty-five minutes to get there. I had to get my e-ticket, and the train station was also pandemonium, with lines of twenty-five people at each kiosk. I headed out to the cab line, where there were at least fifty people. I found a gypsy cab and asked him how much and he said "100 euros" ($1.60 = 1€—you do the math). We haggled, but he wouldn't budge. As you may have heard, this was happening all over Europe, so I bolted for the metro.

All of the machines were out of order (of course) and there was a line that would take forty-five minutes to get through. So I put my best New York City head on and went to the front of the line. In my best French, I told the two women who were next in line that I'd be happy to buy their tickets, if they'd buy me a ticket for Gare de Lyons. Voila! Success! This is a great travel tip when you are in a hurry.

Now to figure out how to get there. Eight stops to Châtelet, a transfer on the 14 line for one stop, and off I went. Counting every minute at every stop, and of course the Paris Metro is subterranean, I arrived with six minutes to go as I climbed the stairs to the main train station. Oh yeah, remember that I needed that e-ticket! While the lines were ridiculous, there was this one lone machine over in the corner with only six people in line. I asked all six of them in my best voice, *"Excusez-moi, mais j'ai six minutes, s'il vous plait"* I

took a deep breath and the second person in line did a sort of grunt, but let me in, and all I could say was *"Merci, merci."*

And of course the machine didn't work on the first try, and then I had three minutes—and let me tell you, the train station is filled with everyone trying to get out. It was like the fall of Saigon. Well, my running paid off—it was quite a sprint (with two bags in tow), and I finally stepped into Voiture 11 and the door closed! All aboard! I swear this is all true!

Is your heart racing? Well, don't forget, there is no reservation and no ticket between Lausanne and Milan, so who knows what will happen? Four and a half hours later, I pulled into Lausanne (more pandemonium) and made my way to the ticket office to learn that the train to Milan was booked. *Merde* again!

Again rattling off in my best French, I tried to sweet talk a very stoic Swiss ticket agent, who has seen and heard it all; I tried to convince him to give me a ticket that would allow me to stand. Meanwhile, behind me, I heard a group of Italians ranting about how will they get back to Milan. Long story short, he sells me ze ticket, but tells me zat I might have to pay a supplement on board (sniff sniff) and zat it might be very uncomfortable (yeah, yeah). Once again the running paid off as I headed off to Voie C and jumped on board. And as the train pulled out of the station, I spied an empty seat—fate again!

Now, if you've ever been to Lausanne, you know that it is beautifully situated on Lake Geneva. It's now dusk and the train runs along the water. The Alps are in the distance, and I'm en route to Milan! All in all, it was a fifteen-hour journey from start in London to finish in Milan. *La vie est bonne!* Along the way, I talked to Brits, Americans, and Italians, all refugees of The Volcano. They told their stories as they headed south, having heard that there were flights from Rome and Athens to the U.S. and abroad. Ahhh, now I know what it must have been like when people tried to get out of Europe in 1939!

So, what did The Volcano teach me? Well, life happens when you travel, and you have to work every available angle to move it forward. Assume the worst when disaster hits and have three back-up plans. Realize that as much as some of us (me?) are control freaks, there are some things you cannot control. As you figure it out, take in what's around you (great food, museums, theatre). Embrace that being stranded in London or Paris sure beats being stranded in Dayton!

Have lots of magazines to read and some good books, paper or electronic. I read *The Big Short* by Michael Lewis. Keep your running up to speed; you never know when you may need tap into it. Tell all of your friends the story; it's a lot better than talking about the weather—or is that what we're talking about here?

So there I was, happily ensconced in the Park Hyatt Milan. The duomo is right outside of the hotel. *Va Bene!* I have a few days of business in Milan, while Fran figures out when and how I'll get home.

TIPS

PAMELA FIORI

Former Editor-in-Chief, *Town and Country*, Author

- Travel alone on occasion. You'll meet more people, be extended generosity and friendship. Plus, you'll learn resilience, independence, and ingenuity.

- Don't go cold. Bone up, do your homework, find out as much as you can about your destination.

- When in comes to tipping, learn the customs of the country.

- Use long flights for deep, creative thinking or for making plans. Consider time aloft as a gift.

- Don't pass it up. If you see something you want to buy, don't let it slip through your fingers. You'll regret it later.

Rome, Italy

ROAMING ROME

How do you even begin to explain a place that has been inhabited for 14,000 years? While there is archeological evidence that life existed in Rome that long ago, many historians would suggest that it is only the past 2,800 years that are relevant. Regardless, every piazza, structure, fountain, and monument has a story to tell. In Rome, you can stand in one place for two hours and you learn about the layers and layers of history that took place on that spot. Rome is a city that can take your breath away at every turn, multiple times per hour. There's no other place in the world that is like it, and no other city in the world that can claim to have had a spot on the world stage for millennia. Which is why they call Rome the Eternal City.

When people ask me where they should go in Europe, my first question is usually, "Have you ever been to Rome?" For the first-time visitor to Europe or for the perennial traveler, this is a place that should be visited time and time again. In my twenty or so times there, I've come to realize that I've barely scratched the surface of everything that this city has to offer, and on each trip I discover something new. (Note to self: When the day comes that I can go and spend six months living somewhere, this place is on the top of my list.)

Here are a few things that you should know about Rome. It's expensive. It's filled with tourists. Watch your wallet. Try to avoid the hotels for breakfast, unless it's included in your room rate, and definitely avoid the hotel bars, where it is not unusual to be charged $25 for a vodka tonic. But you can get beyond all that. This is a city where you have to wear your savvy traveler hat. The local economy is fueled by this constant influx of people from around the world and everyone is on the make. At the same time, there are charming coffee bars and shops with great prices and restaurants that are reasonably priced. There are also some of the best gelaterias in the world, like the Gelateria del Teatro, off of the Piazza di S. Salvatore in Lauro.

Rome is a walking city. If you don't walk, you can miss an ancient ruin that you might pass on a busy street, or miss an incredible side street that has that special gallery or shop or trattoria. The simple message is this: You have to roam in Rome. The guidebooks will give you a three-day itinerary or a five-day itinerary for seeing Rome. I'll give you the five spots that will capture not only the spirit of Rome, but will make you appreciate Rome and its way of life. I know what you're thinking! In a city that has an over-abundance of riches, how can I distill it down to just five spots? Anyone could easily come up with a list of twenty, right? Well, it's true, but on my list you won't find the Vatican or the Spanish Steps or Trevi Fountain. I'm not saying that you shouldn't go there, or that these spots won't bring you fulfillment. Inevitably, in your roam through the city, you'll get there, and savor every moment when you're there.

My first stop in Rome is usually Campidoglio. To me, this is the center of everything. Better known as Capitoline Hill, it has long been a religious and political center of the city, but also the starting point for all of ancient Rome. Tucked slightly behind the Victor Emmanual Monument, a huge white monument sometimes called the wedding cake of Rome and a tribute to Italy's first king. You can reach Capitoline, which is one of the famous seven hills, by walking up a long, beautiful sloping staircase known as the Cordonata. Be sure to make note of the large classical statues of Castor and Pollux at the top. When you arrive you'll stand among a variety of temples, including the Temple of Jupiter Optimus Maximus or Capitolinus, the preeminent temple in ancient Rome. It is on this site that Michelangelo designed what is the Piazza del Campidoglio, and this is where you'll stand when you arrive, greeted by Marcus Aurelius at the center. Take a moment to absorb the Palazzo Senatorio, the seat of the Roman Senate, the Palazzo dei Conservatori, the seat of the city government during the Middle Ages, the Palazzo Nuovo, the site of the first public museum, and the Santa Maria in Aracoeli, a church with origins in the sixth century. This compact world of history is a great starting point to get your perspective on ancient Rome.

From here you can walk to the left or the right of the piazza and in two minutes you'll arrive at the Roman Forum, the Palatine Hill, and the Colosseum. This is where you can spend the day, although there's so much to see that it is overwhelming. It's really better to go back to this area several times during your visit to Rome and it's also best to hire a local guide who can give you the full story, as opposed to fumbling through a guidebook trying to get a full understanding of the Curia Julia or the Temple of Saturn.

Local guides are skilled and you'll thank yourself that you used them. What I can tell you is that the Palatine Hill (the centermost of the seven hills of Rome) is where it is said that Romulus and Remus were found by their she-wolf mother, and it is here that it was decided that the Rome as we know it would be built. You'll find temples and ruins and gardens and palaces. Roam over to the Circus Maximus to see where the famous Roman chariot races took place, as well as the occasional gladiator battles. And, of course, always in sight throughout this tour of ancient Rome is the Colosseum, often voted the number one place to visit in the city and an iconic structure that is recognizable around the world. This elliptical building built in the year 80 AD could accommodate over 50,000 spectators. It was here that the early Romans were entertained with games like the famous fights to the death between gladiators and wild animals. And it is here where hundreds of thousands of tourists continue to visit each year.

One of the most charming and coveted neighborhoods in Rome is a short walk from the Colosseum. It is called Monti and it's a great place to stroll either during the day or the evening. Walk along Via Madonna dei Monti and the streets that surround it and you'll see a local part of the city with great restaurants and shops. This is one of neighborhoods that most people visiting Rome never spend any time in and it's the place to capture the everyday spirit of the city. And while on the "Roam Rome" theme, I constantly study the map of the city, even though I know my way around pretty well. From Campidoglio, I usually head to the Pantheon via the Corso Vittorio Emanuele and make a right turn onto Via del Cestan, which leads right to the Piazza della Rotonda. Stay here for a meal, lunch or dinner, as you gaze upon the Pantheon, a magnificent structure built 1800 years ago. Within lies the tomb of Raphael, but as you enter the structure, study the marble floor and then look up at the 43-meter- (47-yard-) high dome, one of ancient Rome's most significant contributions. Here you'll hear every language in the world. Step back against one of the walls and just watch the global parade in front of you.

A five-minute walk will take you to Piazza Navona, an oval shaped square that is my personal favorite for people watching, whether dining or just having coffee. In this square you feel the pulse of Rome in its purest sense. Make sure to walk around Bernini's famous fountain, the Fontana dei Quattro Fiumi, representing the Nile, Ganges, Danube, and Rio de la Plata.

84

To my mind, this is the most significant fountain in the city. Pick any of the restaurants in the piazza or wander off to a side street in the antiques district, which is a little quieter. But on Navona, you'll meet new friends, enjoy time with old friends, and maybe just meet the person that you're meant to spend the rest of your life with—it's that intoxicating.

A couple of great side trips from Navona are Campo de' Fiori (go on Saturday morning) and the Palazzo Farnese. That's all I'm going to say. Just roam there and look around and you'll know why I sent you. Ultimately I end up walking along the Tiber River and when I'm there, it's usually with two destinations in mind: the Castel Sant'Angelo and the neighborhood of Trastevere. First the Castel. If you read Dan Brown's *The DaVinci Code,* then you'll know it. This place, built by Hadrian in AD 123, has been a mausoleum, a fortress, and a papal residence. It's the best spot to get a view of the city and particularly of the Vatican. Go to the roof for the view and while you're there, make sure to look at the Angel Statue, an icon that stands high above Castel Sant'Angelo, looking out over the city.

The thing about roaming Rome is that it's always a history lesson in the making, which is why a moment of relief in one of the trattorias or restaurants is always a welcome moment. But the perfect antidote for absorbing all of Rome's life is the neighborhood of Trastevere. Approach it from the Ponte Sisto and enter it via Piazza Trilussa. Whether you are eighteen or eighty you'll be energized by it, and if you're eighty, you probably experienced it when you were eighteen. It's the spot in Rome that every young person knows about. Every time I'm there, I see my own eighteen-year-old self standing there, meeting fellow students from around the world. Walk into the neighborhood, but no earlier than 9:00 p.m. Walk into the Piazza Santa Maria in Trastevere and just open up your senses; you'll smell the true Rome, taste the true foods, and rub shoulders with the Romans and the would-be Romans. And you'll see and hear opera singers on the corner, an elderly woman who will let you pet her cat if you reward her for her dancing, and a bearded man may let you see his pet python. You can have your palm read and you can stumble upon shops and start to figure out how you can open a similar business at home. Be prepared to spend hours into the night here, just taking it in.

With all that Rome has to offer and all of its hustle and bustle, there is a respite, a place to go that is easy and quiet and will let you store up your energy for the next round. For me, it's a walk or a run or a cycle on a two- or four-man *bici* in the Garden of the Villa Borghese. This is the park that will calm the mental exhaustion of trying to absorb all that Rome has to offer. Stop at one of the local food wagons and sit on a park bench to watch the locals enjoy their downtime.

So, there it is, one roam in Rome. There is so much more to learn, so many more cobblestone streets to explore, and so much more food to taste. Whenever I leave Rome, I feel like I need to start planning my return. (Note to self: maybe six months isn't enough. A Year in Rome? Why not become an expert? Why not perfect the roam? Why not become a Roman?) I think about it constantly.

Riga, Latvia

BALTIC INSPIRATION

The time had come for me to explore my Lithuanian roots. Although both of my mother's parents had been born in the United States, their parents came from Eastern Europe, and as with many such stories there was some confusion about whether it was Poland or Russia or Lithuania. But one thing we knew for sure was that my grandfather's parents were from Lithuania. And as the story goes, they apparently moved back there after making their fortune in America.

Yet this was just family lore. No one had any idea where and how they returned, nor did anyone ever have any contact with them afterwards. It all seemed a bit mysterious, but then again many families have murky stories in their background.

My father's parents came to America via Ireland and England and met in New York City as young adults. That side of the family had an equally murky story, as my father's father supposedly escaped through the Irish Underground after the Easter Rising. It sounded like a romantic idea, but there was no real proof. And that was the whole point. Destroy the proof—America was a new beginning.

While I'd been to the birthplace of my Irish grandfather and had seen the building that my grandmother lived in during her years in London, I'd never been to Lithuania. The time had come, and with Estonia and Latvia being right there, it seemed like the perfect three-country sweep to see what was going on in that part of the world.

A lot had happened since these three countries declared independence in 1990 and 1991. They'd joined the United Nations and the European Union, they'd competed in the Olympics as independent nations and they'd all created a bit of a go-go economy with their emergence.

Getting to the Baltics is easy, with flights departing from many major European cities. We flew from New York to Stockholm and hopped a Baltic Air flight to Vilnius, the capital of Lithuania. From there we would drive around the country, working our way to Riga, the capital of Latvia, where we'd hop another flight to Tallinn, the capital of Estonia that sits on the Gulf of Finland.

Vilnius has been called the new Prague and the hidden jewel of Eastern Europe, but this is a city that's been around since the early fourteenth century. Established by the Lithuanian Grand Duke Gediminas, the dominant hill over the city is still named after him. By the sixteenth century, Vilnius was one of the biggest cities in Eastern Europe with thriving artisan guilds and trading centers. The university was established in 1579 and the city thrived for centuries. It wasn't until the twentieth century that Vilnius and all of Lithuania fell on tough times, with occupation from both the Germans and the Soviets. Today that's part of the history of Vilnius, which is once again a dynamic city with a youth culture that creates the energy of a modern town, respectful of its past, but always looking forward.

On my first day in the city, what struck me the most was the look of the people. On the streets I saw men and women who looked like they belonged to my family. Fair-haired, light-skinned, and with blue eyes. There was a woman who could have been my grandmother's sister and a man who could have been my uncle David. The city had a homogeneous look to it, unlike other European cities that have experienced waves of immigration from all parts of the world. In fact, most of the Baltics still seemed untouched by immigration. Throughout our nearly two weeks in the region, we were hard-pressed to find anyone who wasn't blond and blue-eyed. For someone like me, who lives in the culturally diverse city of New York, it was noticeably different.

A few days allows one to take in this lovely city, especially the Old Town that was built in the fifteenth and sixteenth centuries and has retained the feeling of an old city, complete with narrow streets and unique architecture. The Old Town was also home to one of the most important Jewish communities in Europe. Here you can see the vestiges of what was called the Jerusalem of Lithuania. Like many Jewish communities, Vilnius was devastated during the Holocaust and there are important remembrances in the Old Town.

If you get to visit Vilnius, go to the top of Gediminas Hill for a view of the city, head to Cathedral Square, spend some time at the National Museum of Lithuania, and go to the university area to visit the local bookstores, galleries, and cafes. Then head to Trakai, the old Lithuanian capital, which has two lakeside castles. Spending the afternoon there and at Trakai National Park is a great way to mingle with the locals and watch daily life.

Throughout Lithuania, you'll experience an upbeat sense of what tomorrow might bring. A drive across the country is easy and friendly, and our goal was to head west, ultimately to a place that I'd always heard about called Klaipeda. The third largest city in Lithuania, this town has been controlled by the Teutonic Knights, the Prussians, the Germans, and the Soviets. And while it boasts architecture as far back as the thirteenth century, the real draw to this part of the world is the UNESCO site of the Curonian Spit.

Here, where you'd least expect it, is a long sand dune that runs sixty-one miles (ninety-eight kilometers) north to south with peaks from thirty to sixty feet (nine to eighteen meters) high. Shared by Lithuania and the city of Kaliningrad, which is part of Russia, its natural beauty is conducive to long walks or climbs for views as far as the eye can see. Along the Spit are small towns like Nida that have attracted artists and writers from the German expressionist painters to Thomas Mann, who lived and worked here for several summers. With its quiet, lovely atmosphere and long, sandy beaches, it's easy to see how this part of the world could be an inspiration for artists of all types.

While the main purpose of my visiting Lithuania was to try and get in touch with my ancestral roots, it's almost impossible to trace a family history here. Especially if your family left during the nineteenth century. There's been so much turmoil in the political and social system in this part of the world since then that records and communities have been lost and broken apart. As I walked the streets of Vilnius and Kaunas (where my people supposedly came from), I could only imagine what life was like here and how daunting it must have been to travel across Europe to get on a boat to a place that was foreign and faraway. So many of us have this story to tell, intrepid tales of how our forefathers came to America to find a new life and a new future for their family. Maybe they didn't have that life, but they paved the way for it. Three generations later, I appreciate that I was born an American with choices, opportunities, and hope. While *as nekalbu lietuviskai* (meaning I don't speak Lithuanian), I can always say *aciu* (thank you) to the Wenslovas family for making the trip across the ocean. They made it possible for our family to have the life that we enjoy.

From Klaipeda, we opted to drive north to Riga, the dynamic capital of Latvia. With all due respect to my Lithuanian brethren, Riga is happening in a way that's different than any other Baltic capital, with more of a cosmopolitan energy in the air. The old quarter, called Vecriga, is a UNESCO World Heritage site, with large gracious parks and a world-renowned Art Nouveau neighborhood.

The city, to be named the European Capital of Culture in 2014, boasts a great National Opera, National Theatre, and more than a dozen museums. This is where it's said that the very first Christmas tree was displayed in the Town Hall Square over five hundred years ago. Throughout the city there are noteworthy monuments and architecture to view including Riga Castle, the famous Laima Clock, Freedom Monument, The Cat House, and the series of guild halls. Elizabetes and Strelnieku Streets is the home of the famous Art Nouveau section, a must-see on any visitor's itinerary.

The Latvians are fun-loving and helpful people, and this all came to life for us when we had a bit of a travel mishap at the Riga airport. Arriving for our flight to Tallinn, we learned that there actually wasn't a flight. We discovered a scheduling mishap that would've had us spending another twenty-four hours in Riga. And while we might have enjoyed it, we only had two days left for our trip and we wanted to see a bit of Estonia.

After exploring our options, we learned that we could hire a taxi to drive us to Tallinn, four to five hours away. After a negotiation with a driver (for $400, including his trip home), we headed north and ultimately arrived at the famous Three Sisters Hotel. There was only one problem: one of our bags was missing. More specifically, a camera bag with lots of equipment. In the rush at the Riga airport, one of my fellow travelers accidentally left it sitting there.

After hearing the story, the Three Sisters concierge had the idea to call the airport in Riga and, sure enough, the bag had been found and turned in to the lost and found department. When we asked how we might get the bag back, the concierge said, "No problem, we'll send one of our porters down to Riga to get it and bring it to the hotel." Now that's what I call brilliant concierge service. And from that moment on, it set the standard for what we now expect from any first rate hotel. It doesn't get better than that. Sure enough, the bag arrived safe and sound, ready for a day of photographing this city that was rebuilt after WWII, complete with a beautifully restored Old Town.

In Tallinn, we climbed Toompea to see the castle and to get a view of
the city below, but the main attraction is strolling through Riga's Old Town
called Vanalinn. There are two parts, the Upper Town and the Lower Town.
Your best bet is to roam the streets, poking your head into courtyards and
alleyways. Town Hall Square, a marketplace since the eleventh century, will
give you a great sense of history and modern Estonian life, along with its
side streets that are filled with churches, shops, and museums, some that
have been around since the thirteenth century.

Throughout all of the Baltic states, there was a sense of rebirth. But there
was also a sense of resiliency of spirit that was inspirational. Prior to the
breakup of the Soviet Union and the independence of these three countries,
they all went through a lot of hardship and misery. It's a testament to the human spirit that we can overcome our past to reinvent our future. In talking
to people in the Baltics, I sensed this with the older people, many of whom
had experienced the difficult times, as well as with the youth who had big
expectations for their own futures.

Time and time again, world cultures show us this lesson. Cambodia is
being reborn, as is Uganda after the atrocities of Idi Amin. Someday, Libya
will become more of a tourist destination, as will Afghanistan. And if you
go there, you'll see the cycle of life that I saw in the Baltics. It only under-
scores that a free people can create miracles for themselves, their families,
and their country. All of us need to go to these places, not only to support
the efforts, but to bring needed foreign currency into the market to make it
stronger. Unlike my Lithuanian forefathers, and perhaps yours, who didn't
have the option of staying for a better future, these people do. So make a list.
Go to places that are struggling to re-emerge. They need you.

My friend Peter Godwin is doing his part with regards to Zimbabwe.
He is the preeminent Western writer relating how Mugabe is destroying
his own country. Godwin keeps the real issues in the forefront for world
leaders and government to see. Someday, Mugabe will fall and those of us
who have seen the beauty of Zimbabwe will be able to return there to help
that nation restore itself. I hope that I can be there with my friend Peter,
who will continue to lead the charge. Zimbabwe will regain itself. And the
Zimbabweans, like the people from the Baltics, will show us how people
working together can create a new destiny.

Rome, Italy

STRANDED, PART 2

When I last left you, I had just arrived in Milan and was getting ready for two days of business there with the usual suspects (Armani, Prada, Dolce & Gabbana, etc.).

Early Monday morning I started with breakfast at the Four Seasons and it was one of those (unusual) sunny days in Milan. And for some reason, the cappuccino was particularly good. As we worked through the day, our Italian office was searching for flights home to New York for Wednesday or Thursday, since planes were flying out of Rome (and not Milan). About midway through the day, we learned that you couldn't even make a reservation until the following Sunday, and that was a maybe. In fact, Alitalia wasn't even taking reservations! How do you say *merde* in Italian?

So I suggested flying Rome-Athens-New York, or Rome-Istanbul-New York. But then I had to put my foot down and say no…that is *pazzo* (crazy in Italian)!

By my fourth appointment of the day, it was becoming very clear that it would be at least a week before I could leave. Now, spending an extra week in Italy—I could deal with that. Visions of Ravello, Tuscany, and walking the streets of Rome eating gelato filled my head! *La Dolce Vita,* baby! Why not?

Meanwhile, back in London, at least eight other execs from my company were stranded, including our CEO, and they were trying to figure out how to get home. Note: There were forty thousand Americans stranded in Europe during the volcano crisis. Late that day, I learned that our CEO had secured a private charter from Barcelona that would leave around 4:00 p.m. on Tuesday. So it was executive decision time for me. By 6:00 p.m., I was in a car en route to Barcelona (621 miles [1,000 kilometers], eight hours). *Ciao* Armani. *Arrivederci* Prada. I had a plane to catch.

There is something romantic about being driven past Monte Carlo, Nice, and St. Tropez, and then Marseille and Perpignan as the driver went 100 miles (161 kilometers) per hour on the highway. It was pitch black by 7:30

or so, but the road signs looked very inviting, especially the one that was for Arles and ultimately, Provence. Oh, well. I settled in and read my book, *The Island in the Center of the World,* all about the Dutch settling Manhattan and the ultimate takeover by the English. We arrived at Las Ramblas at 2:00 a.m. and, Spain being Spain, there were many people out. I checked into the Meridien and ran into several other Americans who had traveled from Copenhagen, Prague, and Berlin, attempting to go south and fly out. One guy from Chicago was going Barcelona-Madrid-Caracas-Miami-Chicago! *Estoy cansado, pensaré en el día*

Tuesday morning began as another beautiful day, and I managed to take an hour-long walk through this beautiful Spanish city, where I spent a long weekend a few years ago. Since I had been taking Spanish lessons, I was *hablando espanol!* Well, trying to *con las chicas y los chicos.*

My colleagues had left London on Monday by van, and twenty-six hours later we all met at the Barcelona Airport and, well, there was fog rolling in—unrelated to the volcano I might add!

We fly? *Si,* we fly! Onto the plane and onto the runway, and three hours later we touched down in the Azores to refuel.

Now, here's what you need to know about the Azores: For those of you who count countries, it counts. (Go to travelerscenturyclub.org for the full list.) So I realized that I would pick up a country count, getting me to 120!

The other thing you need to know about the Azores is that they normally get five to ten flights landing each day, and on Tuesday they would get seventy. This was the underground private jet service taking the southern route to and from the United States. I'm the first to admit that I was very lucky to be in Europe on business and for all of this to fall into place. But then again, what happened to my week in Italy? I could have been *parlando Italiano,* and maybe even have changed my name to Guido!

The small Embraer jet is fast and sleek, and we touched down at Teterboro, New Jersey, six hours later. I entered my apartment twenty-six hours after leaving Milan, and fifteen minutes before a possible doorman strike in New York.

Oh yeah, and one more thing: A pilot at Teterboro said that there was a report that the other big volcano in Iceland may erupt. Who knows? I was supposed to head back to Europe in a couple of weeks, a trip that I did make. Where was I heading? To Iceland. Hey, you can't make this stuff up.

TIPS

VALERIE CHAPOULAUD

President, Louis Vuitton, USA

- Always start your day early.

- Travel by yourself or with very good friends.

- Book early so that you have your trip well planned with time to visit the key places that interest you.

- Have a specific objective for your destination. Do you want to ski, scuba dive, or take in cultural activities?

- Try to pick a place to visit where you have friends, relatives, or friends of friends so you can get an inside view.

Author at the top of Mt. Kilimanjaro

REACHING NEW HEIGHTS IN AFRICA

Africa. It seemed like the perfect place to spend my fortieth birthday. It also seemed like the perfect springboard to my grand pronouncement that my forties were going to be my adventure years! I'd spent my thirties building my publishing career, and my travels up to that point had been pretty mainstream: Europe, Mexico, Hawaii. I needed to start spreading my wings, and the adventure years would be launched on the continent of Africa.

I'm happy to report that in fact my forties did become my adventure years, as I discovered the wonders of places like Bhutan and Myanmar, Madagascar and the Arctic Circle. But in my typical Type A behavior, I had to not only launch my African adventure, but I needed to do it with a big statement; climbing Mt. Kilimanjaro was the goal, followed by a trip into the Ngorongoro Crater and the Serengeti.

I've now traveled to a dozen countries on the African continent: Morocco, Tunisia, and Egypt in the North; Namibia, South Africa, Botswana, Zambia, Zimbabwe, and Mozambique in the south are now among my travel trophies. In our family, we play a game called "Geography." All of the kids get a tablet and pen and have three minutes to list as many countries as they can on the continent of Africa or Asia. Sometimes the game is to name mountain ranges of the world or U.S. capitals. It is "Geography Africa" that is always the most fun, as there are so many countries there. And it always makes me realize that this is the continent that I need to focus on in the future.

Who wouldn't want to go to Mali, taking the boat up to Timbuktu? Or to Rwanda to see the gorillas? Or to Libya now that it is liberated from Qaddafi? Then there's Ethiopia and Ghana and Zanzibar.

It's hard to explain a first impression of Africa, especially east or South Africa. On that first trip, we flew to Nairobi to travel overland to Arusha, home base for the climb up Kilimanjaro. How do you explain passing giraffes along the roadside, or seeing brightly clad Masai tribesmen trotting in a group off in the distance? And how do you describe the first glance at the African light that has mesmerized people for centuries? Or the first glimpse of Kilimanjaro in the Tanzanian distance?

Mt. Kilimanjaro (19,340 feet [5,895 meters]) is one of the Seven Summits. It's the highest peak in Africa and the tallest freestanding mountain in the world. It has been climbed by people from all over the world and was memorialized in the Ernest Hemingway story "The Snows of Kilimanjaro," first published in *Esquire* magazine in 1938. This majestic mountain sits entirely in Tanzania just south of the equator. It has three volcanic cones at the top—Mawenzi, Shira, and Kibo—and it is daunting.

This was the first major climb for our group of seven people, so we opted for the easier route, called Marangu. As in a first marathon or a first triathlon, the goal was to finish. In this case that meant to stand at Uhuru Peak, the highest point on the continent. We had all prepared ourselves with aerobic training and taken Diamox, a pill that would help in high altitude. We had all the right gear, but more importantly we had the right attitude, because we all knew that altitude sickness could happen even to the fittest people. It can hit you at any time and can cause an aorta or brain edema. And if that begins to happen, the first thing that you have to do is head down the mountain, as this is a life-threatening situation.

For extra insurance, we decided on the six-day climb, which gave us a day of acclimatizing to the rising altitudes. We were excited and anxious all at the same time. A great adventure was in front of us, and we made a pact to stick together and get to Uhuru as a group.

Our first day was an easy six-hour hike into the rainforest. We wore shorts and carried daypacks, while our guides took our sleeping bags and larger packs ahead of us. Every group climbing the mountain is assigned a guide and a group of Sherpas to help them get to the top. And all of this is registered with the local government before you begin the hike and then re-registered when you are down from the mountain. Our guide was a large Tanzanian man wearing a New York Giants hat that he'd scored from a previous climber. His English was perfect and he had climbed the mountain at least fifty times. Along with him was a quieter guide, a bit older and more serious, whom we came to realize was the real experienced one. The friendlier one was more of a social director, keeping us happy with stories and songs, while the other made sure that we were all okay.

Day Two was another six-hour hike out of the rainforest into a big open moorland, and here we got our first true sight for how far and high we had to go. We hiked to Maundi Crater and ultimately to Horombo Hut, where we'd spend two nights. Simple A-frame huts dotted the trail, each one housing several climbers, and it was here that we began to feel how cold it would become, especially at night. And it was here that we realized that water for bathing would be limited, the end result being that for the six days away we barely washed. Our Sherpas would give two of us a basin of hot water to share each morning and each of us had to decide what body part or parts would be washed that day. Needless to say, there'd be no shaving. As for drinking water, we carried our own bottles, refilling them in the water creeks along the way. Iodine pills were added to the bottles to purify the water, so we never had any problems with drinking it. The food was pretty basic: Breakfast was eggs, bread, and fruit with coffee or tea, while the main meals were stews or packaged casseroles. We'd packed our own snacks, nuts for protein, candy bars for energy, and fruit lozenges to help in the dusty air.

Day Three was for acclimatizing. We took day hikes, played card games, and just got accustomed to the growing altitude. It was here that we began to feel the anticipation of getting to the top.

On Day Four, as we left Horombo, we began a long seven-hour hike up through steep desert-like terrain. As we got higher, the wind began to pick up and we layered on clothes for more warmth and to protect us from the elements. Along this route we began to meet up with hikers coming down from the summit. They looked dirty and exhausted, and some of them walked in a trancelike state. Here we were, all bright-eyed and full of energy and these folks were like zombies. "What happened up there?" I wondered. Is it really that bad? No one could say—they just said we would have our own experience. Odd.

Arriving at Kibo hut is an important moment on the climb, as it's the last stop before the final ascent. Up to that point we'd all done well. The hikes weren't that strenuous, although each day we moved for five to seven hours. But at Kibo it was cold, and this was the night that lights-out was around 7:00 p.m. After an early dinner, the guides got us ready. We had to sort out our gear and make sure that we had enough layers, headlamps, and ski poles, and more importantly, that no one was feeling the affects of the altitude. All of this was in preparation of a sixteen-hour hike that would begin at midnight and go on until the next afternoon—this was the key part of the climb.

At around 11:00 p.m., we were roused from our short four-hour sleep to begin the ascent. I remember putting on the layers and layers of clothes, anticipating what it would be like to arrive at Gilman's Point when the sun would begin to rise over the continent. In single file we began crisscrossing the mountain through shale and light snow. We were lucky in that there wasn't much snow on our hike—sometimes it can be above your ankles or a foot deep, but not much snow had fallen in the weeks before our trip.

But while we didn't have snow, we did have howling cold winds, and with only our headlamps it was hard to see beyond our own few steps. About three hours into the hike, a person in our group began to get sick. Then another one did. Headache, vomiting. "Not good," I thought as we all stopped to have our main guide check on them. Was it an edema? I realized that I had a slight headache too, but nothing that I couldn't deal with.

We'd said that we'd travel as a group to the top of Kilimanjaro. All for one and one for all. But this was a moment of truth. If one or two of our group couldn't make it, what would we do? Of course we would honor our code, but I secretly hoped that should they fall back, they'd give us a pass to go on without them.

At 3:00 a.m. our two friends were deciding whether or not to continue on to the peak. Finally, they decided. We'd all continue on together. For the next several hours we hiked up the mountain, battling the wind and the cold, checking on our friends and occasionally glancing at our watches to check on our progress.

Around seven hours after the start of our hike we arrived at Gilman's Point, and it's here that you can claim that you've climbed the mountain. And it's here that you begin to see the sun rise above the African continent, and for the first time, you can see the world around you. The rush of adrenaline was what we needed to spark our second wind and make us continue on to Uhuru, the highest peak on the mountain.

Off we went on a magnificent hike along the crater of the mountain with a high wall of ice to our left. And what glory we felt when all seven of us stood on Uhuru Peak with the spectacular African vistas before us. It was a photo moment for sure, as well as the chance to sign the book that's kept in a wooden box at the top to memorialize our visit.

Once you get to the top of Kilimanjaro, it's a fast turnaround and you begin the decent with a rest stop at Kibo and then ultimately a night stop at Horombo. As we hiked down, we realized that we'd become the dirty, tired, and zombie-like people that we'd seen on the way up. Bright-eyed hikers

looked at us on our way down, and like sage advisors, we gave them tips on **101**
how to best conquer the mountain.

Climbing Kilimanjaro was a great way to celebrate my own special occasion and our group still talks about it years later. It has led to other hiking trips in Patagonia, the Himalayas, and Australia, opening up a whole new chapter of adventure in my life. The climb up Kilimanjaro consumed our first week in Africa, and it was followed by a week on safari. We'd selected Hemingway country: Lake Manyara, Serengeti, Ngorongoro Crater. Here we would see all of the Big Five in their natural habitat. For the uninitiated, these are the lion, the leopard, the buffalo, the rhino, and the elephant. If you've been on a safari, you'll remember that first sight of a pride of lions or a herd of zebras. The rush that you feel is combined with disbelief at what you're looking at. To see elephants and rhinos in their natural habitat is one of the great joys in life. And to watch a kill in action is one of the more sobering moments, seeing nature unfold in its most basic form—feeding.

This trip would be life changing for me. Discovering a place like Africa is humbling. You don't realize what you don't know until you actually experience it. And that is something that I learn time and time again. New places just peel another layer back and we come to appreciate how much there is to discover in the world.

Going on safari is a very disciplined experience. Generally, it's two drives per day: one in the early morning, when the animals are out and about, followed by a return to the lodge for a midday rest, and then another late afternoon drive. What many people don't notice are the rifles carried in the enclosed Land Rovers, there just in case something goes awry.

On one drive, our van came between a mother elephant and her baby. Not a good situation and one that made our guide move quickly to get us out of right away. Safari guides are well experienced in the nuances of wildlife behavior and filled with knowledge that will put it all in perspective for you. And there is no better place for a first safari than Tanzania.

During our week in Tanzania we discovered the magnificence of being out in the bush. A trip into the Ngorogoro Crater, considered Africa's Eden or the Eighth Wonder of the World, was our first stop. Descending down into the crater, through rain forests and vegetation, we arrived at the base where thousands of animals from zebras to lions roamed. When we stopped our van, a pride of lions wandered over to catch some of the shade we created. At this moment we were relieved to be in a closed Land Rover, as one of the lions decided to jump onto the car's hood! Starting the engine up again combined with a toot of the horn gave him his cue, and he jumped off and scampered away.

Not far from the Crater is the famous Olduvai Gorge, where the oldest remains of human skeletons have been discovered—over 1.8 million years old. We spent the week in tented camps and drove from the Crater past Lake Manyara with its spectacular bird life into the Serengeti.

My multiple trips to Africa have afforded me the opportunity to take many safaris, but I have to put the Serengeti at the top of the list. This famous World Heritage site is the home of hundreds of thousands of zebras, Thomson's gazelles, buffalos, eland, wildebeest, elephants, and more. Crisscrossing the open plains will give you the fullest experience that you'll ever want on a trip to Africa. You'll see the red and orange sky as dusk settles in. Just sitting there and taking it all in is a moment that you'll never forget.

There are many ways to experience a safari in Africa. There are high luxury camps complete with cable television and hot tubs. There are ensuite tents with built-in bathrooms, or there are more basic tented safaris, which have shower stalls and bathrooms a few feet away. No matter what you choose, you cannot go wrong. I've done safaris in South Africa and Botswana and Namibia, and each one was a different experience. But for your first, I suggest a tented camp. It's authentic and will get you as close to nature as possible. You'll sit around a campfire and eat as a group—the storytelling can't be beat.

Many outfitters specialize in Africa trips and word of mouth is the best way to find one. I've used Abercrombie and Kent, Wilderness Experiences, and Mountain Travel Sobek. What's great about safaris today is that they can be completely customized to your interests and include such things as ballooning and gourmet food. And they can fit any budget. Whatever you decide, be prepared for unexpected moments that will surprise and delight you. We had one of those moments in Chobe National Park in Botswana. As we floated down the river, we came upon the amazing sight of hundreds of elephants charging down a hill into the river. Each elephant would attach its trunk to the tail of the elephant in front of him, and within minutes an orderly line of swimming elephants appeared before us! These special moments make the magic of safari.

Africa has many different dimensions beyond the bush. A visit to the city
of Cape Town will show you modern Africa at work. Its cosmopolitan flair
and exciting youth culture put energy in the air. The beaches, restaurants,
and nightlife rival any major capital in the world, and day trips to the tip
of the continent or into the wine-growing region of Stellenbosch will only
add to what could be an easy five-day trip to this sparkling city at the base
of Table Mountain.

The coastal areas of Africa have some of the most beautiful beaches in
the world. On one trip, we spent five days on the Bazaruto Archipelago
off the coast of Mozambique. Crystal white beaches, dunes, and clear blue
water—perfect for a getaway vacation.

Yes, the continent of Africa has many problems, from the AIDS crisis to
famine in parts of Somalia. It's a huge, overwhelming continent with many
stories to tell. A trip there can focus on adventure, preservation of endangered species, or humanitarian efforts. Perhaps nowhere else in world will
you see the human plight in its fiercest dimensions. The plight of hunger
and disease and the circumstances of man versus animal. It's important for
all of us to go there. Not just to see what issues the world faces, but to con-
tribute in our own individual way.

During a visit to a village in Mozambique, we saw that while there was a
school for the children, the children had no clothes except for worn, tattered
fabrics. Upon our return to the States, we held a clothing drive and shipped
three big boxes to the village. This was our way to give something back for
our visit to their continent.

Bringing to Africa foreign currency and open eyes will help this continent move forward in its own growth and development. Bringing home
from Africa the stories, not only of the glories of the African plains but
the need of the people, may stimulate your own small actions, or help to
stimulate others.

Africa is the place where you can see mankind in a different way. It is
also the place that makes you realize that we all have a responsibility to
help. You'll go there and enjoy a unique and special place in the world. And
hopefully your visit will make you want to come home and do good. Once
you've been to Africa, it will never be far from your mind and your heart.

Sossusvlei, Namibia

I'LL ALWAYS HAVE NAMIBIA

Not that I needed an excuse to plan an adventure, but it seemed appropriate to usher in the new millennium at some exotic location, and the invitation to a New Year's Eve party in Cape Town seemed perfect. While I'd been to the stunning city of Cape Town before, it gave me a reason to think about finally planning the trip to Namibia that had always been in the back of my mind. The Skeleton Coast. The Namib Desert. Swakopmund. It all sounded so exotic, especially when I learned that we'd have to charter a Cessna 210 to get us around this vast country. And while we'd need to hire a local pilot, I'd get to use my flying skills on the African continent. I was in, as were a few friends who also signed up for the trip. We'd spend a week in Namibia before heading off to a quick visit to Victoria Falls, then on to Cape Town to ring in the New Year.

Just exactly where is Namibia? Most of my family and friends had no real idea. One of the last African nations to shed its colonial status, Namibia became independent in 1990 and has grown into a democratic and safe nation. Formerly called Southwest Africa and governed by South Africa, it is situated just northwest of South Africa, bordered by Angola, Botswana, Zambia, and a 994-mile (1,600-kilometer) Atlantic coastline. Though four times the size of the U.K., Namibia has only 1.6 million residents, leaving hundreds of miles of unspoiled land. And for a pilot, hundreds of miles of open skies.

A bit of advice for those of you who travel on small airplanes: Make sure your traveling companions are okay with six-passenger planes. One of our four arrived at the local airfield to announce that he was afraid of small airplanes. A little late for that, since we were about to embark on six or seven flight segments within the next week. (He ended up just fine). Another friend threw up on the very first leg, requiring that we hose him down, along with the plane, once we landed. Nothing that a little Dramamine couldn't help for the next segments.

It all starts in Windhoek, the capital city, which is a two-hour flight from Johannesburg. The city sits smack in the middle of the country. Its architecture, food, and customs still resonate with the influence of its 1890s German settlers; although English is the official language, one can hear German spoken by many locals in shops and restaurants. Our plan is to fly to four distinct regions of the country: the Namib desert, one of the oldest in the world; along the Skeleton Coast; Damaraland; and the famous Etosha Pan.

Seventy minutes from Windhoek, we begin our bumpy descent into a vast 11,000-acre scrubby flat plain. The desertscape below is sprinkled with shepherd bushes and the famous quiver tree, a spiky and almost prehistoric-looking tree indigenous to Namibia. In the distance, we spot a short airstrip with a lone Land Rover parked alongside it. After deplaning, we're driven a few miles to the Sossusvlei Wilderness Camp, with nine huts built 2,500 feet (762 meters) above the desert, resting in a granite formation (complete with individual plunge pools).

From the campsite we drive to the Sesriem and Sossusvlei, areas in the Namib-Naukluft National Park. During our two days here we make forays in search of oryx, springbok, and the Tok Tokkie beetle, and then close each day with a gin and tonic in hand, watching the brilliant African sun descend into the neighboring foothills. The park, massive even by African standards, covers more than 19,216 square miles (49,769 square kilometers) and is one of the continent's largest. Running along the Atlantic Coast, it offers some of the most haunting and sensuous scenery anywhere.

At the main jump-off point for Sesriem there are curving and swerving dunes some 1,148 feet (350 meters) high. We set off to climb "Big Daddy," a dune that surrounds Deadvlei, an old saltpan with dead acacia trees, some more than five hundred years old. At first the climb looked like a fifteen-minute scamper. But we soon learned what an intense workout it is as we sank at least eight inches with each step. An hour later we were at the top, triumphant and exhausted, but rewarded with a view that has to be one of my top ten ever. For miles and miles before us we saw dunes and hundreds of the dead acacia. This was like a place that none of us had ever seen in our lives.

The next day we flew north toward the Skeleton Coast, named for the treacherous seas that have created more than a few shipwrecks over the centuries. The coastline's ancient hulls resemble steel corpses in the desert sand. Descending to get a better look, we came across abandoned diamond camps and saltworks. Wild flamingos glided below us, and every minute or so we flew over seal colonies on the rocks along the coast. Ultimately, we landed in Swakopmund, a resort town on the coast that the actress Charlize

Theron once told me was a place that she went to as a child. On the beach
was a tented picnic set up for us, complete with lobster and champagne. This
was a different Africa than any of us knew.

As we moved farther north toward Damaraland, we flew over Brandberg,
the highest mountain in Namibia. Our destination here was D-Camp, a
safari camp made up of nine step-in tents with en suite bathrooms that had
stone floors! Here is where we'll search of the famous desert elephants. Rising early, we take to the sands, past the poisonous milk bushes that dot the
landscape. Our local guide takes us on an elephant-tracking journey, and
within the first hour we find our first desert elephant. D-Camp is a beautiful
spot to stay for a couple of days, hiking in the neighboring hills or searching
for Welwitschia, a species of plant found only in Namibia that lives for more
than a thousand years but produces just two leaves.

Leaving this interesting part of the country, at 1,000 feet (305 meters) or
so we look down to see a herd of ten elephants running along the dunes, and
it's yet another reminder of what a special place we have discovered.

Etosha, our next stop, offers the spectacular scenery and animals you'd
find in most African parks, but without the usual crowds. We encounter
giraffe, zebra, cheetah, lion, and rhino, along with black-faced impala and
the Damara dik-dik. This was an Africa that was more familiar to us, but
Namibian style. What we learned as we moved around this still undiscovered country is that there is a lot to see. The Fish River Canyon, which is
second in size only to the Grand Canyon; the Waterberg Plateau Park area,
with its dinosaur footprints; and Bushmanland, a conservancy where small
groups can take hunting trips into the bush are just a few possibilities.

Once in Cape Town, we learned from many of our South African friends
that even they hadn't been to Namibia yet, although they were familiar with
London and Sydney. Of my many trips to Africa, Namibia always stands out
as special. It is a place that's hauntingly beautiful. At times, when I'm feeling
stressed or overwhelmed, I simply close my eyes and imagine flying along
the Skeleton Coast, over the dunes and the flamingos, along the coastline
where the sand meets the water. It's a form of mediation for me. And when I
open my eyes, I'm ready to continue. It's those moments of a travel memory
that can enrich your life and make you feel whole again. For me, I know that
I'll always have Namibia.

Burmese Dusk

YOU CAN TRAVEL OR STAY AT HOME

People often lament that they can't travel because their spouse or partner doesn't like to travel. Or that they have no one to travel with to their dream destination. I have to admit that I have very little patience for these complaints because, as your grandmother may have said, "Where there's a will there's a way!" So if you suffer from this malady, stand up, shake it off, and start planning. Leave that cranky husband at home, or that live-in girlfriend who would rather spend her time near her family. Every couple knows about negotiation. Let the games begin!

It's true that some people enjoy traveling alone, and I don't mind it for short trips. But for the big life experiences, I want my family and/or friends to join me. My sister Peg and I are seeing the world together as we run seven marathons on seven continents. My family has congregated in New York City, Long Island, and Santa Fe, as well as in Mexico to share time together.

But it's the establishment of a travel club that has given me the richest experiences, and finding the right people to travel with can make all the difference. How do you find the right mix of people? Well, some of it is trial and error. Some of your best friends are disasters when it comes to travel, while mere acquaintances can surprisingly be the best travel companions. I've found that my high-maintenance friends are actually some of the best people in the travel club, while those that I'd think would go with the flow are the biggest travel pains. Experiencing a trip together is the best way to decide who will get invited back versus who will be politely omitted from future trips.

I've been traveling with the same group for almost twenty years, so at this point we have it down to a science. I instinctively know who the right candidates are for a rental in a Tuscan villa versus those who I know can rough it on a mountaintop in Bhutan. I have my luxury travel group and my adventure travel group. Mixing in people who love to cook is perfect for a week in Umbria, while mixing in great storytellers is perfect for wilderness trips. Our total group is about fifteen people or so, although on any given trip we number six or seven. We've endured break-ups, divorces, weddings, and babies; yet one thing we know for sure: We are good travel partners!

I couldn't have asked for a better group than those who traveled to Argentina for the wine harvest. Tom, Andy, Martha, Haideh, Jack, Amy, and Mary were the perfect group. We spent a day in the vineyards, attending winemaking camp, horseback riding, hiking in the Andes and enjoying great Argentine food and wine in Mendoza. For ten days, we were a harmonious group, with only a couple of minor clashes, all to be expected when you put a bunch of Type A personalities together.

My friends Penny and Jay are part of the luxury group. They are happiest in Cabo San Lucas or Los Angeles and would never plan to join us in the small village of Sayulita on Mexico's West Coast. On the other hand, there are friends who wouldn't be caught dead at a five-star luxury resort.

For the house in Italy, you'd want Tom, Andy, Mary, and the other Tom. With that combination you get the magic of great sous chefs, cooks, and clean up crew. The cooks are inventive, using local foods and produce to create amazing meals.

Many of my group trips have been adventure trips, and those can be a bit challenging. Imagine spending two weeks with a group that is hiking in Nepal, followed by camping and whitewater rafting down the Trisuli River, and ending up in Chitwan National Park. This kind of trip requires a certain laissez-faire attitude because anything can go wrong while you're in this part of the world. Our group did pretty well, until one of the people was interested in buying marijuana from the local guide. I felt that this was reckless and that it endangered the welfare of the group. That person has not been invited back on any of our trips since.

There is a hardcore group of us who like high adventure, which has included hiking trips in Patagonia, to the top of Mt. Kosciusko in Australia, and up Ben Nevis in Scotland. We've been on multiple safaris, into the wilds of Madagascar, on the archipelago off of Mozambique, and in the waters off Antarctica. These are my true people. Tom will go with the flow anywhere, as will Frank and Cap. Never a complaint, always a high degree of curiosity, and always an appreciation that we are experiencing things that the average person doesn't get to experience in a whole lifetime.

A walk at dawn to look for lemurs with our local guide is something that Frank and I will always remember. Tom and I will always remember the walk into the local village in Mozambique, which led us to go home and establish a clothing drive to send clothes and shoes to the children of the village. Some of my friends don't go all the way. It's true that I ended up hiking to the top of Ben Nevis on my own, but I respected that my group just didn't want to go for the summit in the lousy weather that we encountered. And when I could only rustle up one other in the group to sleep in the open air on the Antarctic ice, I also appreciated that we all have to make our own decisions. Dan and I took the zodiac out to the ice with a few other intrepid travelers from our Russian icebreaker. We dug a hole in the ice, lined it with tarp and our subzero sleeping bags, and nestled in under the open stars, while a local sea lion slept only a few feet away. What an adventure!

Planning our trips is always one of the most fun parts of the group coming together. We try to plan a year in advance so that people can opt in, clear calendars, and figure out if this particular trip is right for them. And as life goes, some people can't be on the same trip due to a variety of circumstances. So like any family, we navigate around those nuances. One person might get the Christmas trip, while the other gets the summer trip. Or vice versa. Somehow it all works out and everyone is happy. Since keeping the group together is my charge, I like to ask everyone for input on the future trips, and we do have a running list of destinations. But life or events can get in the way. We had to abandon a trip to Syria, Lebanon, and Jordan due to the unrest there, opting instead on Thailand and Laos. We have to decide if we want a grand adventure like a trip to Rajasthan, India or a simple trip to Santa Fe for a Southwestern adventure. But whatever we do, we generally plan a year in advance, and the majority of the time we all make the trip happen.

Sometimes there are offshoots of our group who take other trips, and while I'm invited, there are certain destinations that just don't appeal to me. I'm not big on the Caribbean, particularly St. Barts, where many of my friends like to go on a regular basis. And that's okay too because we all have our trip list and our travel to-do list. Mine includes Mongolia, the Everest Base Camp, Mali, and Papua New Guinea, to name a few.

Somehow, after years of traveling together, everyone in the group takes on a special task. One person is responsible for culture, another for restaurants, and another for finding a way to meet the locals. Chris was perfect for this role during a trip to Iceland. Using social media like Facebook and twitter, he lined up a group of people from Reykjavik who we all had drinks with and got a full understanding of life in that Northern European city. Over many years and many trips there have been very few arguments and very few moments of high drama. But when they have occurred, we have this knack as a group to sort it out pretty quickly and keep the trip momentum in a positive direction. It's a great way to resolve conflict at home too: Don't hang on to problems. Sort them out quickly and move on.

Having a tight travel group is one of the greatest gifts that anyone can have in their life. When our group gets together during a regular work week, we find ourselves talking about the time a wild boar ran in front of the car on a local road in Umbria, or when we turned into the Ngorongoro crater to confront thousands of wild animals. We've stood at Uhuru Point, the tallest point in Africa at the top of Kilimanjaro, and we've sailed along the Turkish Coast. We once awoke on Christmas morning on the island of Nukubati in the Fiji islands to see the most magnificent rainbow of our lives, and we've flown along the Skeleton Coast to witness the marvels of Mother Nature in Namibia!

I could go on and on, but I think you understand: To have experienced this with the most important people in my life is a great gift. In the end, it's not about what material goods we amass or about keeping up with the neighbors. It is truly about experiencing the world and all of its glories; it's the memories that we make that will fill us to the brim of satisfaction.

TIPS

MARTHA MCCULLY

Lifestyle Expert

- For creature comforts, travel with Dr. Dre Beats headphones, a pashmina for warmth, eye covering for darkness, and Greens Plus bars for sustenance.

- Sit as far forward in the plane as possible, even in coach. It makes getting on and off the plane easier.

- Keep one map and mark every place you go on it. You'll begin to become familiar with the area and easily identify the places you want to return to.

- Find a local market. Saturday mornings are best. Buy a little cheese, prosciutto, and fruit and keep it in your hotel room for snacks. Buy water in local markets to avoid the mini-bar.

- Use your frequent flyer miles only for international flights. Take mass transit to the airport to avoid traffic jams and carry anti-bacterial towelettes throughout your flight.

Khatmandu, Nepal

THE WONDERS OF NEPAL

I will always remember the sound of the brain popping. It is only a moment of the cremation ceremony, but it is a jarring moment. We're standing across the river from Pashupatinath, Nepal's holiest Hindu temple, located on the banks of the Bagmati River in the small town of Deopatan. Dedicated to the God of Shiva, the temple is off-limits to Westerners, but there are places to stand on the opposite side of the river that allow you to take in the whole scene.

We are watching cremations in the tradition of the Hindu religion. Jutting out across the river are concrete platforms called *ghats* where the rituals take place. A body is wrapped in a white sheet and placed within a stack of firewood and straw, the mourners are dressed in white and have shaved heads. When the funeral pyre is lit, the family is prepared, Buddhist monks chant, devotees of Vishnu work on the scene, and snake charmers and holy men called *Sadus* with long, braided hair below the waist gather around the scene. Monkeys and goats fill out the tableau, as multiple bodies burn and plumes of smoke fill the air. A cremation takes four to five hours and the brain pops sometime within that period. When the ashes are cooled, holy men sweep them into the river as part of the ceremony. It couldn't be a more surreal experience for a Westerner, but then again, in Nepal there are many things that you'll not see elsewhere. When you're there, you're about as far away as possible from your everyday life.

A group of us had decided on a visit to this fascinating country, high in the Himalayas, neatly tucked between India and China. There, you can have an experience that blends Hinduism and Buddhism. You'll learn that eight of the world's highest mountains exist there with 240 peaks over 20,000 feet (6,096 meters), including the granddaddy of them all, Mt. Everest, known here as Sagarmatha. Nepal is the birthplace of Buddha and home to thousands of Tibetan refugees who fled their home country when the Chinese invaded.

For centuries, Nepal, one of the only countries in the world to have never been dominated by a foreign power, was governed by a monarchy, which came apart in the early twenty-first century. In the mid 1990s, a

Maoist group began an effort to replace the monarchy, leading to a civil war that claimed over twelve thousand lives.

In 2001, a Royal massacre that killed the king and queen, along with seven other members of the Royal family, was a turning point. The killings perpetrated by the Crown Prince Dipendra, who then killed himself, set in motion the ultimate replacement of the monarchy. While his brother Gyanendra inherited the throne, it all came apart as Nepal moved into a secular state and then a republic in 2008. Today the government is stable and Nepal is safe again for the adventurous traveler.

A trip to Nepal usually begins in Kathmandu, the exotic capital city that is an easy ninety-minute flight from Delhi, India. We are met by our guide, JK, who will be with us over the next two weeks, as we take a trek into the Himalayas, raft the Trilusi River, and pay a visit to Chitwan National Park, a great wildlife refuge and home of the elusive Bengal Tiger. A visit to Kathmandu itself is worth several days, as the experience is a rich one. What you cannot avoid there is Bodhnath, the largest Buddhist stupa in the city. Shaped like a massive bell, it is the center of Tibetan life. Displaced Tibetans living there, as well as pilgrims from other parts of the country, from Ladakh, Bhutan, and Tibet all come there to pray. They circle the stupa clockwise, spinning their prayer wheels. Built in the fourteenth century, this massive structure has a lot of symbolism at work, including its nine levels that represent the mythical Mount Meru, the center of the world. It is a multi-level structure topped by a pyramid of thirteen steps, representing the ladder of enlightenment. At the top are hundreds of prayer flags that flap in the wind. This is a place where you can easily spend a few hours just taking it all in—sights, sounds and smells that will remind you that you're not in Kansas anymore!

Daily life in Kathmandu is filled with religious prayers and visits to shrines and temples, as well as going about the everyday activities of making a living. Although nearly 80 percent of the Nepali workforce is engaged in agriculture, the country's main activity, the towns are filled with local craftsmen and merchants.

One of the greatest experiences that a traveler can have is to be connected to someone local who can give you some special insights into the place that you are visiting, and it's worth it for you to put your feelers out before you go anywhere. My advice is to tell everyone you know where you're going and see if there are any connections that they have there. I've also posted my destination on Facebook to get connected to the locals. In **117** this case, a colleague of mine connected me to a husband and wife who had moved to Kathmandu to live, study and set up a business. Luca, an Italian who was studying Tibetan Chinese, and his English wife had brought their young family there and had also managed to set up a business trading in Tibetan carpets and restored furniture. Visiting them in their spacious apartment with views of the stupa was a special treat, along with the local cakes and tea that they served us. With them we learned about the plight of the Tibetans, along with the unique craftsmanship that goes into Tibetan furniture. An afternoon with them included a visit to a restoration facility, where local Tibetans produced cabinets and thangka boxes that were spectacular. Under the headline of "strike while the iron is hot," we found ourselves negotiating with them, Luca acting as our translator. Soon we'd committed to a couple of dozen pieces that we arranged to have shipped to the U.S. While it took several months to happen, today in my New York apartment sit two or three pieces that conjure up great memories of that day in the local life of Kathmandu. Throughout our trip, we added to the cache with leather boxes, old coffee urns, incense burners, paintings on silk, and brightly painted ornate masks, all great memories of our visit.

A must-see spot in Kathmandu is Swayambhunath, or the "monkey temple." This large temple complex that is the most important Buddhist shrine in the country was built over two thousand years ago. As you approach it, you'll see the 365 steps to get you to the top, but it's the activity around the temple that will put your senses on overload. In fact, here you'll find five shrines for each of the senses, as well as huge painted Buddha statues and the Harati Devi Temple, a place devoted to the protection of children. Praying monks, pilgrims, prostrating women, *Sadus,* incense and prayer flags, and hundreds of monkeys that roam the site all add to the local color. But it's the eyes gazing from the top of the temple, representing the all-seeing Buddha, that attracts so many people to this spot. On a separate note: Don't feed the monkeys. Just let them go about their business because once you attract them, you'll never shake them.

From the temple, walk to Durbar Square, the hub of the old city that was established in the eighth century. This is a collection of over fifty temples and monuments surrounded by vendors selling fruits and vegetables, as well as the ever-present monks, who are always on the streets of the city. Just roam the streets, taking in the sights of the brightly colored mountain peo-

118 ple who've come into the city, the flapping pigeons and monkeys and stray dogs. The Kumari Bahal, the eighteenth-century temple of the Kumari or living goddess, will be one of your first stops. Just sit on the sidelines, camera ready, zoom lens in place, and snap away. I promise you that you'll wow yourself and your friends—it's a photographer's paradise.

But to take it up one more notch, head out to Bhaktapur, one of the three royal cities in Nepal (Kathmandu and Patan being the others). There, twenty kilometers (twelve miles) from Kathmandu, the "City of Devotees," located on the ancient trade route between India and Tibet, will sweep you away into yet another place. Founded in the twelfth century, it is a feast of history and religion, home to nineteen Buddhist monasteries and Durbar Square, which is a UNESCO site that will enthrall you for hours. Imagine a spot with no cars, where you enter through the Golden Gate, erected in 1753 and seen as one of the greatest pieces of Nepali art anywhere. You'll find a temple to Shiva, the Royal Palace with fifty-five windows, and the National Art Gallery. Women in traditional saris with tattooed ankles go about their everyday business, carrying baskets on their heads and children on their backs. Don't miss Taumadhi Square, home of the five-story pagoda temple and Dattatreya Square, a complex of Hindu monasteries, temples, and museums. Although we weren't there for one of the festivals, there are many to choose from, including Dashain, a fifteen-day festival honoring the goddess Devi Durga, Gai Jatra, the cow festival that is for bereaving families, and Bisket Jatra, the Nepalese New Year's celebration.

Even if you're not a great photographer, this is a place where you can't miss. Whether you have a point-and-shoot or a more sophisticated camera, just let it follow your eye to what you're experiencing. In my travels, I've converted completely to digital. Each night, I download my photographs onto my laptop, allowing me to see what I captured that day. The beauty of instant digital gratification is that it allows you to go back to a spot the next day if you feel you missed some important shots.

Another memorable moment on this trip that excited me from the photography perspective was the flight above Mt. Everest. From the local airport there's a forty-passenger turbo prop that ferries people on a one-hour sightseeing visit to the world's tallest mountain. Maps are passed out so that the passengers can identify different mountain peaks along the way. Once Everest was in view we circled the peak, with a select group of us taking turns going into the cockpit to get a bird's eye view and to take some photographs. Our day was crystal clear and the view was awe-inspiring, making me wonder if I'd ever get to the top. Well, maybe to the base camp. Put that on the bucket list. This is what I mean about accumulating a wish list when you travel. Each new place spawns a new idea and the list goes on. Someday I'll make it to base camp, and in my fantasy life to the top of Everest. There's a lot to do in the Kathmandu region including stopping at the Yak and Yeti, a gathering spot and hotel for travelers from around the world who will be happy to share tips with you about what to see and do.

On a foggy morning, we head out to the airport for a short flight to Pokhara, the jump-off point for our trek into the mountains. We are a group of eight people and we will have twenty-one porters and six Sherpas who will carry our gear, tents, kitchen equipment, stoves, food, and other essentials for our five-day hike into the Himalayas. We start the first day with a three-hour hike into the hills and past small villages with thatched houses and terraced farms for mustard, potatoes, and other crops. The trekkers' life is one of serenity, finding the rhythm in the surrounding beauty and the simplicity of village life. In the hills, there are no roads, but rather dirt paths we use to follow our route. Each day we hike for several hours, stopping at a local school one day to meet the students, giving them crayons, paper, and sweets, sharing "Namaste" along the way. Locals in local garb pass us on the path, carrying water cans, food, sticks or twigs, and smiling at our group. Occasionally, someone will stop and talk to us in broken English, or ask us if we have an aspirin to help a toothache.

Meals are simple. Eggs, potatoes, and toast for breakfast and local dishes made with rice, spices, chicken, and vegetables for lunch and dinner. Simple as it is, it is plentiful throughout the trip and we augment it with the power bars, nuts, and trail mix that we brought from home. At night, we sit around the campsite sharing stories, playing cards, and sharing the scotch that someone carried in their backpack. Lights out came pretty early, as we rise at 5:30 each morning. Along the trail we're on winding paths that go up and down and around hills, across farms and small settlements, and up a hill that has 2,200 steps, according to our guide. At the top there is a great view of the Fishtail Mountains in the distance, followed by a view of the Annapurna range that include Annapurna I through IV, Hiunchuli, Machhapuchhre, and Lamjung Himal, all noteworthy mountains that poke majestically into the sky.

120   One thing about several days in the mountains is that it clears your head and calms the soul. It especially gives you perspective when you have the opportunity to visit with a local family. Late one afternoon, we were invited into a home, a two-story clay structure with a thatched roof and intricate woodwork around the glass-free windows. The main floor has one room with a dirt floor, a fireplace, and cooking utensils scattered in a corner. The second floor also has one room with clothes hanging from the ceiling along with stalks of corn stored in a corner. In the front yard are a pig, a cow, a rooster, a goat, baby chicks, and a dog to add to the camaraderie. And the dwelling is home to three adults—husband, wife, and grandmother—and four children, who all sleep in the second floor room. This is a happy family, smiling and offering us drinks while the kids laugh and point at my blue eyes! These are medieval conditions, a reminder that there is a world out there that lives in the most basic form possible.

Our group moved in a harmonious way, winding our way to a point where we had a van waiting for us to drive us to the Trisuli River, where we would do a three-day, sixty-mile (ninety-seven kilometer) whitewater trip towards Chitwan Park. Loaded into two rafts, we headed down the river that runs through a gorge with mountain villages on either side. Along the river, there are pulley systems for the locals to utilize in crossing the river. The water is fairly tame, but fun nonetheless. And it was on this part of the trip when our group had a blowout argument, never good on an adventurous trip, especially in a third-world country.

It all started when one of our fellow travelers, a physician no less, asked our guide if he could buy some marijuana from someone. Generally, I don't pass judgment on people, but in this case, I thought it was an irresponsible act that jeopardized the whole group. Trying to buy drugs in a third-world country is just stupid. First of all it's illegal, and in many countries in can result in years of imprisonment. But more importantly, it could have affected the whole group's well-being. I took on the role of challenging this guy, who became indignant and thought that I was overreacting. But I held my ground and rallied support from the rest of the group.

What's the lesson here? Know whom you are traveling with and set some ground rules to follow while you're away. You'd think that you wouldn't have to put "Don't buy drugs in a foreign country" on the list, but you just never know what people might be thinking. As a result, it's not a bad idea to review some travel etiquette when traveling with a group, especially in places like Nepal. It can prevent stupid mistakes and also tense moments **121** during a trip. With that incident behind us, we all got on track again and finished up the whitewater rafting trip to be met by land rovers that took us into the jungle to Chitwan National Park.

Arriving at Tiger Tops Tented Camp has its own sense of romance. Set among a beautiful ridge, our tents are seven feet (two meters) tall by twenty feet (sixty-one meters) wide with plenty of room for two beds decked out in white linen, comfortable blankets, and duvets. Side tables hold flashlights and potable water, as well as kerosene lanterns. Each room has an outside deck with tables and chairs to look out over the Western sky, but the pièce de résistance is the bathroom. The room is about nine square feet (three square meters), complete with flushing toilet, a shower with hot running water, and a sink and mirror. Now this is luxury in the jungle!

From our tents we have views of rhinos and elephants grazing in the distance, and nearby is the elephant-mounting stand, the place where we get on elephant back. Chitwan is 360 square (932 square kilometers) and while on elephant back moving through the tall grasslands we spot more rhinos, barking deer, wild boars, bison, crocodiles, and sloths, but not the elusive Bengal tiger. We spend three days on elephant back in pursuit of the tiger, and during that time we all learn to bond with the elephants, the oldest living mammals in the world. We visit them at their sanctuary where there is a breeding station. We jump in the river with them and the guides, to help bathe them and watch them play in the water.

Elephants can live to be sixty to seventy years old, but ultimately starve to death once they lose their three sets of four molars. On an average day, they eat 400 pounds (181 kilograms) of grass and drink 40 gallons (151 liters) of water. Their famous trunks have more than forty thousand muscles and serve many purposes including feeding, washing, and protecting themselves. Of all of the wildlife that I've ever seen in Africa and parts of Asia, I'm most mesmerized by the elephant. If you are too, then you'll be in heaven at Tiger Tops. There are 106 tigers in all of Chitwan, and while we've been able to track footprints and hear them in the distance, we did leave the park without spotting this rare creature. Ah, the marvels of nature and what you might or might not see.

Throughout our trip to Nepal, it became clear that this was a place that was incredibly different from anywhere else. One of the great realizations that I've had as I've traveled the world is how many distinct cultures continue to thrive on the planet and how little appreciation there is for them. Talk to the average American, for example, and they'll have no idea of the distinction between Peru and Argentina. They just think of them as down there in South America! But the countries couldn't be more distinct. Thailand is very different from Cambodia, which is very different from Vietnam, though all three countries border each other.

Maybe this helps to feed my relentless quest to see the world. Yes, there are influences that one country can have on another, especially if they've been dominated by the former. England and India are a good example, as is France and Southeast Asia. Nepal hasn't had that kind of influence. So if you want to visit a purely indigenous place, put this on your list.

From Kathmandu, we flew back to Delhi to spend a few days, as well as to take a side trip to Agra to see the Taj Mahal. After a day there, I realized that there was so much to do and see in India that it was frustrating just having a small bite of it. Ultimately, I went back to Rajasthan to see the cities of Jaipur and Udaipur, and their majesty deserves a story of its own. And then there's Varanasi and Mumbai and Kerala and Chennai. There are at least two to three more trips to India in my future.

Travel is intoxicating. Having the privilege of seeing the world and making it a life priority will expose you to things that will change your perspective and give you memories that will serve you for a lifetime.

Sitting across from Pashupatinath observing the cremation ceremony will be with me forever. There are probably hundreds if not thousands of different kinds of death rituals around the world. After all, death is a universal experience. Having that understanding also helps to understand a culture and what makes it tick.

When you visit somewhere, learn about it. Not just the death ritual, but also the birth ritual and the family values and the dreams of the people that you're visiting. In some ways they are very different from us, but in many ways they are similar. It will show you the family of man with our shared human experience. Therein might lie the secret to how we can all get along. Mutual understanding can go a long way. Each of us can bring home this message from our travels.

TIPS

MELISSA BIGGS BRADLEY

Founder, Indagare.com

● Keep connected. Register as a traveler and update your travels with the State Department website to get alerts or for help should a crisis arise.

● Recheck reservations. Many times there are slight mistakes. The transfers are slightly off, the room category is wrong, or they forgot to make the rooms connecting.

● Don't settle for the first hotel room you're shown if you don't like it. This should be decided by you.

● Wander. Be prepared but leave time for serendipity. Wander a neighborhood or a beach path to discover the daily rhythm and heart of most places.

● Network globally. Reach out to friends of friends and acquaintances. It can lead to family dinners, private parties, or just tea with the locals, making it a more memorable stay.

Tiger's Nest, Paro, Bhutan

A LESSON LEARNED IN BHUTAN

If you're in search of a place on the road less traveled, search no further than Bhutan. In a certain way, this kingdom, tucked deep in the Himalayas between India and Tibet, has been with me on many of my travels. Veteran travelers that I've met around the world have gotten misty-eyed relating their experiences in Bhutan. When I heard that the country aims for a standard of "gross national happiness," that education and medical care are free, and that the air is purer than anywhere else on earth, I knew that it was time to head to this place that has been compared to Shangri-La!

Also known as Druk Yul (land of the dragon), this country is half the size of Indiana, with an estimated 810,000 inhabitants. It is currently ruled by King Jigme Singye Wangchuck and has existed as a political entity since at least the seventh century. During the eighth century, holy man Guru Rinpoche established Tantric Buddhism in Bhutan. Today, the Tantric form of Mahayana Buddhism, a kind of Tibetan Buddhism, is the official religion and imbues Bhutan's daily life.

The country began to modernize in the 1960s, and tourism emerged in the 70s with the introduction of currency, paved roads, media, and hospitals. Television and the Internet arrived in 1999, the same year a terminal was built next to the Kingdom's single airfield.

Getting to Bhutan isn't easy—in more ways than one. First of all, there's a government mandated minimum fee of $200 a day for food, lodging, transportation, and other essentials. Second, there is only one airline, Druk Air. It operates in and out of the country several times a week from Delhi and Bangkok to the country's airport, in the western town of Paro. The sole landing strip runs along the bottom of a deep valley, and as a pilot myself I marveled at the skill required to maneuver a plane through a roller-coaster maze, over and around the mountaintops.

At the airport, we met our guide, Phurba, who, with a driver, would escort us in a Land Rover during our ten-day stay. He wore a *gho*, a cotton wraparound garment that is the traditional national dress for men, and spoke

English, which is taught in all of the schools, impeccably. Besides Paro, we wanted to see Thimphu, the capital, as well as some surrounding towns and villages. We also planned a four-day trek into the Himalayas.

Today, the Aman resort has established several small inns throughout the area that hikers travel between over the course of several days. But when we were there it was very Spartan, especially in the mountains, where we had Sherpas who set up our camp and cooked meals for us in the open air.

The first thing you'll notice upon arrival in Bhutan is the silence. There are very few cars and very little industry, so the only sounds you hear are gusts of wind, flapping prayer flags, cowbells, and the laughter of children. People move quietly and gently amid the towns' simple wooden homes and shops with their beautifully painted windows and doors. My advice is to leave your electronics and technology at home and completely unplug when you're here. It will put you back in touch with yourself in the most human way. Throughout our stay, we remained liberated from our phones and Blackberries (which probably wouldn't have worked anyway), and we didn't worry about what was happening elsewhere. Our focus was on the simple life the Bhutanese enjoy and on trying to figure out how to extract that for ourselves.

Bhutan's cultural heritage is wonderfully displayed in Paro's National Museum. Housed in a round watchtower built in the 1650s, the museum boasts six floors of art, costumes, *thangkas* (religious banners) and silver work. Also in Paro is a massive *dzong,* or fortress, which, like those in the countryside, was once used for protection but now serves as a school for monks. Within the walls of Paro Dzong, we observed the monks, many just five or six years old, in their dark red robes both at prayer and at work. Whether they eventually leave or stay in the order for life, the experience brings great honor to their families.

From Paro we continued on to Taktsang Lhakhang, or "tiger's nest," the burial place of Guru Rinpoche. Getting to it requires a literally breathtaking one-and-a-half hour hike from 7,500 to 10,000 feet (2,286 to 3,048 meters) above sea level, with a stop at around 9,200 feet (2,804 meters) for lunch with a spectacular vista. Westerners are not allowed inside the temple, but it's worth hiking to a point that offers a bird's-eye view of the structure, built right into the mountain. Happily, many of Bhutan's *dzongs* (temples) and *chortens* (Buddhist funeral monuments) are open to Westerners and we experienced many of them. One of my favorites was Drakarpo, or "white cliff," carved out of the side of a hill. To get there we traversed a narrow path, and then climbed a twelve-rung ladder to the entrance. Inside were ornate altars with offerings of fruit, flowers, unbaked wheat dough, and *torma* (butter sculptures). The temple keeper invited us to lean into a human-shaped depression in the wall, a ritual said to bring good luck.

Our tech-free experience continued as we began our trek into the countryside. Three of us had a guide and a crew of five, including a cook, as well as eight packhorses. We set out on a trek toward Dongkola Pass and it was one of the more spiritual experiences I've ever had. Along the way, the sights and the friendliness of the people inspired us. We had stunning views of looming Kanchenjunga, the world's third highest mountain, on the border between India and Nepal, and of Bhutan's highest peak, Gangkhar Puensum, which is never climbed out of respect for the spirits believed to inhabit it.

Our nightly surroundings were astonishing, my favorite being a campsite that was actually above the clouds. We pitched our tents in a circle and, surrounded by thirty fluttering prayer flags, enjoyed the panorama for hundreds of miles. After dining on *datsi,* a hearty stew of cheese and chili peppers, we listened to monks chanting in the distance and enjoyed our simple act of reflection.

This is the kind of experience that allows you to clear your head and to determine what's important to you and your life. On these kinds of trips it's great to keep a journal, review goals and priorities, think about relationships. And it's on this kind of trip that you can get a better appreciation for what you want or don't want in your life. You're there alone with your thoughts, with no distractions of twenty-first-century life, and the voice inside you becomes sharper and more distinct. I've made many life decisions on these types of trips. They've given me the strength to end friendships that had gone sour and to enrich friendships that had big potential. I've made career decisions and focused on how I wanted to participate in my own community, ultimately setting up a foundation that grants random acts of kindness to individuals and families in need.

Up in the mountains, we saw very few Westerners and met young monks who'd never seen a Westerner before. We communicated in the basic ways with smiles and small offerings, underscoring the importance of very simple human acts.

128   Many people have asked me why I seem so calm when there is chaos around me at work or in life. The source of my calm is oftentimes the perspective that I've gotten on trips like this one. I've trekked in Nepal and Patagonia and the American West, and all of those trips are the source of my inner fortitude. Learning to be alone with your thoughts and your own spirituality is a powerful cure for the stress of modern life.

Once out of the mountains we headed to Thimphu, the capital. Here we found wonderful handicrafts, the impressive National Textile Museum, and the famous philatelic store at the main post office. The small town seemed urban to us after having spent many days in the mountains.

We worked our way back to Paro for what would be our flight out of this magical country. The silence followed us, and we bathed in our own reflections. As we boarded the flight back to Bangkok, I got a clearer understanding of the meaning of gross national happiness. In Bhutan, it is a cultural priority, rooted in the basics of life. It's not about the external, but more about the internal. It made me realize how much work I still needed to do on my internal life.

As we lifted into the air to navigate around the mountains that would take us out of the valley, I knew one thing that was for sure. Our life's journey never ends. We are always thinking and learning and pursuing what it is that we think will bring us happiness and satisfaction. Maybe there isn't an end state, but the pursuit of it keeps us open to all of the possibilities that might await us. That was the lesson from my days in Bhutan.

TIPS

NANCY NOVOGROD

Editor in Chief, *Travel and Leisure*

- Never skip the nuts on the plane. They may be the best food you'll have on your flight other than the hot fudge sundae.

- For overnight flights, have dinner at the airport so that you can sleep after the nuts are served.

- Always bring a small travel steamer. Bring enough underpinnings and soap to avoid the hotel laundry. Only send out workout clothes for laundry service.

- Pack in your head first, then pack on a spare bed or sofa, then edit before you put it in the bag. Start two nights before you leave.

- Check out the local offerings at your destination in advance of the trip. Ask the concierge to reserve tickets to events that require them (not unusual for blockbuster museum shows).

Marrakech Bazaar

IF YOU LIKE IT, BUY IT

How many times in your travel life have you lamented that you didn't buy that one item you admired when roaming the souks of Marrakech or the galleries of Soho? The one that got away. The one memento or piece of art or rug that would have been perfect in your house, or made the perfect gift for someone.

Here's what I have learned in my travel life: If you like it, buy it!

Like many of you, I learned the hard way. I'd think about buying. I'd circle back. I'd debate with myself. By the time I made up my mind I was on a flight to the next stop and, well, it was a lost opportunity. Yes, you can follow up online or with a phone call, but sometimes that isn't possible. When I acted quickly, I felt rewarded. I remember stumbling upon a gallery in the Le Marais district of Paris to find a small piece of art that I admired. It really spoke to me and it was very affordable. That was twenty years ago, and it still hangs in my bedroom. The same goes for two small oils of beach scenes that I bought on a beach in Rio for $2 apiece. They sit in very fancy frames and some of my very fancy friends think that they're true works of art. Well, they are—by a street painter in Rio.

On a trip to Nepal, I connected with an Italian couple living in Kathmandu who had started a small business restoring Tibetan furniture and thangka boxes that the local Tibetan community had been able to smuggle out of the country. They were able to keep them out of the hands of the Chinese, and by restoring them they could sell them to foreigners and get much needed currency both to live and to fight for a Free Tibet.

When we got to the small workroom of Tibetan workers, my friends and I were astonished at how beautiful the works were and when questioned our Italian friend Lucca about purchasing some of them, we were amazed at the reasonable cost. That was a pivotal moment for me. We were getting ready to leave in the morning for a trek into the Himalayas, then on to a rafting trip on the Trisuli River, and then to visit Chitwan National Park. There was no time to contemplate, as Buddha might say. But there was time to act.

132   On the spot, our small group decided to buy about twenty pieces that we would ship to New York, hoping that maybe in six months everything would arrive, if it arrived at all. We knew there was risk, but we went for it. Two months later our carton arrived and we got it released from customs. Today many of those pieces sit in my New York apartment, admired by many who visit. And I get to tell the story of how I came by them.

Now when I travel, I'm as decisive as a surgeon. Here's what I look for. No tchotchkes. I went through that during the early stages of my traveling career, and with rare exception, a lot of this is junk that doesn't amount to much once I'm home. My rule is if I want to help a local vendor in a third-world market, I give them some the money and ask if I can take their picture. It works most times, and I get a great photo—I can live without the beaded macramé hanging basket.

Some of my most fun times have been in the bazaars and souks of Morocco, Turkey, and Tunisia. These are a shopper's paradise with some amazing finds. But you have to be as shrewd as the vendors. Play their bartering game and be willing to walk away unless you can get to the bottom price that you are willing to pay. It's all part of the sport.

I found myself at the place of a rug merchant in the Bazaar in Istanbul. My friends and I walked in and before we knew it, the back and forth had begun. We threw out prices, we laughed, we called each other crazy, and when the merchant knew we might be serious buyers, out came some thick Turkish coffee and sweets, along with two of his helpers, who ran around pulling out rugs for us to look at. We walked out. We walked back in. We pulled out the calculators. And we ultimately walked out with five rugs, all neatly packaged. My friend Cap obsessed that he paid way too much, until he got back to the States and learned that he could sell the rug here for nearly three times what he bought it for. But you have to know when you have a bargain in front of you and what you are buying. That day, the rugs were a good buy, as were the old metal Turkish coffee urns that we also bought.

Some people like to go to Milan or Paris or New York to shop the sales at the designer boutiques. Some people go to wine auctions or to major art and photography fairs, or even to the famous Concours d'Elegance to pick up a vintage car. That is for the fortunate few, but you can have those experiences in a different form.

Along with fellow serious travelers, I have a taste for finding unique products that have value or a special meaning to the travel experience. At a wine tasting in the Vines of Mendoza wine room in Mendoza, Argentina, I had the opportunity to join a wine club and get a shipment of great Argentine wines four times per year. You can find great photography at the annual AIPAD show in New York; don't be shy to ask the dealer for a better price. As your mother may have said, if you don't ask, you don't get.

On a hiking trip two hundred miles (322 kilometers) above the Arctic Circle in Norway, I came across a local shop that sold reindeer skins that were a great reminder of our ten days of hiking and camping near Tromso. Two of them are on the beds in a guestroom and they inevitably bring back the memories of that special trip into nature.

I don't usually seek these items out; I just come across them. I'm not much of a serious shopper when I travel, but the local markets or shopping areas almost always offer something of interest that stops me in my tracks.

In Bangkok, I was wandering around a local shopping area when I entered a store that had some unique looking items. Standing in the corner was a wooden horse on a pedestal, maybe three feet high (about one meter), colorfully painted with some ornamental touches. I learned that it had been a puppet in a children's theatre show at the turn of the twentieth century. It was one of the most unique objects I'd ever seen. When I found out how affordable it was, I immediately asked about shipping costs and how such a fragile thing could be packed. It all seemed doable, and like the items from Tibet, I acknowledged that if it arrived in pieces, I would have to chalk it up as not meant to be. But sure enough, a month later the horse arrived in one of the most airtight packages that I'd ever seen, and to this day it stands at the end of the hallway, a reminder of that day in Bangkok.

Most of my travel friends have now picked up on my way of thinking. When a few of us went to Gem Palace in Jaipur, India, my friend Dan wondered if the two precious stones that he wanted to buy to have made into cuff links were too expensive. After some consideration, he bought them, and when he got back to New York, the jeweler who would make the links told him that the finished cufflinks would cost twice as much in a New York store.

Do you like it? Then buy it!

Above the Arctic Circle, Norway

THE A TO Z OF GLOBETROTTING

A IS FOR AIRCRAFT. Find out what aircraft options you may have for your upcoming flight. There's nothing worse than an MD-80 on a four-hour flight when you could be on an Airbus. Get to know airplanes and their seat configurations, and get your seat assignment early. It can make all the difference for a comfortable flight.

B IS FOR BEGINNING your travel as early in the day as possible. That 6:00 a.m. flight might mean a brutal wake-up call in middle of the night, but you'll know that your airplane is there and it'll be one of the first flights out before the airport gets too congested. You'll have no traffic on the way to the airport, you'll get through security faster, and there will be no lines for your morning latte.

C IS FOR CARRY ON. I don't care if you're flying for one hour or for twelve hours, do your best to consolidate everything into luggage that you can carry on the plane. Think black, think washables. When you're at home, pack your bag and then take out half of what you've packed. You'll be amazed at how you can get by with just that amount. The side benefit is no waiting at baggage claim, not to mention dealing with a lost piece of luggage that the odds say you'll never see again.

D IS FOR DEALS. There are so many of them, you should never pay top dollar. Work the sites like TravelZoo.com, where my friends got a week in Kyoto with airfare and hotels for $2,000 each. You should never pay top dollar—you can get amazing travel experiences at great savings.

E IS FOR EARLY. Book as far in advance as you can. You'll get frequent flyer mile seats easier that way, as well as your choice of hotels and resorts. I work a year in advance. Yes, plans change, but at least you're locked in if they don't.

136 **F IS FOR FLEXIBILITY.** When you're traveling, especially in third-world countries, you just have to go with the flow. Leave your Type A behavior at home and learn how the locals work. Flights get cancelled, plans change due to strikes, and vans break down. When our boat wasn't allowed to cross the border from Vietnam to Cambodia, we hired a local fisherman to take us to Phnom Penh. Get on the phone, get online, and remember that money talks. Tips can work wonders.

G IS FOR GLOBETROTTING. There is no better time to start than today. Put down this book and plan your trip. Go somewhere that you've always dreamed about visiting. Why are you waiting? There are people who dream and there are people who do. Be the dreamer and the doer. You deserve it.

H IS FOR HEALTH. It amazes me how many people do not check to see if they need shots or malaria pills for their destination. Having all of your inoculations is critical and can save you months of recuperation that is time-consuming and expensive. Do a Google search for "international travel shots" and you'll get information on places in your local area that specialize in knowing what shots are needed for what destination.

I IS FOR INSURANCE. Forget flight insurance, but do buy cancellation insurance, especially if you're taking a pricey trip. If you're traveling to a remote place, buy medical evacuation insurance, especially if you have health issues. You'll want a medical evacuation out of the jungle if you find yourself in bad physical shape.

J IS FOR JPEG. The beauty of digital cameras is that you can photograph to your heart's content at a much lower cost than with film. I went cold turkey from film to digital and my travel photography has never been better. Plus, you can edit, work PhotoShop, email pictures to friends, and even have a gallery showing of your work. Digital photography has become the traveler's best tool. I always travel with my laptop to download every day, editing along the way.

K IS FOR KIDS. Make sure that you get their input on your destination. I've heard too many stories from parents who had a miserable trip because they were interested in visiting a place, but their kids didn't want to go there. It depends on the age of the kids, but I recommend places like the Galapagos, Costa Rica, and the Hawaiian islands that have something for everyone. Get buy-in from the kids!

L IS FOR LATE CHECK OUT. If you don't ask, you don't get. Most hotels **137** will be more than happy to accommodate you, especially if you're a regular to that property or to the hotel chain. Become friendly with someone at the front desk, or with the concierge. When you get a note and a bowl of fruit from the hotel manager, call and thank him or her and request the late check out. I've checked out as late as 3:00 p.m. It's all about being nice.

M IS FOR MANNERS. Always be nice, especially to airline personnel. They cannot control the weather or a plane with mechanical problems. The nicer you are, the more they will help you. Know the customs of the place that you're visiting and have the appropriate manners to respect them. What's appropriate in Japan is different than what's appropriate in Greece. Make it your business to learn the local customs.

N IS FOR NEGOTIATING. For everything. Don't assume that any price is the final price. Ask a hotel, a shopkeeper, or a guide if that's the best price. With airlines, I always ask for the cheapest seat on the plane. What's the lowest fare? What's the lowest fare that I can have to upgrade with miles? Learn the restrictions and decide accordingly. In many places in the world, like India or Turkey or the souks of Morocco, vendors expect you to negotiate. It's part of the culture and the fun.

O IS FOR OVERBOOKING. Airlines do it all the time. Check in online. Print out your boarding passes beforehand so that you've secured your seat. On the other hand, if you have lots of flexibility in your travel plans, check in very late and you may find yourself already bumped up in class. Or volunteer to give up your seat. Many airlines will pay for your hotel and food and give you a voucher worth hundreds of dollars for a future flight. Work the system if you have the time.

P IS FOR PREMIUM STATUS. Watch your airline points and try to consolidate your travel on one or two airlines and partner airlines. I'm a three-million-miler plus on American Airlines and it is a major bonus for my travels. As Executive Platinum, I get to board early (and bring my traveling companion with me). I also get lots of upgrades. Once, when my sister and I were flying coach from Sydney to Los Angeles, we were both upgraded to business class due to my status. Qantas is the partner airline to American.

138 **Q IS FOR QANTAS,** one of the best long-haul airlines in the world. Especially on long flights, the airline can make all of the difference. Emirates, Singapore, Thai, British, and LanChile are my personal favorites. If you can, take business class on any of these airlines and you'll feel so pampered that you won't believe you're on an airplane!

R IS FOR RENTAL CARS. Finding the best rates has become like finding the best airfares. It's dizzying. Make sure that you shop around, especially if you're going to popular places like Rome in the summer or Aspen in the winter. And read the fine print. I once returned a rental car two hours late in Italy and they charged me for a full day. None of my charms worked and I got stuck paying for the full day. Had I understood the fine print, I could have gotten in under the time restraint. Extra insurance, bringing the tank back half full, and upgrades all have their idiosyncrasies. One hidden one is that if you pre-pay for gas, some companies won't charge you just to top off, but they will charge you for a full tank. Ask the questions before you sign anything.

S IS FOR SECURITY. I'm talking about your own personal security. Don't swing your handbag around or flaunt big camera equipment in crowded places. If you wear gaudy jewelry and flashy watches, you're inviting trouble. Be smart. Wear simple clothes, look around you. Have your sixth sense working to avoid being mugged. It's all common sense. Also, check for travel advisories at travel.state.gov. It may lead you to postpone that trip to Syria, as I did, due to the recent unrest.

T IS FOR TRAVEL AGENTS. Yes, the web has empowered all of us to become our own planners, but find a good travel agent and stick to him or her. My travel agent, Ken Lewis at Classic Travel in New York, has worked wonders for me in lots of my travels. How do you get from Chiang Mai to Luang Prabang? A great travel agent has all of the answers.

U IS FOR UNDERSTANDING. Learn about the history, art, and people of the country that you're visiting. Don't just show up somewhere without an appreciation for what you're about to see. It will also lead you to places that are off the beaten path. Carthage, outside of Tunis, or Pergamon in Turkey are two places that I might have missed if I hadn't done my homework beforehand.

V IS FOR VISA. Ask if you need one. You'd be surprised at the countries that require them, such as Argentina. Also, make sure that your passport is not about to expire and that you have enough blank pages. Make copies of the opening pages of your passport and of your visas for the country that you're visiting; if you lose your passport along the way, this will insure that you get a replacement faster.

W IS FOR WORD OF MOUTH. I always ask my fellow travelers what must-see place they discovered in a city or country. What restaurants are interesting and who is the local guide? Those who have just gone before you are great sources. I also check Trip Advisor and send an email to my well-traveled friends, who connect me to locals. As we were planning a trip to Luang Prabang, Laos, not only did we get a full itinerary from someone who had just gone there, but also one of my traveling companions was able to connect us to an expat who's been living there for a year. A local connection always pays off.

X IS FOR "XTRAS." Read the fine print. There are lots of add-ons that are free (breakfast, beach services), but there are also a lot of extras not included in the price. Car rental companies are notorious for having lots of hidden extras. Paying for WiFi seems ridiculous. At a luxury hotel, they once charged me for a tip and a service fee when a latte was delivered to my room. That's insane and you should complain.

Y IS FOR YES. Just say yes to opening yourself up to new experiences and ideas when you're traveling. Don't eat in the hotels—go out and explore. Stay away from touristy spots—go to local neighborhoods. Get to understand what the locals like to do and mingle with them. It'll make your trip richer. We once went to a local tango hall in Buenos Aires, where the locals were learning how to dance. Some of our group jumped in and they felt like true porteños!

Z IS FOR ZEN. Step into the present during your globetrotting. Savor every moment and get into the Zen of your experience. If you can travel the world to see its marvels, you are very fortunate. Embrace your good fortune.

Bangkok, Thailand

THE LURE OF SOUTHEAST ASIA

Bangkok. It's chaotic. It's noisy. It's crowded. It's spectacular. And it's my favorite Asian city. Yes, Shanghai and Tokyo are dazzling. Hong Kong is stunning and Singapore is sleek and modern. But give me Bangkok. In fact, give me Southeast Asia. In my dozen or so trips to Asia, I'm drawn to the wonders of Thailand and Cambodia, Laos, Vietnam, and Myanmar.

My advice to any first time traveler to Asia is to fly directly to Bangkok. It's a long flight from just about anywhere, but it's worth it. Thailand is a globetrotter's paradise that offers world-class beaches, beautiful mountain towns, the finest hotels and resorts in the world, and a cultural experience that will fulfill you from start to finish. And take the kids. It's a great family experience too.

Siam, as Thailand was originally called, was first inhabited in the tenth century by the Chinese who came from the Yunnan Province. In 1932, the absolute monarchy ended and a constitutional monarchy was established. In 1939, the country's name was changed from Siam to Thailand, meaning "Free Land." Thailand has the dubious honor of being one of less than a handful of countries in the world that has never been taken over by a foreign power. That's not to say that Thailand hasn't had its internal political issues that have included strikes, protests, and bombings. But the country is consistently safe for travelers.

It's easy to spend a week or two in Thailand, but what makes it so perfect is that it's within two hours of every major Southeast Asian city in what was once called Indochina. In past trips to Thailand, I've flown to Siem Reap to visit Angkor Wat and to Ho Chi Minh City to experience Vietnam. The spectacular UNESCO city of Luang Prabang, Laos, is also accessible, as is Rangoon, the capital of Myanmar (formerly known as Burma). But in the fantasy game of Where Would You Like to Live for Three Months? I'd put Bangkok on my list, specifically to get to know this place called in Thai Krung Thep (City of Angels) better.

Founded in 1782 by King Rama I, Bangkok is built around the river called Chayo Praya or "River of Kings." Home to more than nine million

142 people, much of the city's life takes place on the river, and water taxis and longboats are the ideal way to get around to see the sights. I recommend that you splurge and stay at one of the great hotels like The Peninsula or The Shangri-La. This is where service was invented and sent around the world to so many places. Take the hotel's boat to The Grand Palace and the other must-see places like the Temple of the Emerald Buddha (Wat Phra Kaew), the Temple of Dawn (Wat Arun), and The Reclining Buddha (Wat Pho) to name just a few. On land you can take a *tuk-tuk* around town or hop on the Skytrain, a clean and efficient modern transportation system that is the perfect way to get around the city. There are museums and shopping spots galore, including the amazing markets and antique shops in River City where I once discovered a nearly life-size brightly painted wooden pony that was a marionette. I decided to buy it and ship it home to the states. Flawless. It was packed perfectly and arrived just after I returned home. The stores on Sukhumvit Road are a shopper's paradise, and when you get tired, you can hop a floating taxi and have the driver take you to the Floating Market on the Damnoen Saduak Canal, one of the best floating markets in any Asian city. Make sure that you bring your camera.

Then there's the food. Thai food is so unique in its flavors that it will be hard to resist taking a Thai cooking class when you're there. I don't generally cook, but I was pulled right in and before I knew it I was chopping and dicing and preparing dishes such as Tom Yum Goong, better known as spicy prawn soup with lemongrass.

Here's how my day at a Thai cooking class worked, and I recommend it to everyone. Our particular class was in the Northern city of Chiang Mai, one of the must-visit destinations in Thailand, if only to see the elephants (more on that later). We began our day at around 7:00 a.m. with a visit to the local market filled with fresh vegetables, meats, chickens, fish, and whole pigs heads. We roamed the stalls, picking ingredients for our class, but also sampling a lot of the local fare (although we passed on the french-fried worms collected from bamboo and the deep fried chicken heads). But we did try the exotic fruits and homemade sticky rice pudding, along with some of the best deep-fried donuts that I've ever eaten.

In our class, we were going to learn how to make homemade red and green curry paste along with Pad Thai sauce. We would create Larb Isan Gai, the well-known Thai Spicy Chicken Salad, along with Pha Naen G Ai Pol La Mai, a creamy red curry chicken with coconut milk and mixed fruit.

For each dish, we sat around the instructor chef's table, watching as he explained how best to use lemongrass and the root galangal as well as turmeric and coriander. We learned what utensils to use and how to slice properly. We worked with soybean oil and a wok, and I have to admit that I was entranced. To me cooking was always a mystery. I have great respect for cooks—cooking requires patience, time, and talent, none of which I seem to have for the kitchen. But here I found myself immersed, appreciating how the various pieces of the puzzle came together to create an amazing meal. By the third dish, I was definitely in my groove. Maybe I was a cook after all. Move over Bobby Flay! Our group of seven worked for hours, experimenting with many different flavors and tasting bits and pieces along the way, knowing that at the end of the class, we'd eat everything that we'd prepared—a Thai food feast.

Ultimately, it was my Pad Thai Goong, stir-fried rice noodles with prawns, that won me over. And while I'm not a foodie, I can't resist sharing this recipe with you. If I can do it, you can do it. So, here goes (serving for one).

PAD THAI GOONG

3 tbsp vegetable oil
1 clove garlic, chopped
1 egg
5 prawns
100 g rice noodles, pre-soaked
    in water to soften
¼ cup prawn stock
(you can substitute water)
½ tbsp dried shrimp
½ tbsp dried sweet turnip
2 tbsp dried fried tofu
1 tbsp cashews, roasted
    and chopped
40 g bean sprouts
20 g garlic chives

1. Heat the vegetable oil in a wok.
2. Add garlic and stir-fry until fragrant.
3. Add egg and stir-fry until it mixes in.
4. Add prawns and stir-fry until they're no longer translucent.
5. Add rice noodles and prawn stock. Stir until the noodles are soft.
6. Mix in dried shrimp, sweet turnip, tofu, and cashews.
7. Add Pad Thai sauce (you can buy this pre-made).
8. Add bean sprouts and garlic chive. Stir well.
9. Decorate with egg net (yes, we learned how to make an egg net too!)

144 I recommend a great beer with this dish. It especially helps to soften some of the spicy seasonings in the food.

Now it's true that ingredients like kaffir lime skin and homemade shrimp paste are hard to find, but a lot of it is already packaged and available at your local Asian market or specialty food aisle.

It should be obvious by now that Thai food is my favorite Asian food. Specialties vary from North and South Thailand. In Northeastern cooking, there is no oil, sugar, or coconut. In the Central Region (Bangkok), all of those ingredients are used. This is a country where you should open yourself up to try everything. I'm happy to eat any of it. Okay, maybe not the bamboo worms. But definitely the fish.

There are 2,000 miles (3,219 kilometers) of coastline in Thailand with lots of beaches to visit. The more popular places are Pattaya and Phuket, but I recommend the smaller places like Koh Samui on the Gulf of Thailand or Hin Daeng for diving, swimming, or sunbathing. In places like this, fish are plentiful and prepared in lots of whimsical ways. When you're there, I guarantee that you'll want to sign up for a Thai cooking class that specializes in fish!

Once you've had your fill of sun, make sure you put Ayutthaya, a spectacular World Heritage site, on your list of places to visit along with a trip north to Chiang Mai and Chiang Rai, two of the most popular spots in the country. From here you can visit the hill tribes, hike in the mountains, and feed and ride the elephants. In some of the local elephant farms, you'll be able to feed them sugar cane and bananas, and they'll be happy to wrap their trunks around your waist to thank you for the treats. You can climb on seats secured to their backs and they'll take you to the top of a mountain, up harrowing narrow stretches of paths that seem inches from impending disaster.

I wondered how I'd say it. "Well, I was on this elephant and he slipped and fell down the hill and that is why my body is broken in so many places." Or, "How did I break my shoulder? I fell off an elephant. True story." Of course there was a part of me that almost wanted it to happen, just to watch the reaction from people, especially at some swanky New York party.

Traveling in Thailand does require some precautions, especially on the health front. Never drink the water. Make sure that you have all of your shots for that part of the world. Beware of dengue fever and make sure that you take malaria pills if you're going to parts of Thailand or other Asian spots that require it. It's all pretty simple, really. For the seasoned traveler, this is a familiar precaution. I'm convinced that malaria pills make me dream in Technicolor. I have sharp, vivid dreams that are rich in detail and nuance. Then again, maybe it's the ingredients in the Thai food.

Thailand is a pretty easy place to travel to. Most people speak English, and the Thai sensibility is welcoming and lovely. Most Thais will go out of their way to help you and to tell you a tale or two about their country. In fact, they'll thank you for visiting them.

If you have another week or two after visiting Thailand, consider going to Myanmar. It is still largely undiscovered and a trip on the Irrawaddy River to visit the temples of Pagan will amaze you. But if you only have a few more days to add to your trip, I'd recommend one of two places. The first is Luang Prabang in northern Laos and the other is Siem Reap in Cambodia, the location of the famous Angkor Wat temple.

Having seen most of Asia, I have to say that Luang Prabang is one of the most under-visited places in the area. Only an hour from Chiang Mai or ninety minutes from Bangkok, this UNESCO World Heritage site just opened to tourism in 1989. Situated in a verdant valley between the Nam Khan and Mekong rivers, Luang Prabang has a touch of the old Indochina. Imagine the charm of French colonial architecture mixed in with forty or more temples all within walking distance from the center of town. There are charming cafes and restaurants, along with friendly shops that sell Laotian handicrafts and artwork. Throughout the city, there's still a bit of a French flair that permeates the town and is beginning to attract both worldly travelers and adventurers.

It was here that we met Emi, the sister-in law of my friend and travel group member Frank. An Australian who moved to Luang Prabang a few years earlier, Emi has a charming shop called Mai te sai, which carries handmade products from local villages. Emi and her dog Leon are well known in town and we spent a lot of quality time with her getting to know what life is like there. At her simple Laotian home built on stilts over a pond, we learned how an expat found her way to establish a business and become a part of the local life.

She took us to one of her neighborhood restaurants for Sinda. For this meal, a bucket of hot coals is placed in a cutout in the center of the table. A metal device is placed over the fire and you lubricate a dome-like part of the metal with chicken fat. Then you place strips of meat and chicken on the dome to cook. The drippings fall into a rim that is filled with chicken stock,

146　and here you place fresh vegetables and greens to accompany the meal. All washed down with Lao Beer, the meal was one of our favorite local experiences, costing us around $6 each. We were the only Westerners in the place and it was a treat to watch the locals enjoy their night out, especially a group of teenage girls who manipulated all of the ingredients while checking their cell phones for messages. Some things are the same no matter where you are in the world.

On a beautiful Laotian afternoon, Emi piled us along with a group of friends from London, Brisbane, and Sydney into a long Mekong River Boat to head downstream to the waterfalls outside of town. During the hour-long ride, we took in the busy river life, where sloping farms come down to the water and where locals are bathing themselves and washing their clothes. We nibbled on sushi and took it all in before pulling up to the riverside, where we all loaded into an open pickup truck to take us the five miles (eight kilometers) to the lush waterfall in the jungle.

Luang Prabang is filled with charming guesthouses (complete with Internet access) along the Mekong, or you can stay at the Amantaka or La Résidence Phou Vao, a charming hotel on a hilltop that overlooks the surrounding mountains. Wherever you stay, make sure that you walk to the top of Mount Phousy, where you'll see Buddhist life in local form. Get up at dawn to observe the young monks accept alms as they parade through the city, visit the night market, and stroll along the leafy side streets—all are sure to enthrall. After spending a few days in Luang Prabang, I could have easily stayed a few more. The town is friendly, warm, and welcoming. Put this one on your list as one of the great treasures that can still be experienced in an Asia that has rapidly become modernized. Cap, one of our fellow travelers, did stay on longer and then announced that he'd return the next year, perhaps for two or three months. It's easy to become charmed by this lovely city.

On the other hand, Siem Reap in Cambodia has crossed the line into tourist mania. And while it is true that the country needs the income from tourism dollars, it's developed a bit of a circus atmosphere. The whole reason for going to Siem Reap is to see Angkor Wat, one of the Seven Wonders of the World and the largest religious building on the planet. Built in the early twelfth century by King Suryavarman, it started as a Hindu temple, but transitioned into a Buddhist place of worship. Its stunning Khmer architecture will stop you in your tracks as you take in the enormous temple complex known as City Temple.

Visit Siem Reap as soon as possible, and when you're there, arrange to go to Angkor Wat as early in the day as possible, before the busloads of tourists arrive. Why go now? It's still possible to freely roam Angkor, but the fragility of the place may dictate that it be roped off someday, and visitors may have to observe it from above or from a distance. Today you can still walk around, visiting places like Ta Prohm, the much-photographed tree with giant roots that wrap around the temple. It will not disappoint.

Cambodia has worked hard at moving beyond the devastation brought on by Pol Pot and the Khmer Rouge. One place where this is evident is at the Children's Hospital of Angkor Wat. Founded by the well-known Japanese photographer Kenro Izu, it is now more than twelve years old and has just treated its one-millionth child. Kenro saw a desperate need to help the children of Cambodia, and the Hospital is a beacon of the country's hope and future. It's been my great pleasure to help raise funds for the hospital over the past decade. For those of us involved with the organization Friends Without a Border that handles all of the hospital's needs, it's been rewarding to watch our efforts come to life.

Unlike Northern Asia, much of Southeast Asia is still a work in progress. In the streets of Ho Chi Minh, Phnom Penh, and Luang Prabang, there is the belief that the future will be filled with opportunity and promise.

Perhaps if I was in my twenties I'd venture to this part of the world to participate in the excitement. Getting involved in an NGO or helping young adults establish businesses would be one possible path. In the U.S. today there is much talk about the future of China, and American students elect to study Mandarin and lean into the big future that China will represent on the world scene. While this is all true, I say go south, young men and women. Whether you prefer the big city life of Bangkok or Singapore, or you want something more rural, it's all there in Southeast Asia. You'll have a rich experience that will fulfill your life. I'll be looking for you on a riverboat on the Mekong, or in the streets of Bangkok, or in Luang Prabang, sharing a coffee with Emi.

Perhaps Mark Twain said it best.

Twenty years from now, you will be more disappointed by the things that you didn't do than by the ones you did do.

So throw off the bowlines. Sail away from the safe harbor. Catch the trade winds in your sails. Explore. Dream. Discover.

Above the Arctic Circle

MONEY TALKS IN MANY LANGUAGES

A little bit of cash can go a long way. Dollars, euros, pesos, bhats; they can all work little miracles in a travel dilemma. I'm not talking about slipping a maître d' a $20 bill for a table at that restaurant that you want to try in New York, or the concierge who can get you two tickets to that hit play in London. I'm talking about what you do when you're stranded on the Mekong River at the border between Vietnam and Cambodia, or when you learn that your flight from Riga to Tallinn was actually the day before, or when a policeman stops you in Havana, telling you that you made an illegal right turn even though there was no sign prohibiting it (that happened to me twice).

No matter where you go in the world, the old adage "money talks" is a universal theme. And how to apply it just the right way is one of the best travel skills that you can develop.

On a trip through the Mekong Delta in the southern part of Vietnam, we had ended up in the lovely city of Chau Doc, a bustling market town that is a photographer's delight. You can spend hours in the floating markets taking pictures of stacks of bananas and passion fruit, all being sold by the friendly locals. We'd bought tickets on a boat that would take us up the Mekong River to Phnom Penh, Cambodia, a few-hour journey that had just been approved as a way to improve the relations of the two countries.

It all started out pleasant enough. We were on a small yet comfortable boat that could hold around sixteen people, although there were only six of us that morning. And the hotel had even sent along one of their staff to chaperone us to the border. We enjoyed watching the river life on the Mekong, and all went fine until we reached the border. We handed over our passports to the border patrol and went through a series of checkpoints, while the other passengers and the boat crew did the same.

While we were waiting in the sitting area after the checkpoints, we began to see that there was some type of problem. A thirty-minute wait turned into a an hour, then an hour and a half, and soon we learned that while we

150 were okay, the boat wasn't. The papers, as they say, were not in order, and we would have to go back to Chau Doc. But I was determined to move forward, as we were en route to Siem Reap and Angkor Wat, a portion of the trip that I was not going to miss.

Along the riverfront, I noticed a few fishermen with their small boats. Time for a little negotiation, I thought. Remember that staff member from the hotel? My assignment to him was to help us find a fisherman who would take two of us up river. Within fifteen minutes we'd made the deal: twenty-five dollars for the boat ride and a few bucks for the hotel staffer. With that, my friend Frank and I piled our luggage onto the small boat, no more than sixteen-feet (five meters) long, and began the four-hour journey.

It did occur to me that no one in the world knew where we were, and that anything could happen on a big river; but the fisherman looked friendly enough. Until an hour into the trip, when, in the middle of the river, he shut off the engine, got on his walkie-talkie, and started talking in rapid sentences. Not a good sign. After he hung up the phone, he stood on the edge of the boat, relieved himself in the water, gave us a big smile, and off we were again. The proverbial rest stop, Cambodian style.

The trip was actually magical in the small boat, giving us a very local view of river life as we moved into dusk and ultimately to a public dock in Phnom Penh, where we were dropped off. We jumped out of the boat, paid our bill to the fisherman and gave him and extra $10 for getting us there safely, then hailed a rickshaw that would take us to our hotel, only a few hours later than our original arrival time.

For me, the "money talks" premise counts when it comes to transportation. Once, arriving late on a flight from Tel Aviv to Cairo, where I had to catch a plane to Rome, I explained my situation to the flight attendant, and she said, "Let me see who meets our flight." Pulling in to the gate, I saw her chatting with someone, and she waved me up to the front of the plane.

"This is Abdul, she said. "He's going to take care of you, but you have to take care of him."

"Done," I said.

And off we went, through a variety of passport controls, security stops, and checkpoints worthy of anything that you'd expect on a flight between these two destinations. All along the way, I was handing out twenty-dollar bills as I was ushered through one place to the next, arriving at my gate for the flight to Rome with a minute to spare and a big smile from Abdul as I handed him fifty dollars. The hundred dollars in total was worth every bit, considering that I had an important meeting in the morning with the Italian Trade Commission in Rome.

I've paid my way out of a lot of jams, delays, and chaos. Flying from St. Maarten to St. Barts and vice versa is notorious for having to pay off the gate agents to get on the small planes that go back and forth, and I've done my part. Offering an off-duty cab driver double his meter to get me to a destination works most of the time. I even tipped a baggage desk attendee when our group was stranded in Nelspruitt, South Africa, trying to get to Mozambique. By connecting to the travel agent in Johannesburg who'd arranged the trip, we were able to work up an alternative plan that was actually more convenient than the original.

But perhaps my favorite is when three of us arrived at the airport in Riga, Latvia, for a flight to Tallinn, Estonia, and we learned that our travel agent had made a mistake by booking us on a flight that didn't exist. The flight was actually the day before. After assessing the situation, we realized that the trip wasn't that far (about four hours away by car), so we went downstairs and cut a deal with a taxi driver to take us to Tallinn. For around $400, he delivered us to the front door of our hotel, and we all got refunds on the flight, paid for by the travel agent, who had realized the error.

Most times people just want to help and don't expect a tip, and you can usually assess the situation pretty quickly. But sometimes you have to decide if you want to take a risk. While visiting Havana, a policeman pulled us over to tell us that we had made a right and that it was illegal, even though there was no sign that said "no right turn." He asked for our passports, and when he saw that we were Americans he said in broken English, "I'm going to have to take you to the police station and give you a ticket."

So, I decided to go for it and said, "Can I just pay you directly for the ticket?" After a minute of thinking about it, he said yes, but had no idea what he should charge me. When I offered twenty dollars, it seemed to be the right amount to him, and the deal was done. Ironically, the next day, another policeman pulled us over in another part of town for the same supposed wrong turn. At first I thought, "Could the word have gotten out and

152   now we were going to become the favorite target of every cop in town?" This time, I slipped a twenty dollar bill into my passport when I handed it to him, and sure enough, he thanked me, gave me back my passport, and I was on my way.

Now I don't recommend doing this in a major city like New York or London or Tokyo. But in Havana, or other third-world capitals, it is a practical solution. What we learn when we travel is that we have to navigate through the tough spots. A twenty here or a twenty there will not only help you out, but quite honestly, this extra bit of cash is important to those people who you give it to. Perhaps it's my rationalization of things, but the next time you find yourself at a dead end, think about it. Cash is still king or queen just about everywhere in the world.

TIPS

GLENN AND SUSAN ROTHMAN

Owners, Hearts on Fire Diamonds

- Push yourself outside of your comfort zone. Exploring or experiencing something new opens you up to learning new things about yourself and the world.

- The farther away you travel, the clearer your life becomes. Quiet minds away from day-to-day worries are powerful and can be re-charged by faraway adventures.

- Before going somewhere, ask trusted explorers for advice. You'll discover experiences that you shouldn't miss or wouldn't have encountered otherwise.

- Spend the money. It will create a better experience. Shorten the trip if you have to, but go for it.

- Pack, then take half the clothes out. Wear lots of black and take a Kindle or Nook.

Pudong, Shanghai

SHANGHAI: THE CITY OF THE FUTURE

I had to see Shanghai with my own eyes. Actually, I'd already seen it in the late 1980s, when a walk on the Bund (the local river embankment) turned into a near riot as more than a hundred locals surrounded us in a circle, just to take a look at their first Westerners. In those days, the shimmering skyscrapers of Pudong, across the Huangpu River, where the tallest building in China now stands, soon to be overtaken by a new building that will be the tallest in Asia, simply didn't exist. Pudong was just marshland. The Shanghai No. 1 Department Store was dark and gloomy with lots of empty cases, while today it overflows with merchandise. And as for restaurants, in those days, we often didn't know what we were eating.

That was twenty years ago! Today, Shanghai will dazzle you with its futuristic view of the world, where hundreds of skyscrapers have been built in place of small neighborhoods within the city. And hundreds more are in the works. The transformation has been nothing short of breathtaking, perhaps one of the fastest development works in the history of the world.

What else will you see in today's Shanghai? Mega stores that house Vuitton, Gucci, and Prada, all with multiple locations around the city. GAP, Nike, and Starbucks (there are four hundred Starbucks in mainland China) are in neighborhoods around town. And then there are the two gigantic Apple stores, along with the Maserati, Mercedes, and Audi dealerships. And if you're hungry, Jean-Georges has a restaurant here, and you can find any type of cuisine you crave, although I wasn't able to find a Mexican restaurant (for you entrepreneurs out there). There are still many small family-owned boutiques and dumpling stores on the streets, but parts of Shanghai don't even feel like China. However, one thing is for sure—this town feels rich! And with two hundred million Chinese entering the middle class over the last seven years, it will only get richer.

I'd come to Shanghai in search of old Shanghai. To photograph the crumbling and disappearing neighborhoods for a new book called *Global*

156   *Remains* (Glitterati, 2011). My guide Annie, a local twenty-something who watched *Project Runway* and *Sex and the City* on the Internet (Chinese television would never show it), has a page on the Chinese version of Facebook, Happy, (Facebook is outlawed) and is one of one hundred million Chinese on the site, and who wears one of the hottest fashion trends—UGGs, pronounced here as three letters U.G.G—was as frustrated as I became as we drove around the city looking for vanishing neighborhoods.

Aside from moving into the twenty-first century at warp speed, Shanghai went on steroids a few years ago to prepare itself for the 2010 World Expo, which just ended after greeting seventy-three million visitors. This has been the main catalyst in the city's remarkable evolution.

Over two days, we crisscrossed the city on leads about abandoned neighborhoods, and we did find some great subjects. But I soon realized that I had missed the real opportunity. Shanghai has already metamorphosed into a modern Asian city of twenty-five million. And while you can still see many lane houses, local housing tucked in alleyways off of the main streets, there is more of a feel of Hong Kong here, or Singapore. Vanishing Shanghai has already vanished.

While this town is several hundred years old, it is the 1920s that put this place on the global map. It was then that the city lived up to its legendary status: home of glamour, spy rings, brothels, and commerce. It was then that many of the stunning art deco buildings (many along the Bund) were erected by European businessmen, who came here to create the most Western destination in Asia. To walk along the Bund is to see the famous Peace Hotel, the Shanghai Club, and the famous Customs House. Today those buildings are beautifully restored, housing offices, shopping complexes, and restaurants. Here you'll find Armani, Cartier, the famous M restaurant, and now a Peninsula Hotel. There's also the House of Roosevelt (yes, that Roosevelt), which is a wine bar, store, and three restaurants, boasting the largest collection of wine in all of China (over 2,600 wines). In many ways, the Bund carries on its tradition as the center of the universe. A walk along its nearly one-mile riverbank, on a modern expansive walkway with views of Pudong, says it all. Hello twenty-first century. And by the way, Westerners are now a dime a dozen. No one even looks twice!

Like many big cities, Shanghai is a collection of neighborhoods: The Old City, the Bund, Pudong, Jingang, Xintandi, and more. And getting around is easy; there's a modern, sparkling clean metro system along with plentiful and cheap taxis ($3 for a fifteen-minute ride). But I want to focus on two areas: People's Square and the French Concession.

A microcosm of modern Shanghai, People's Square is an area that was once the home of an in-town racetrack and is now the cultural center of the city. Here, in a massive and leafy park, are walkways, fountains, and flower gardens, along with the stunning Shanghai Museum, The Shanghai Grand Theatre, the Modern Art Museum, and the Shanghai Art Museum. All of this has been built within the past decade, a monument to urban planning gone right. From here it's a twenty- to thirty-minute walk down famous Nanjing Road to the Bund, home to Shanghai's daily life and a great place to people-watch. You'll see stylish young women in knee-high boots (or UGGs) and teenage boys who look like they could be in any mall in the U.S. And what would any major city be without street hawkers? Although here people approach you and ask if you want "watches, iPhone, or iPad." Welcome to Shanghai.

The French Concession, Shanghai's most charming neighborhood, is where I stayed, as recommended by Han Feng, the Chinese designer who returned here after twenty years in New York City to build her fashion and theater costume business. This part of town was literally given to the French when they first came here (the Americans and British got a designated area too), which is why it has the name it does, not to mention the touches of Parisian life, like the leafy trees that fill the neighborhoods of Paris and are also evident here. This part of town has charming streets, alleyways, shops, bistros and, believe it or not, the highest concentration of art deco build-ings anywhere in the world. This is where both Sun Yat-sen and Mao Tse-tung chose to live (what a surprise), and where you'll find many embassies and consulates. Strolling theses streets can feel like walking in the sixth arrondissement of Paris and here is where you'll see the charm of Shanghai that has not been torn down and rebuilt from the ground up.

The Shanghainese people have mixed feelings about the rapid changes going on in their city. In one sense, it's making them prosperous and mod-ern. On the other, the street life that gives a city it's unique character is fading into the past. I guess all major cities go through this at one time or another, but it's making for a more homogeneous place. Shanghai today is more like Singapore, or Frankfurt, or even Houston.

158   The change was inevitable, as China marches forward to become the second most prosperous country in the world. Some say that it will surpass the U.S. in GDP by 2025. China is on the move. Its people are being educated, and they can't get enough of education, success, and hard work. It's inspiring to see and to hear the locals talk about their opportunities and their drive to achieve. There is no sense of entitlement like what has crept into our national psyche. And while the one-child rule has lead to what many say is a spoiled class of young adults, they're all working hard to make it on their own. If Shanghai is representative of the new China, then look out. This is an economic tsunami that's going to continue to ripple across the globe.

All Americans who can should come to China to see for themselves what is happening and perhaps to take a lesson. How do we reinvent ourselves to stay competitive and vibrant? What is happening in China right now is affecting all of us and our future.

At one point, while strolling through the old market area of Shanghai (complete with a Starbucks), Annie and I came across the oldest teahouse in Shanghai. I remember it from my trip here in the 80s. The whole area was subdued and drab and dotted with dumpling shops. Today, the old teahouse is restored, the crowds were buzzing with energy, and off in the distance were towering skyscrapers. The old dumpling shop is still there, but it is now lined up with young, stylish Shanghainese locals coming to the new trendy destination. And while dumplings will always be a mainstay of the Chinese diet, something tells me that these same people would be dining that night at the new Mortons, a sushi restaurant, or at Barbarossa, a Moroccan style restaurant, if that were the mode.

Welcome to the new China. Welcome to the future.

TIPS

ROBBIE MYERS

Editor in Chief, *ELLE* magazine

- When you're on a business trip, always visit at least one place that you haven't seen.

- It's better to dry clean on the road than to over pack.

- Globetrotter (the brand) luggage. It's sturdy and chic.

- Log onto elle.com before you leave. It will give you the inside track for events and shopping on every continent (except Antarctica).

- If you're waffling about a place, just go. It's on your mind for a reason.

Australian Ski Country

THE SNOWY MOUNTAINS OF AUSTRALIA

When most Americans think of Australia they imagine Sydney Harbor, the Outback, or the Great Barrier Reef. Yet one of Australia's true national gems is the Snowy Mountains, better known as the Australian Alps, which are situated midway between Sydney and Melbourne, in the southeast corner of New South Wales. The destination of choice there is Thredbo, an alpine village whose population grows from three hundred to four thousand in the winter and offers access to all of the many sporting activities in the region.

Nestled in a valley in Kosciuszko National Park, a UNESCO Biosphere Reserve, Thredbo was established in the late 1950s following environmentally conscious guidelines for housing, shops, and restaurants. The result is a unique design that gracefully blends into the eucalyptus-rich area. The town has Australia's longest ski runs (there are only five ski resorts in the country), but also offers year round activities including whitewater rafting, horseback riding, fly fishing, and mountain hiking on great alpine trails. One may also hike to the top of Australia's highest mountain, Mount Kosciuszko at 7,310 feet (2,228 meters), which draws climbers from all over the world.

My own attempt to climb the world's Seven Summits is what led me to discover this unique part of the country. The summit is attainable by most; it takes about six hours of moderate hiking and offers the experience of standing on the very top of Australia, complete with majestic views of the surrounding peaks and valleys.

Often compared with Sun Valley, Idaho, many locals and ski instructors spend American winters there and Australian winters in Thredbo. Like Sun Valley, it attracts a well-heeled, sporty crowd both on and off the mountains.

For après-sport entertainment there are several fine restaurants in town, like Santo and Credo, both serving exceptional food from local trout to organic chicken, chef-inspired appetizers and desserts, and an impressive list of Australian and international wines.

162   Accommodations in town range from the larger Thredbo Alpine Hotel to smaller inns. A favorite is the Suncloud B&B, a four-bedroom luxury boutique bed and breakfast. Staying at the Suncloud is like staying with friends in their lovely ski house, yet it also offers privacy. The stylish house boasts a very comfortable living and dining room with a great stone fireplace, a selection of outstanding photography books on Australia, and many videos and CDs to enjoy in your own room or while you're in the roomy hot tub. Guests have tea and coffee service in their rooms and fresh baked muffins every morning, along with a home cooked breakfast. The Suncloud is minutes from the town center, and when you take the nature walk to get there you may spot wild parrots, a family of ducks, and quite possibly a kangaroo or two.

The quickest way to reach Thredbo and the stunning Snowy Mountain region is on the forty-five-minute Horizon Air commuter flight from Sydney, followed by a forty-five-minute drive. The drive from Sydney is around six hours and around two hours or so from Canberra. Auswalk and other local tour operators can arrange all of your hiking and skiing needs. This Australian experience promises a different dimension to a holiday down under, but still captures the fun-loving nature of the Australian people and their commitment to enjoying not only the sun, sea, and beaches, but also the mountains. For any traveler who enjoys this kind of outdoors experience, Thredbo is a world-class destination, worth at least three or four days of an Australian adventure.

TIPS

KATE WHITE

Former Editor in Chief, *Cosmopolitan* Magazine and Best Selling Author

- Create a personalized flight kit that includes a sleeping mask, almonds—whatever is important to you.

- Follow the 80/20 rule. Only plan 80 percent of the trip and leave the other 20 percent for serendipitous experiences.

- Use guides like Zagat and Trip Advisor sparingly. Use these resources for ruling out the duds, but rely on people who know your tastes and interests for recommendations.

- Stay in the best hotel that you can afford. Ignore the people who say, "You're hardly in the room." Waking up and returning each night to a charming hotel can make all the difference.

- Put your itinerary in a flexible binder—it makes it easier to refer to. And when you're back, you can drop it in a folder so that you have a record of your entire trip.

Above the New York City Clouds

THE ZEN OF THE LONG-HAUL FLIGHT

When I learned that Singapore Airlines had scheduled the longest flight in the world (more than eighteen hours from Newark to Singapore), I had an adrenaline rush. It immediately went on my bucket list, and I started to figure out how and when I might experience this milestone flight. I am a fan of the long haul flight—twelve-, fourteen-, sixteen-hour flights. For most people this is inconceivable; for me it's as good as the destination itself.

There's a long list of long-haul flights in my repertoire. New York to Johannesburg, Los Angeles to Sydney, Buenos Aires to Paris, London to Cape Town, and New York to Dubai are just some of my trophy flights.

When people ask me how I cope with such long flights, I tell them that "I get into the Zen of it." The first step is to wrap your head around the idea that you'll be on an airplane for a while. Being anxious won't help. Plan it out, just as you would plan the trip itself.

How do you plan? The answer is, it depends. Is it an overnight flight? Is it non-stop (preferable)? Are you in coach? I've flown the sixteen-hour flight from Los Angeles to Sydney in coach. I've also flown it in first class (always preferable), and I've even flown on a private G-5 from Cairns to New York, with a refuel in Honolulu (definitely preferable). Are you crossing multiple time zones or just one such as New York to Buenos Aires?

Regardless of the situation, the long hauler is a mini-vacation for me. In a constantly wired world of smart phones, blackberries, e-mail, Facebook, Twitter, and Foursquare, a long flight actually gives me time to think, reflect, relax, and catch up on sleep, books, and movies. And even though a long flight across the world can be tiring, I usually arrive feeling like I've accomplished something.

On a flight to Sydney I wrote a speech that I had to give in New York a week later. I've worked on major work presentations, organized photos, and even wrote out goals for the following year. And while many of my friends debate what sleeping pill to take, for me sleeping on a plane is pretty much a no-brainer. A glass or two of wine with dinner, and I'm usually out for at least a six-hour power-sleep. Obviously, I don't subscribe to the idea that you shouldn't drink on a plane.

In a particular Type A move, I once ran the Buenos Aires Marathon and six hours later boarded a flight to Paris. I have to admit, I wondered if it was one of the dumbest things I'd ever done. But ultimately it was one of the best eight-hour sleeps I ever had. So on these long overnight flights, plan to sleep as much as possible. If you need a pill, then so be it.

For every long haul, I wear loose clothing, take off my shoes immediately, and check out the amenities pack, filled with eyeshades, toothpaste, and a razor. I drink lots of water and moisturize regularly, as well as brush my teeth. And I always eat every meal offered. Actually, the food is pretty decent on these flights.

I prefer flights that leave at 10:00 p.m. or later, and I always try for non-stops. And for upgrades. Nothing beats a sleeper! On a recent non-stop fifteen-hour flight from New York to Shanghai, I decided to keep a mini diary on what I did on the flight. The Continental 777 left Newark Airport at 11:00 a.m. and landed in Shanghai at close to 3:00 p.m. on what was the next day. The time zone for Shanghai is thirteen hours ahead of New York so this fifteen-hour flight took place during what was waking hours. I did manage a two-hour nap, but what about the other thirteen hours? Well, here goes.

On this particular flight, I used earned miles to upgrade to BusinessFirst, which allows ample room to stretch out, roominess in the cabin, and an entertainment system that you'd love to have in your home. There were 198 movies (yes, 198) to choose from, 116 television shows, ten different music genres, games, and a first rate flight tracking map. This is what I call airplane heaven.

Most airlines that fly long hauls—Singapore, Thai, Emirates—really know how to pamper their passengers and I'd put this flight right up there. The attendants were an attentive multi-lingual group that made everyone feel at home. And they had a great menu. I passed on the Mongolian beef and opted for the Chinese noodle bowl, shrimp and scallops in oyster sauce with sui-mei dumplings as the main course with sumptuous appetizers, salad, and desserts. For breakfast there were five different choices from omelets to congee. And there was espresso and cappuccino and snacks along the way.

I decided to do some cultural catch up. So, here's my lineup for this flight:

- Three movies (*Gandhi, X-Men,* and *The Reader*)

- One book (*The Wave,* by colleague and friend Susan Casey), hardbound

- Half a book (*Freedom* by Jonathan Franzen), iPad

- Four magazines (*Economist, Esquire, AOPA Pilot,* and *Conde Nast Traveler*)

- *Time Out Shanghai* (a guide to help plan out some of the visit).

Periodically I'd check the flight progress; three hours out at 35,000 feet (10, 668 meters) and 596 mph (959 kph), we headed past Davis Strait into Baffin Bay in Northern Canada, heading to fly over the North Pole, across Northern Russia, Mongolia, and ultimately Shanghai. The 7,868-mile (12,662-kilometer) flight was tracked well, and I swear I didn't wonder what would have happened over the Pole if there had been some issue with the flight. I think that's when I put Gandhi on.

Anyway, it was a cultural explosion. And, did I mention that I wrote this story too? And made a Christmas list.

And since this is a four-day trip to Shanghai to take photos for a book project, *Global Remains,* I'm already looking forward to the flight home. Although I haven't gotten my upgrade yet.

I still haven't done the longest flight in the world, but I'm well trained and you will be too, if you just settle in and go to the Zen of it. The long hauler may just become your favorite kind of flight. See you at the airport.

Nukubati Island, Fiji

TAKE ME TO FIJI

Bula! For any visitor to Fiji, this is usually the first word you hear upon arrival at this South Pacific paradise. It's a happy greeting meaning hello, welcome, and good health; far different from how visitors must have been greeted two centuries ago, when Fiji was known as the Cannibal Isles.

Today friendly to outsiders, the tropical Fiji Islands, an archipelago of over three hundred islands situated between Vanuatu and Samoa, deep in the South Seas, are fast becoming a destination of choice for international travelers weary of big, overcrowded island resorts. Still unspoiled and un-developed, Fiji is what many people say Hawaii was like one hundred years ago. You won't find big, inclusive resorts overrun with tourists, but instead smaller hotels along the Coral Coast and scattered throughout the islands. A collection of private island resorts has emerged, creating a unique travel experience. While there are a couple of dozen of these resorts, only a hand-ful are considered truly exclusive. Some of them offer only seven to ten bungalows or *bures,* and many of them can be rented exclusively for a whole family or group of friends.

Our travel group usually looks for something with a little edge or adven-ture. We'd recently been on camelback in the Tunisian Sahara, and had been on one of the first boats from Chau Doc, in the Vietnamese Mekong, to Phnom Penh, before moving on to Siem Reap and Myanmar. But this time we wanted something a bit more tame and relaxing for unsettling times.

I remembered that when I was a child, my aunt and uncle, then living in Melbourne, would stop in Fiji overnight before heading home to the U.S., but none of our well-traveled group knew anyone who'd actually gone to Fiji for a vacation. After some research, we were convinced that we'd found a place not yet overtaken by either the traveling masses or big developers.

For centuries, Fiji existed as a collection of fishing and farming villages, mostly made up of tribes of Melanesian and Polynesian influences. Not until the Europeans arrived in the seventeenth and eighteenth centuries, followed

170 by European missionaries in the nineteenth century, and ultimately gaining British colony status in 1874, did Fiji begin to evolve into the exotic melting pot that it is today. An independent nation since 1970, and with a new, stable democratic government elected in August 2001, modern Fiji is a flavorful mix of native Fijians, Europeans, Indians (who came as indentured servants in the last century), and Chinese. Considered the most multi-racial country in the South Pacific, this fact is felt in the unique foods, customs, and traditions that make up modern Fiji. Yet with a population of approximately 800,000 covering an area of 7,056 square miles (18,274 square kilometers), there are still many local social and religious customs that remain only in certain parts of this scattered island nation.

We decided on the private island resort approach and explored options with Lynette Wilson, owner of Santa Barbara-based Destination World and a 140-trip veteran to the islands. The choices were plentiful, from one of the top luxury resorts like Turtle Island, where parts of the film *Blue Lagoon* was filmed, or Wakaya Club, owned by David and Jill Gilmour, also founders of Fiji Water, where you can spend over $3,000 a night or more.

Ultimately, we decided on Nukubati, situated just inside the Great Sea Reef, the third largest reef in the world, just north of Vanua Levu, the second of the largest two islands. Nukubati offered an authentic experience, as opposed to feeling that we might be at just another luxury resort anywhere in the world. One of the most appealing features was that it is the only Fijian owned and operated resort. Our hope was that it would give us a personal connection with the Fijian people. Personally, I was also intrigued that the island's power was from its own solar plant, fresh water was filtered rainwater, and all fruits and vegetables were organically grown. The setting seemed totally idyllic, yet still offered all of the creature comforts that would make it special.

"If you're going to the South Pacific for the first time, you should have the genuine experience," Wilson said. "On Nukubati, you'll feel like you're in another time and place."

We arrived on Christmas Eve morning, losing a day during our ten-hour Pacific Air flight from Los Angeles. The Fijian national airline, operated by Qantas, and Air New Zealand both operate non-stop flights from L.A. All international flights land in Nadi (pronounced Nandi), a sleepy town on the west coast of Viti Levu, the larger of Fiji's two major islands. While many visitors head directly to the Coral Coast two hours away, we decided to spend at least a week on Nukubati, followed by a few days of sailing in the Mamanuca Islands. After clearing customs in Nadi, we took the short walk to the domestic terminal, arriving at the Pacific Islands Counter, a seaplane charter service that would take us one hour north to Nukubati. Above the counter, a sign read, "We Fly You To Places Others Only Dream Of."

"Bula and g'day," our Australian pilot, Tony, said, asking each of us to step on the scale, so that he could determine the weight and balance for our own dream flight. Soon, six of us were on board the ten-seat DHC-3 Otter, given our safety check, provided with headphones for inflight music, and asked to buckle up. Within minutes, our barefoot pilot maneuvered the plane onto the active runway, and soon at 5,500 feet (1,676 meters), we nestled in for our smooth ride over the lush hills and valleys of Viti Levu.

"There's Nukubati," yelled Tony above the engines, as he circled in from the north, gently settling the plane onto the water, taxiing towards the island. A small motorboat approached the plane, taking us to the island, where a group of Fijian men and women in native dress, or *sulus,* sang welcome songs while covering us with hibiscus leis.

"Bula and welcome," said Jenny Bourke, the owner of the island, as she led us through the seashell-lined sand walkway into the resort's main open-air pavilion, where we would have our meals.

Of Fijian and Chinese descent, Jenny, along with her Australian husband, Peter, founded Nukubati in 1993, while thinking about their own future retirement plans. Raised in nearby Labasa, Jenny went to college in Sydney, where she met and married Peter and where they continue to spend most of their time, raising three teenagers.

"My father had a trading store in the area, so I knew its natural beauty," said Jenny. "When I was young, I couldn't wait to leave the area, now I can't wait to get back here. I know everyone who now works for us on the island, and in most cases I knew their parents or grandparents. We are one big extended family," she laughs.

Nukubati, a thirty-five-acre (fourteen hectare) island, was originally occupied by a Fijian warrior clan. In the mid 1800s, the warring chief Ritova gave the island to Jacob Steiner, a German gunsmith. And after five generations, some of his descendants still live on the island. Nestled in a former coconut plantation, the resort has only seven bures, each facing the Western

Pacific sun. During our stay, we were a small international group of adult Americans, Australians, and Russians, both friends and strangers.

When we first arrived on the island, I must admit that I thought to my-self, "How am I going to do this for a whole week?" I imagined island fever, marooned on such a small place.

"Isn't that the whole idea?" asked my friend Tom, a fellow New Yorker. Not to worry, because in less than twenty-four hours, after absorbing the magnificent setting of mangroves and fruit trees, I quickly adapted to the rhythm of daily island life. There are no phones, televisions, or videos on the island. And although the small office has two-way radio and Internet ac-cess, we all agreed to stay out of touch with the world. We wanted to create our own private Fiji.

For the twelve guests on the island there was a staff of forty-five, yet we never had any sense that they were around. We were flawlessly cared for throughout each day. Our meals were prepared for us when we wished, and we selected from daily menus that offered such selections as Urau Ni Tulei, or poached lobster in Mornay sauce, or fresh local octopus cooked in coco-nut milk and accompanied by snake beans, Bok Choy, fresh breads, and corn pancakes, always finished off with a homemade pineapple meringue pie or bread pudding.

Snorkeling and diving was available, also at our own schedule, as was sailing or fishing in the area, all arranged by Matai, the island's charming activities director. Our own catch of the day, often times *walu* or coral trout, was happily prepared for us Fijian style in citrus or cucumber and ginger salsa by the resort's chef. Daily exercise included kayaking around the island, swimming in the warm Pacific, or playing the occasional game of tennis or volleyball with the staff. And for relaxation, the island offered a library of several hundred books and a massage hut where Eta, a local woman, soothes muscles with her own mix of coconut oil.

The only truly scheduled activity was the daily champagne and caviar each afternoon, delivered beachside or to our own private bure, usually with a big smile and greeting from Sarah, one of our personal favorites. Aside from the traditional kava ceremony, a social ritual that involves a pre-pared drink of local root and water shared as a spirit of friendship and wel-come and an oft-repeated event, most evenings were spent listening to sto-ries about life in Fiji, learning about life in Moscow from our new Russian friends, and sharing fishing tales with Jonathan and Annie, who had joined **173** us from Australia, or strolling the beach under the well-lit sky. The simplicity of studying the wide-open skies of the South Pacific could take an hour, reminding us that this was what a real tropical experience was meant to be. For a family, or great friends, it's the place for both quality time and a chance to rediscover relationships and even yourself.

On Nukubati, as in all of Fiji, dress is casual. If you prefer to wear native sulus and no shoes for your entire stay, my choice for Day Three, you'll feel comfortable and welcomed. Each bure is equally casual, furnished with wicker furniture, straw mats, and tropical patterned fabrics, creating a South Seas atmosphere. Fresh flowers, a replenished beverage bar, and the daily laundry service all create a sense of home. The spacious bedroom and bath area, a generous seating area, and a wraparound porch all provide plenty of room for writing, dreaming, or napping. During our week stay, our only foray to the mainland was to visit the village of Niurua, home to two hundred people, fifteen minutes away by boat.

On Christmas morning, we were welcomed to the local Methodist church, where we joined in on the one-hour Fijian service, complete with Christmas songs sung in local dialect. The preacher gave us a special English welcome, and we were asked to speak to the small congregation, offering our own Christmas best wishes. Like Thanksgiving in America, this day in Fiji is for family gatherings and does not include gift giving or decorations. In that spirit, after the service we were invited to visit the village, where we met the local people who lived in houses that were more nineteenth century than today. More importantly, the genuine warmth and openness of the Fijians, still untouched by years of tourists descending upon them, made us appreciate the special nature of life in these tropics. Like Jenny, who told us that Nukubati was her home and wanted us to feel as if it was our home, the villagers took us onto their porches, offering kava and tea, showing us their gardens, and even performing dance recitals for us.

Throughout all of Fiji, we felt the special warmth of its people, and a welcome lack of constantly being harassed to buy souvenirs or take local tours. In fact, aside from the local craft markets operated for visitors and shops in the main cities, there is no real evident tourist trade that so many developed resorts have in full evidence. To visit Fiji is to feel and experience authentic island life indigenous to the South Pacific.

174 By the end of the week, the Fijian ways had captivated us. Without the distractions of everyday pressures and the frenetic days and crowds that resorts can often times create, we had been able to transport ourselves into their world, and we left Nukubati feeling that we had all reclaimed our lives in our own unique way. As we flew south to join our sailboat, leaving Nukubati was like leaving a home that we had discovered as our own, and our goodbyes with Jenny and her staff were as emotional as saying goodbye to family. My dream was to stay marooned a bit longer.

Yet I was soon to discover that sailing through the Mamanuca and Yasawa Islands is one of the great pleasures of the Fiji Islands, and that there are a number of ways to approach it. While it's easy to charter your own boat in Nadi, both Captain Cook Cruises and Blue Lagoon Cruises operate three-to-seven day cruises throughout the area, either by tall ship sailing, motor yacht, or luxury yachts of up to thirty-six staterooms. While Blue Lagoon offers the more luxurious way to travel, we opted to keep with our theme of a more authentic experience. The Captain Cook four-day sailing safari on the SV Spirit of the Pacific promised daytime sailing with overnight stays in simple bures on Drawaqa Island. A bit Spartan, with outdoor showers, Africa style, no electricity, and simple, but plentiful home cooked meals, this approach is for the more adventurous traveler. Whether open-deck sailing or cruising in an air-conditioned yacht, the simple beauty of experiencing life in these waters is the same. Whether sailing around the spectacular White Rock Island, snorkeling in Yalobi Lagoon, or visiting Waya Island to hike to the top of the Yalobi Hills, this is the South Pacific at its best, from azure waters to sparkling, cloudless blue skies.

Although these are the most popular islands to sail around, there are many different places to choose from, like the remote Moala or Lau Group, a collection of over fifty islands to the east, midway between Fiji and the kingdom of Tonga. Sighted by Captain Bligh of Mutiny on the Bounty fame, these island groups can be reached by local Air Fiji flights from Suva or Nadi, and you can either stay on local islands or on charter boats. A little further research can uncover many different places to explore in the islands, depending on your time and the type of experience that you may want.

A few months after I returned to the U.S., Jenny traveled stateside, and I welcomed her into my home in New York, where she agreed to spend the weekend. As she arrived in her winter clothes, she looked so different, yet as we embraced, I could smell the fragrances of Nukubati, and it transported me back to that special tropical experience. We reminisced, had a great reunion with some of the group who shared that Christmas week on Nuku-bati, and in that same Fijian warmth, Jenny invited all of us to her home in Sydney, but only if we agreed to stop in Fiji along the way. It was then that I realized that there are certain places that capture you, even if you've only been there once. In that odd way, Fiji had seeped into my soul, and in talk-ing to Jenny I found myself talking about the next time that I'd be able to go home to Fiji for a visit. She smiled, knowingly, her eyes sparkling. "The islands have that kind of magic. You just won't be able to stay away," she said.

With that, it seemed that my destiny awaited me.

San Telmo, Buenos Aires

RUNNING THROUGH BUENOS AIRES

When you're reading a story about Buenos Aires, you probably don't expect to read about a sports bra, but in this story one plays a role in the plot. But before we get to that, let me say "hello" from Palermo Viejo, one of the great neighborhoods of Buenos Aires (think Soho meets the West Village), where spring is in full bloom. This is my fifth visit to Buenos Aires, but the first time that I've stayed in this part of town. Part of the reason is that it's closer to the starting line of the Buenos Aires Marathon, a 26.2 miler (42 kilometers) through the city that my sister Peg and I are planning to run on Sunday morning. And as crazy as it sounds, I need to cross the finish line, go back to the hotel, shower, and head to the airport to fly to Paris. More on that later.

Argentina. What can I say except that it has become one of my favorite countries in the world? And I've managed to travel all over the country, from Ushuaia at the tip of Tierra del Fuego to the Perito Moreno Glacier in Santa Cruz province to the Valdes Peninsula, Bariloche, Iguaçu, and Mendoza. This is an achingly beautiful country with vast expanses of land, mountains, lakes, and glaciers to enjoy.

But of course, it all started in Buenos Aires, a place that was established in the sixteenth century by Europeans, mostly from Spain with a few Portuguese thrown in. From that beginning, this city (and country) has been plagued with some of the most volatile political and economic sagas to hit the Americas. Boom and bust, boom and bust, the cycle has continued from its early days to independence in 1810 to today.

My first trip to Buenos Aires was in 2002, when the country was reeling from yet another cataclysmic economic meltdown. The country went into default, unemployment rose to 20 percent plus, the country had four presidents in eleven days, and the peso was ultimately devalued by double digits! Those were the days when you heard stories about North Americans stockpiling amazing four-bedroom apartments at $50,000 each, as the dollar reigned supreme. At the time, the *porteños,* as the locals are called, seemed to take it in stride as just another part of the Argentine saga. Let's not forget that Juan Peron and Eva Peron were part of the country's colorful past, not to mention the dark days of the 1970s, when thousands were kidnapped and disappeared for opposing the government.

Buenos Aires has always had big ideas for itself. And you can see it in the streets; literally. Back in the 1880s, one of the city fathers, Torcuato Alvear, had the vision to create the grandest city in all of South America. Grand boulevards like Avenida de Mayo and Avenida 9 de Julio were conceived, and grand buildings of government and culture still dot the city. Many have compared Buenos Aires with Madrid or Paris, and they're not wrong, especially with the abundant plazas and parks. But unlike those cities, Buenos Aires does suffer a bit from neglect, and parts of the city could use some upgrading to give it the shine that it deserves. Still, the city is alive with over twelve million residents that create energy unrivaled in this part of the world.

To walk the streets of Palermo, Recoleta, or San Telmo, a gentrified neighborhood filled with antique stores, cafes, and restaurants, is to see Buenos Aires at work. Along the way, you'll find countless shops filled with everything from Cuban cigars to the delicious Havanna cookies to bras.

Yes, back to bras.

When my sister realized that she'd forgotten her sports bra, there was an all-out effort to find one somewhere in Buenos Aires. And here is what you need to know. Do *not* forget your sports bra when you come to Buenos Aires. Now there are many lingerie and bra shops here. In fact, they might be as plentiful as Starbucks in New York; there seems to be one on every corner. And in each one (we stopped counting at five), there was not one sports bra to be had. There were lots of other bras; pick your needs—pushup, sexy—well, you get the drift. Even the sports shops didn't sell them. Finally, we found ourselves on Florida Street, one of Buenos Aires's main shopping streets, when from behind the counter on the bottom shelf under a box, a saleswoman found what might be the last and only Reebok sports bra in the whole country. With only eighteen hours before the start of the marathon, this could have become a national incident.

Since the country was stabilized in the mid 2000s, Buenos Aires has been on a confident rebound. Each time I'm here, the city seems stronger. A trip to the Puerto Madero area is symbolic of what I mean. This dockland district went through a major facelift when the red brick port buildings and grain warehouses were restored to become a series of shops, restaurants, and clubs. Today the area is a dazzling example of the new Argentina at work. Here you will find Puerto Madero Este, a modern city within the city of glass and steel high rises that include some of the most expensive real estate on the continent. Here you'll find a super modern footbridge designed by Santiago Calvatara, as well as the world famous Faena Hotel + Universe. On the other side of Puerto Madero Este is a spectacular Ecological Reserve that boasts four lakes and a wide variety of birds and butterflies. One could almost come to Buenos Aires and never leave this part of town. But then you'd miss a lot of what there is to see and do.

Buenos Aires offers culture to rival any world capital (although most don't have tango), and maniacal sports, i.e. soccer, to rival any major American city, and all kinds of architecture that stands out in every neighborhood, though it exists alongside the requisite ugly South American box architecture. There are amazing restaurants such as Sucre and Patagonia Sur with every kind of food, although due to the heavy Italian influence here Italian food rules. But so do grilled steaks. And of course, all this needs to be washed down with Malbec from the Cuyo Valley near Mendoza. One can easily fill a week here, including a side trip to Iguaçu, a visit to an estancia, and maybe a hydrofoil ride over to Uruguay to walk the cobbled streets of Colonia, a World Heritage town.

Although Buenos Aires is a sprawling city like London, it is a city that you can walk in. But unlike London, the taxis are cheap, as are most things; this is one of those places where you get a lot for your dollar. And this is why Argentina has become one of the go-to places for Americans in the last few years.

I know that I'll return here again and again, as the country seems to be on a great track of growth and prosperity. There is a strong middle class and the government seems more stable than it has been in a long time. And even if Argentina has another of its political or economic hiccups, it won't daunt the *porteños* as they move it forward through the twenty-first century.

Now about that marathon. It was a stunning spring day and we ran a spectacular course that traversed every gorgeous part of the city, including the best parks, the rim of the ecological reserve in Puerto Madero, and all the important sights. Whoever mapped this course had one thing in mind: Show off the beauty of Buenos Aires.

180   The course is flat, at sea level, and extremely well organized. There were kilometer marks at every kilometer, ample water and Gatorade stations, as well as stations with water-soaked sponges to wipe your face, even bananas, oranges, raisins, and figs along the way! There were not a lot of crowds, as in other marathons, but there were groups that appeared at different intervals to cheer you on. Tell your marathon friends to put this one on their list.

I crossed the finish line at 3:49:53, and took a taxi back to the hotel to prepare for my 5:00 flight to Paris for a business trip; Peg would fly home the next day. A three-day weekend in Buenos Aires is a short stay, but with flatbeds and 777s, it all seems easy. And aren't we lucky to live in a world where this is even possible? *Abrazos!*

TIPS

MAX RYAN

Actor

- Carry your own antibiotics and tablet water purifiers, as you never know when you might need them.

- European airlines have different luggage weight and size limits than U.S. airlines. When you fly the low-cost European airlines with all of the add-ons, it's sometimes the same price for a mainstream airline, which is more comfortable.

- Photocopy your passport and zip it away somewhere on your body. Don't open your wallet in public. Carry limited credit cards and have some local money when you enter the country. Carry a card with your blood type.

- Learn some of the local language; please and thank you is a great start.

- Carry a spare phone with your local carrier service. Back it up with all of your phone numbers. It comes in handy if you lose your phone.

Mendoza, Argentina

MENDOZA, A WINE LOVER'S HEAVEN

It all started with love. And a wedding. If Alexia hadn't done her junior year abroad in Argentina and followed it up with a Fulbright there, perhaps she would not have met Diego. More importantly, they wouldn't have fallen in love and planned a wedding in Santiago before moving back to Boston, where Alexia would enroll at Harvard Law School.

The occasion was a perfect excuse to plan a trip and some of us, including Alexia's Uncle Tom, decided on a trip to Buenos Aires, a day in Iguaçu, some time in Bariloche, and some wine tasting in Mendoza before heading to Santiago for the celebration.

But this is really a story about a different kind of love. It's about how I fell in love with Mendoza and the Argentine wine country and how a small group of us became winemakers, growing our own Malbec—The Accidental Winemakers. But, I'm getting ahead of myself.

It all started with an innocent three-day trip to this lovely, leafy city that was founded in 1561. What makes Mendoza so special is the combination of lovely squares and wide boulevards that underscore its colonial feel, along with the sophistication that the wine world brings to the city.

In Mendoza, an intricate web of canals runs through the city and carries runoff water to all of the side streets. This has led to a wonderful commitment to planting trees all over town and this creates the special leafy characteristic that is unique to Mendoza. One place to see a concentration of greenery is in the main central park in town. It competes with any great urban park and it is great for a stroll, a run, or a quiet time to sit under a tree and practice your Spanish.

Argentina has long been a producer of wines, but it wasn't until the early part of the twenty-first century that there was a boom that was heard round the world. Much of it came from the *terroir* of the area surrounding Mendoza, the wine regions of Mendoza, including the Uco valley.

Still, some of the best-known names in Argentine wines were established in the late nineteenth and early twentieth centuries, including those

184   from the family of my Mendozan friend and great winemaker, Federico Benegas. For a great understanding of the history of this region, I'd recommend Laura Catena's book *Vino Argentino*. As a descendant of the famous Catena wine-making family, she brings great color and knowledge to the explanation of the whole wine region in this part of the world.

That first trip to Mendoza took me to a place that, unbeknownst to me at the time, would play an ongoing role in my growing love affair with Argentina. Following are just some of the reasons.

About thirty minutes out of town, we turned off of a main road onto a gravel road that began to wind through wine and olive vineyards, past a gathering of sand owls who sat on posts, blinking at us along the way. (The owls will take on an important role in this story, so stay tuned). As we wound our way through the intoxicating acres and acres of grapes, we arrived at a turn to see seven modern "vignettes" or villas poking their heads above the vines. Driving under a huge set of willow trees, we pulled into the Cavas Wine Lodge.

Owned by a young, stylish couple from Buenos Aires, Cecilia Diaz Chuit and Martin Rigal, Cavas is set on a thirty-five-acre (fourteen hectare) piece of property that was bought in 2003. Since then, this couple has built a most welcoming and warm spot that is always filled with international guests who mingle together at group breakfasts, wine tastings, and dinner. Since there are only fourteen rooms, spending time there tends to be an intimate experience, especially in the common areas, which are Spanish inspired, yet modern, filled with art from all over Argentina and with truly magnificent views of the Andes off in the distance.

Our stay there was magical—fine dining, open fires on the villa rooftop as we sat among the vineyards and watched the sunset over the Andes. We felt like family was taking care of us, as we headed for days of horseback riding in the foothills of the mountains, floating down the whitewater, and visiting some of the great local wineries, like Achaval-Ferrer. We were totally mesmerized by the beauty of the area and the warmth of the people, not to mention the delicious Malbecs.

On our last night, we drove into town to have dinner at Francis Mallmann 1884, an open-air restaurant in the heart of town, owned by the famous Argentine Chef, Francis Mallmann. And then I knew that somehow Mendoza play a part in my future.

Off we went to Santiago for the wedding, but my heart stayed nestled in **185**
the vineyards of Cuyo. I couldn't get it out of my head. What I'd discovered
was a magical spot that was like Napa Valley twenty years ago—a burgeon-
ing area of winemaking that wasn't yet overrun with commercialization.
And here it was in one of the most spectacularly beautiful parts of the world,
complete with many of my favorite outdoor activities. Not to mention
Aconcagua, the tallest mountain in South America, which is a climb on my
bucket list. I just had to find a way to be connected there.

So back in the U.S. I became the unofficial Publicity Director for Mendoza and the Cavas Wine Lodge. Before long I'd sent multiple sets of people
there for vacation. And with each group I talked to I'd sigh and say, "Come
back with some ideas for me. How can I find an investment there that would
make me an honorary Mendozan?"

Marlene came back with some thoughts. So did William. And finally,
when Martha went there, I sent her on a reconnaissance mission.

Bingo.

The report from the field was that Martha had discovered an idea and as
she presented it, I thought, "This could be it; this could be the one."

American Michael Evans, a former political strategist, had been traveling
in the region and, like many of us, he was inspired not only by the area, but
by the possibility that was emerging there. Before you know it, he'd linked
up with local Argentine businessman Pablo Gimenez Riili and famed winemaker Santiago Achával to establish a new type of business model for winemaking. Vines of Mendoza would be a five-hundred-acre (two-hundred-
two-hectare) operation that would produce their own wines and sell land
to commercial producers, including restaurateurs who might want to create
their own house wines, as well as making three- to ten-acre (one- to four-
hectare) parcels available to private investors. The idea was that you could
contract with the main company in a land purchase, pick your own desired
grapes, and then they would take it from there. You could be involved as
much or as little as you wanted to be. In the end you'd have your own wine,
for your own consumption or for sale. It seemed too easy. It seemed too
perfect. It seemed just right.

Before Martha could finish the whole story, I was on the LAN Chile
website, booking a flight to Santiago with the thirty-minute hop to Mendoza (the preferred route, by the way), and was soon in a Land Rover en

route to the Uco Valley to pay a personal visit to Vines of Mendoza. And, of course, I stayed at Cavas with Cecilia and Martin.

A day with Michael Evans and his team, which included horseback riding throughout the property and an Argentine asado (barbeque) on a small hilltop, and I was hooked. Damn! It was now inevitable—I just needed to figure out the details.

Fortunately for me, I have a lot of friends who love the taste of wine, and several in particular, Jack and his wife, Amy, and Jay and his wife, Penny, have impressive wine cellars. So when I returned home, I called a meeting. I sold my heart out to have them join me by forming a small consortium to invest and become winemakers thousands of miles away in a place that they had never been with people that they'd never met. I had hit a cord with Jack and Jay, and before I knew it we were drawing up papers, calling lawyers, emailing Michael Evans, and establishing what would be JMJ Vines, LLC (Jay, Michael, Jack).

When Martha got wind of it, she said, "What about me?" So after giving her a hard time because Martha is the person whom we love to tease, we did invite her into our group, and she shares the M with me in JMJ.

We were winemakers in Argentina!

Once we closed on the purchase of our land, we had to decide what type of grapes we would grow. How much fun do you think is it to sample as many Malbecs as you can? Not to mention the Malbec blends. We knew that we'd choose Malbec for its unique taste, not to mention that the Uco Valley is the only place in the world where Malbec can be grown successfully.

With the day of the planting set, there I was—the designated emissary for JMJ—flying down once again, along with some friends, for the ceremonial planting of the vines, baby plants that would become part of our future wine tastings, dinners, and memories.

On our hands and knees, we spent a few hours learning how to plant the vines into the rich earth of the region, and there is nothing more soothing than having your hands in the earth, feeling that connection with nature. I looked around at the sweeping views and the majestic Andes once again, and knew that I belonged here in a way that soulful. I was fulfilling my destiny.

Periodically we'd get reports from Vines of Mendoza on how our plants were doing, and everything was going well. For the uninitiated, the first harvest of grapes is a three-year process and in South America the prime harvest season is in March. As the time approached, I knew that this would be a truly festive occasion and so, as the true scout leader that I am, I began to put a group together. Jay couldn't make the trip, but Jack and Amy could, along with Tom, Martha, Mary, Andy, and Haideh. The eight of us would visit Buenos Aires for a couple of days and then head to Mendoza where we'd stay at Cavas, spend days at the Vines to attend Winemaking Camp and, of course, pick our grapes.

Harvest day was one of the most memorable days of my life. Under the hot, sunny skies with a group of great friends, we clipped and piled into bins the plump, happy grapes that would become our wine. And as we carted our grapes to the winery, we tested the level of sugar and learned that we had beautiful grapes. We sorted out the leaves and twigs and watched as the grapes went into the maceration process. Here we were, experiencing the core of winemaking and seeing the various steps that the grapes would take over the next nine to twelve months, when we'd have our first wine. The day was interspersed with horseback riding, an *asado,* and, of course, the tasting of various wines. It was one of those days that you dream about: long, luxurious, and filled with happiness.

We began to think about what we might call our wine and, depending on how much wine we'd drunk during any of these discussions, we'd have some crazy ideas, like Jam Jam, But it wasn't until one day when we were returning to Cavas and saw our friendly owls waiting for us that our name began to take form. Asking the driver to stop the van transporting us, I quietly stepped out to take a picture of the owls with my zoom lens. There in the frame was a short owl with big eyes sitting on a post; and there were vines climbing up the post.

When I asked about the owls, we learned that part of the lore is that they are the protectors of the vines. Something clicked. "What's the Spanish word for owl?" I asked.

Lechuza.

And this is how the debate began. As we moved back and forth on different names, we kept coming back to Lechuza. Over dinner one night, the deal was done. Lechuza it would be, and from Mendoza we began emailing graphic artists to start working up the label.

188   As I write this story, our grapes are in their bins getting ready for us. We await the bottling and the ultimate shipping to the U.S., where we hope to wow all of our friends with our rich Malbec from Mendoza.

Cavas owners Cecilia and Martin have become part of our extended family, visiting us in New York, now with baby Martina. Our U.S.-Argentina connection grows every year.

When people ask me where I'd like to live someday, I know that I'll always live in New York City. But now I know that I'll spend more time in Mendoza, on the leafy streets of the city, and out in the vineyards of the Uco Valley. I'll be the accidental winemaker for years ahead, and I'll continue to be the unofficial ambassador to the area. I hesitated in writing this story, afraid the area would become too well known, but we're now beyond that. The region has had many write-ups in major newspapers, magazines, and travel websites. The seduction of Mendoza has gone global.

My early connection to this part of the world came through the celebration of love, and it continues on. The beauty of travel is like love. Sometimes it's right around the corner, unexpected. It shows up on your doorstep and you have to decide what to do with it. That first spark of discovering Mendoza has now led me to a rich life there. It has become a part of me, in my heart and in my soul. And after all, isn't that what love is?

TIPS

EMILY HENRY
Interior Designer

- When traveling with kids, always have a laminated card with all of their information on it and some cash in their pockets.

- Have a driver meet you at the airport and take you to your destination. It takes a lot of anxiety out of car rentals, directions, finding your way around a new place. Sometimes, we'll have the driver for the full day.

- Go to a local park for a quick game of soccer or a picnic. The kids will meet some local kids and you'll meet some local parents who will give you some great hints on their city.

- Go to the local farmer's market, not just to pick up some fresh food but to see what the local community is like and what the locals sell and eat.

Antarctica

ANTARCTICA AND THE ARCTIC CIRCLE

One of the greatest adventure trips in the world has to be a trip to Antarctica, the Blue Continent. I'd been saving it so that when I did set foot on it I could claim it to be my seventh continent and my one hundredth country at the same time. In fact, this goal had become my magnificent obsession!

When I learned about the Travelers Century Club, an organization that you can join once you have visited one hundred countries, I was hooked. The TCC has a unique way of counting countries in that they have a separate count for territories, enclaves, and island groups, as well as places that are geographically, politically, or ethnographically different than their parent country. Greenland is a good example, as are the Faroe Islands. As a result, the TCC lists 321 "countries" that are eligible for counting.

Once I learned the ground rules and counted up my own countries and places on the list, it had all rolled up to around eighty-five. Let the frenzy begin! Making one hundred countries was in striking distance, and if I plotted it out correctly, I thought that I could achieve it with a five-year plan. (Don't you hate it when work gets in the way!)

In my most efficient manner, I began to plot out my travel clusters. The three countries in the Baltics could be collected in one trip, some island hopping in the Caribbean could rack up a few countries, and how about a trip to Cambodia, Laos, and Vietnam? It all seemed doable.

Okay, I admit I did become a bit annoying at times. A beach vacation? Sorry, I have to hop a plane to collect some countries. Christmas with the family? But it's a good amount of time to put a few more places under my belt. The race was on and the trophy would be Antarctica.

As I read more about TCC and its members, I realized that I was a real amateur at this game. The race was on among hundreds and hundreds of its members to break 200 and 300. In fact, there were a few individuals who were crisscrossing the globe to get to all 321 to claim the seat of the world's best-traveled person. But while I knew that I was way out of their league, I sure was having fun playing this game. Hey, some people collect cars, some collect antiques, some collect sports memorabilia. I collect countries! And reaching one hundred countries also led to the publication of my first book, *Wanderlust, One Hundred Countries.* And as of publication of this book, I've been to 122 countries and still counting. I don't expect to break the 200 mark, nor am I that interested. Hopefully, I'll reach my own personal goal of 150 countries, with visits to Mongolia, Papua New Guinea, and Malawi in my future.

In my planning for getting to Antarctica, I thought, "Why not go somewhere in the Arctic too?" I didn't have the time (or the funds) to commit to going to the North Pole (or the South Pole for that matter), so I'd have to figure out how I'd get to Antarctica and the Arctic on my own terms. Part of that planning process is choosing a country to use as the jump-off point. For Antarctica, the easiest access points are from Argentina, Australia, or New Zealand. To get above the Arctic Circle, there are many choices: Norway, Sweden, Finland, Russia, Alaska, Canada, and Greenland.

The more complex of the two trips is definitely Antarctica, and the natural choice for a New Yorker is Argentina, as it is a straight shot south. A flight to Buenos Aires is followed by a four- to five-hour flight to Ushuaia, in Tierra del Fuego at the tip of the continent. Here at the bottom of the world is the gathering spot for globetrotters from around the world who board ships to take them on a journey into the wild frontier of Antarctica.

Gondwana. That was the original name of Antarctica when it was a landmass that included South America, Africa, Arabia, Madagascar, India, and Australia. The continents began to break up 180 million years ago, and while the other continents went on to greener pastures, Antarctica has remained the coldest and driest place on earth, covered with snow and ice, and a place where the sun never completely sets. It is truly at the end of the world.

The terrain of Antarctica is about 98% thick continental ice sheet and 2% barren rock, with average elevations between two thousand and four thousand meters (6,562 and 13,123 feet). Mountain ranges rise up to nearly five thousand meters (16,404 feet), and ice-free coastal areas include parts of southern Victoria Island, Wilkes Land, the Antarctic Peninsula area, and parts of Ross Island on McMurdo Sound. The incredible glaciers form ice shelves along about half of the coastline, and floating ice shelves constitute

11% of the area of the continent. At the center of it all is the South Pole, the southernmost point in the world, where Earth's axis of rotation intersects its surface.

It was in the late nineteenth century into the twentieth century that man began the race to get to the Pole for the first time, and while there were expeditions led by Scott, Shackleton, and others, it wasn't until December of 1911 when the Norwegian explorer Roald Amundsen reached the Pole. A mere one hundred years ago was the first conquest, and since then many others have set foot at the bottom of the world.

But that wasn't our goal. For the layman with limited time, a two-week trip to the Antarctic Peninsula is the best way to get a taste of this continent and to claim the trophy of your seventh continent. Getting a group of friends together for this trip was a bit of a challenge. Let's see, two weeks in icy terrain on a Russian icebreaker, looking at ice all day. Fortunately, I do have some intrepid friends who are open for adventure, and soon the six of us were flying south to Ushuaia over Christmas break (the best time of year to visit Antarctica is December through March) to board the Akademik Ioffe, one of the better scientific boats that travel these waters.

The accommodations were comfortable, as were the dining hall, library, and lounge, which had a constant supply of coffee, tea, and snacks, along with videos and board games. The one hundred or so passengers on the ship enjoyed meals together, along with lectures and special presentations on what Antarctica was all about. To our surprise, there was much to learn about this amazing place.

The continent is governed by The Antarctic Treaty, established in 1961, which states that it can only be used for peaceful purposes. Forty-two countries have signed the Treaty, and in 1991 the Protocol on Environmental Protection was established, designating the continent as a place devoted to peace and science.

How do I best describe this place? Otherworldly. After traveling through the Drake Passage, we began to spot enormous icebergs floating past us, and as we approached land, we saw thousands of them of all shapes and sizes. Some were as tall as ten-story buildings, while others had shapes that were molded by the winds, resembling all sorts of configurations from sailboats to mini versions of the Alps. What we began to appreciate is that every day was a symphony of ice that never bored us. With each day, we would speculate about what types of icebergs we would see on that day. It was a pastime that kept us excited at all times.

What is particularly enlightening is how the light played off of the ice, creating completely different visual experiences. As the skies turned blue, then gray, with corresponding cloud coverage that ranged from high to low, each piece of ice became a prism of changing colors from white to various shades of blue, the light refracting itself in ever-changing ways. While we could have easily stood on deck to watch the icebergs all day long, what made the trip extra special were our twice-a-day trips out onto the continent. Wearing our boat-provided wet suits to keep us warm throughout the visit, we loaded ourselves into Zodiac inflatable boats, and then we hiked the glaciers, watched penguins in their rookeries, or walked among the sea lions resting on the shore. All I can say is that the scenery around us was spectacular—it was as if we were on another planet. In my life, I haven't seen anything as unique as the geography of Antarctica.

One of the highlights had to be the penguins. Just to be clear, Antarctica doesn't have terrestrial mammals, meaning no reindeer, wolf, or fox as are found in the Arctic. And while there are marine mammals such as whales and seals, there are no polar bears, as are also found in the Arctic. As a result, I would say that the penguins rule. They have the stage to themselves and they are quite the performers.

Most people know penguins from their local zoos, or from the movie *March of the Penguins,* but imagine seeing thousands of them in their natural habitat. There are seventeen species of these unique birds (that don't fly!), but in Antarctica four species—the Emperor, the Adelie, the Chinstrap, and the Gentoo—rule the roost (so to speak). At any given moment you might see thousands of them in one spot, all waddling around together, or posturing (displays of courtship), or feeding (they eat fish), or regurgitating for their young. As they went about their everyday business, we were a bit of an annoyance, as rows of them had to navigate around us. But one thing is for sure, they will put a smile on your face, especially as you watch them slide down the ice into the water, sometimes on their bellies and sometimes on their backs.

The Emperor Penguin is probably the best known, yet they are one of the smaller groups with an estimated population of five hundred thousand. My favorite are the Chinstraps because they have what looks like a permanent smile on their faces, a distinctive thin black line that runs from ear to ear through the white of their throats. With an estimated seven million pairs on the continent, they are the noisiest of them all, infusing the colony with a high pitched sound, and they are the least intimidated by humans; but don't get too close, or they may strike out at you.

Sea kayaking is a great way to get even closer to both the continent and the wildlife, as is sleeping out in the open air. As I've said many times, when I'm an old man and reflecting on my life, this will be another one of those moments that I'll remember as a globetrotter. One night about twenty-five of the boat's passengers opted for the adventure, and we headed out for the landmass where we would spend the night. Upon landing, each of us dug a three-foot plot in the snow on which to lay out tarp and thermal sleeping bags. Since the continent experiences twenty-four hours of sunlight during the summer months because of its location on the planet, we were more concerned about light making sleep impossible than with the cold being the main deterrent. As we all nestled into our sleeping bags, we found ourselves toasty inside, actually enjoying the clean, clear air. It wasn't until 4:00 a.m. when I awoke to see a few sea lions sleeping ten feet (three meters) away that I realized what a special experience we were having. I'm not sure if they thought we were just part of their group, but it was a perfect example of our harmony with the locals.

There's a lot to learn about Antarctica, and I believe that the best book out there is *Antarctica: The Blue Continent,* written by David McGonigal and Dr. Lynn Woodworth, whom I met on our trip. Their knowledge and love of the place comes through in the book, which covers everything from the history of exploration to the environment and wildlife. Many people only get to Antarctica once in their life, and that was certainly my plan, but now I'm already booked for a return visit. This time it will be to run my seventh marathon on a seventh continent. You'll find me there in early 2014 and I'm already thinking about the experience. One thing I know for sure is that I'll plan to wear black and white to blend in with my penguin friends. I may even draw a Chinstrap line across my face. So if you happen to be there at that time and see a strange looking six-foot penguin running by, don't be surprised if he waves back at you!

After conquering my seven continents, it only seemed natural that I should head north to the Arctic. For that trip, we opted for Norway, as it

196 was the only Scandinavian country that I hadn't visited, so it allowed me to add a country to my count as part of an experience north of the Arctic Circle. Unlike Antarctica, the best time to visit this part of the world is in the June-through-September period. That is unless you want a freezing winter experience that might include some dog sledding across the ice. We opted for August.

Frank, one of my travel buddies, and I flew to Oslo as the starting point of our trip. There we would meet up with a few other travelers before heading north. As it turns out, Oslo became one of the more interesting cities that I've ever visited in Scandinavia. It has museums and galleries, a royal palace, castles, charming neighborhoods, and one of the most interesting parks I've visited in the world. Here you can stroll Karl Johan, home of the Norwegian Parliament, the Royal Palace, the University and the National Theater. Ultimately, as you walk past the plentiful shops, you'll come to Studenterlunden, one of the great parks in the city.

In Oslo, you can see Munch's *The Scream,* learn about Ibsen, the father of modern drama, and visit the area called Bygdøynes, where there is a phenomenal Viking ship museum, the Kon-Tiki Museum, with the actual boat that Thor Heyerdahl used when he sailed the world. You can also visit the Norsk Museum and the Frammuseet, a small museum dedicated to the polar expeditions of Roald Amundsen and others.

However, if there is only one place that you can visit in Oslo, or you only have a few hours there during a stopover, my suggestion is to go directly to Vigelandsparken, one of the most interesting spots that you'll visit anywhere. Named after Gustav Vigeland, this is the largest park in Oslo, filled with 212 sculptures by Vigeland, depicting humanity in its many forms. It can be a bit overwhelming, but it is inspiring and there is no better spot to take it all in than at the Monolith, a fifty-six-foot- (seventeen-meter-) tall stone that is surrounded by thirty-six different groups of granite statues that depict all types of relationships from families to children. It's easy to spend half a day here and it's a photographer's delight. Do a Google search Vigelandsparken in Oslo and you'll see what I mean.

Although we only spent a couple of days, we could have easily spent two more in Oslo. It's a delightful city with lots to see, and of course lots of unique foods to sample from *kokt torsk* (codfish) to *reinsdyrstek* (roasted reindeer) and lots to buy from great knit products to Sami crafts (more on that later).

Our real goal in coming to Norway was to spend a week hiking above the Arctic Circle, and we started our journey by flying to Bardufoss in the north, above the Circle. Upon our arrival we were met by our guide, Espen Prestbankno. Think right out of central casting: six-feet-two-inches (188-centimeters) tall, blond, with solid muscles and a charming singsong accent in English. He lives on a mountainside with his Swedish wife in a home that he rebuilt with his own hands and where he keeps his sixteen dogs for his winter dogsledding expeditions. Get the idea? In the week that he led us through the wilderness, we camped out in tepee style tents.

It was interesting to watch Espen at work. It made me realize that so many American men, or at least New York men, have become so fussy about themselves. Espen had the natural masculinity that many men think they have, but don't. Over the week he explained what life was like where he lived. It didn't entail lots of concern about grooming, diet, or workout habits. His genuine ideas about family and friendships were important in life and he exuded a quiet confidence as he took us over mountains and through fast waters. When we met his wife, Lena, I teased her that it was a good thing that she got him because if he came to New York, the women would go insane. No manscaping here—Espen was all guy.

And it is a good thing because he had to lead four of us on five- and six-hour hikes past raspberry, blueberry, and lingonberry patches to vistas that were the purest anywhere. Each day we found ourselves camping along glacier lakes and drinking water right from the source. We hiked around the lakes to stand beneath waterfalls and we walked on the underbrush of moss, heather, and crowberries, eating them along the way.

We traveled by van and canoe and we fished in the Arctic Sea for coalfish and *bromsa* that we would cook in our tepee hut or along the waterfront, washing it down with Mack Beer. We learned about the great Norwegian adventurers and Espen told us stories of the local towns like Mefjordvaer with only 230 people or Husøy, a lovely fishing village of 250 people located on Senja, the second largest island along the Norwegian coast.

Senja is the kind of place that you'd escape to if you had to get away from civilization, and it was here that we met a psychologist from Oslo who works via a telemedicine practice. He treats his patients via Skype and moonlights as a commercial fisherman. He said that he wanted to move here with his young family so that his children had a different type of experience than most. I can guarantee you that this will be the case, as they are home-schooled and live surrounded by the stunning scenery in this part of the world.

Throughout our week, we also stopped at Sami villages. This is where the indigenous people of northern Norway live within their own culture, speaking their own dialect, and working in fishing and fur trapping businesses. Some of the Sami are semi-nomadic and are involved in reindeer herding. It was there on a hilltop in the middle of nowhere that I negotiated with a local to buy two reindeer skins to bring home to the States, and today they sit in a bedroom across twin beds. It makes a great story for both adults and kids when I explain their origin. One Christmas, my friend Emily showed up with reindeer collars and attached them to the bedpost to complement those natural skins. The Samis produce jewelry and silver spoons and many different crafts that are unique to their culture too; some of them found their way into my bag and became gifts for those at home.

Many people have asked me what the weather is like in August above the Arctic Circle and it was there that I learned about the true effects of global warming. In August, it was in the 40s or even low 50s, but more importantly, many of the local fishermen and loggers and townspeople told us that it was getting warmer and changing the fish life as well as the vegetation. A lot of the ice continues to melt and they wonder what the future will bring to this part of the world. Yet the raw beauty here continues to inspire outdoorsy people from around the world, as well as the people who live there. If you like the outdoors and camping and breathing clean air and having an experience with nature, this is the place for you.

When we traveled above the Arctic, I came to learn about the thriving world that exists at the top of the world. For centuries, there has been life and trading among the people of Norway and Murmansk in Russia. And it extended to what is called the New Siberian Islands to Baffin Island in Canada and to Greenland. Here, above it all, towns and cities existed and people traded and moved around the Arctic Ocean as part of their lives. I'm embarrassed to admit that I was clueless about how much life there is in this

part of the world. Ask any Norwegian and they have a good understanding **199**
of this, but ask any American and I'll bet you'll get a blank stare. It was all a
part of my globetrotting education.

Going to this part of the world created the same issue that I always have
when I discover a new part of the globe. Now I wanted to get to Svalbard
to see the polar bears. A friend in London had gone to the North Pole to
run a marathon. Should I put it on my bucket list? I had a long list of books
to read about the Arctic explorers, and of course I fantasized about taking a
boat trip around the circle of the Arctic Ocean.

Back in Oslo, it all reminded me of how much I don't know about the
world. And while we can read about places, it's hard to envision them. How
would I describe the feeling of living in the Arctic wilderness for a week,
finding antlers along the way, or fossilized flowers embedded into rock?
How could I really explain what it felt like to paddle across a wide-open
lake, where the mountains in the distance caused a reflection in the water
that captured the whole scene? The stillness. The freshness. The midnight
sun and the ability to clear my head. I had no laptop, no Blackberry, no cell
phone. No technology of any kind. And I realized that this gave new definition to luxury, a tech-free experience.

Every now and then we need to completely unplug. That is the lesson
that I learned above the Arctic Circle in Norway. It's now part of my travel
repertoire, and any time I can make that happen, I work it in. It's the best
tip that I can give you and it lets you get reacquainted with yourself. I call it
being "Espen-ized." Try it.

Peruvian Local Life

EXCUSE ME, HAVE YOU SEEN INDIANA JONES?

As we roam the world, the globetrotters among us have our fantasy about whom we'd like to meet or whom we would like to be. I have friends who vote for Lawrence of Arabia. Some would have liked to be crossing Asia with Marco Polo, or climbing Mt. Everest with Sir Edmund Hillary. My more urbane friends want to be James Bond at the tables in Monaco, or they romanticize about the life led by Beryl Markham, as written in *West with the Night*.

There's no question that we all have our heroes, real or fictional, and mine would have to be the character of Indiana Jones, or more precisely, Colonel Henry Walton "Indiana" Jones, Jr. PhD, the globetrotting archeologist who has prevented the Nazis from capturing the Ark of the Covenant, traveled to India to the Temple of the Doom, searched for the Holy Grail, and swashbuckled his way into the Kingdom of the Crystal Skull. Maybe the Crystal Skull is what motivated me to head to Peru in search of ancient civilizations and all of their mystery. Or maybe it was there that I thought I might run into Indiana on one of his adventures!

I really knew that Cusco, Machu Picchu, The Sacred Valley of the Incas, and the famed Lake Titicaca all offered a bit of adventure for my inner Indiana. It did not disappoint, and I think I even had a glimpse of the man himself, somewhere high in the altiplano of the Andes.

Only six hours from Miami, Peru is tucked into the West Coast of South America, sharing a border with Ecuador, Colombia, Brazil, Bolivia, Chile, and the Pacific Ocean. Only 496,225 square miles (1,285,217 square kilometers), it is bursting with ancient cultures, is a jump-off point to the Amazon, and it holds the mysteries of Nazca and the haunting beauty of Arequipa. A week or two in this country that was the home of the Incan Empire in Pre-Columbia America will offer you adventure, history, and a travel experience that you will talk about for years.

Usually you'd arrive in Lima, the capital city that is located on the Pacific Coast, but to me that is not where the true Peruvian experience exists. Unlike other South American cities like Buenos Aires or Quito or Sao Paulo, this city does not have any dramatic or charming elements to its cityscape. Yet a few days on its beaches, or in Miraflores, the chic part of town, to sample a Pisco Sour is pleasant enough. The city has a great Indian market in the Pueblo Libre section of town on Sunday mornings and there are some awesome museums, including the Gold Museum and the Museum of Anthropology and Archeology (I think I saw Indiana there) that are worth a visit. But generally, it's not a city that to my mind deserves more than a couple of days.

My advice is to hop the flight to Cusco or Cuzco, as it is sometimes spelled, as soon as possible. Stepping off the plane that has taken you from sea level to over 11,000 feet (3,353 meters) will create a bit of "soroche," as you get light headed from the instant hit of altitude. It will make you a bit woozy and it may require a nap, or a special "cocoa coffee" to settle you down, as you swear you have just seen Indiana walk by you in the airport. But all of this is natural and worth the momentary feeling, as you have just stepped into another time and another place.

Cusco is the historical capital of the Incan Empire, a World Heritage site that is nestled within magnificent scenery that is lush and verdant. Upon arriving in the city center, you'll feel as if you're on a movie set, where all of the actors have been dressed in brightly colored, native costumes and getting ready for the scene that is about to be filmed. But here it's real, as indigenous Indians go about their everyday business in brightly colored serapes, stovepipe hats, and multi-colored dresses. In the Plaza de Armas, the center of the city, where Pizarro conquered the lands and the massive cathedral sites, you'll be able to spend hours watching the incredible faces of the Peruvians as they carry their babies and packages. Bring your zoom lens and pay special attention to the elderly people and the children, who will usually be willing subjects (sometimes for a small fee) of your photographs.

The Incans were a spectacular culture that thrived in this area until the Spanish Conquistadors arrived in the sixteenth century, initially to conquer and then to destroy them. Today Peru is an independent country (since 1821), predominantly Catholic, with an Amerindian, Euro, African, and Asian population (Peru had an ethnically Japanese president), yet there is still a large presence of its Incan history in its streets and historical sites.

While there are lots of places to stay in Cusco, settle on the Libretador, which was once the home of Pizarro. It is an oasis in town constructed around two establishments: Casa de los Cuatro Bustos, a very old Spanish colonial home built over original Incan walls, and a new wing. The old part has a very serene cobblestone courtyard, complete with fountain, benches, and big earthenware pots filled with local greenery and flowers. The modern part provides all of the comforts that you'll require, and also houses a great collection of Indian artifacts.

Roaming the streets of Cusco will provide you with many surprises that will make the point that you are in a very different place. In the cathedral, for example, the statues of Christ, Mary, and the saints are all fully clothed with ornate costumes, as well as hair! There are hundreds of paintings hanging in the church, including a painting of The Last Supper with Christ and the Apostles looking very Spanish with the subjects dining on guinea pigs—the Incan interpretation.

Calle Loreto is a must-see street that runs out from the plaza and is lined on both sides with high Incan walls, on top of which adobe homes have been built. Also check out Calle Hatun Rumiyuq for a splendid display of ancient stonework, as well as a visit to the Barrio de San Blas, the home of artisans and craft workshops. And as you take it all in, have a dining experience at one of the local *chicherias* or *picanterias* for some local food and review what you plan to do while you're in the area.

Our plan was to visit the Sacred Valley of the Incas, head to Machu Picchu and take the train from Cusco to Puno on Titicaca, and eventually arrive in Bolivia, with a final stop to the Capital city of La Paz before heading home. For our ten days we had to make the choice not to go to other parts of Peru, but instead to concentrate on this area in the Southern part of the country. And it was the right decision, as there is so much to experience and do there.

Throughout the surrounding area of Cusco, you'll find Sacsayhuaman, the fortress of Ollantaytambo; Tambomachay, a sanctuary dedicated to the cult of water; and Kenko, the spot for the adoration of animals. Getting to these places requires a drive from town into some of the most beautiful scenery imaginable, not to mention sightings of interesting and mysterious locals and foreigners (all looking for Indiana, no doubt or at least their version of the Crystal Skull).

Take a day-trip into the Valley to see Chinchero, the picturesque "Town of the Rainbow;" Urubamba, the Archeological Capital of Peru (Is that you,

Doctor Jones?); and to Moray, site of one of the most unusual and fascinating experimental methods of farming that was created by the Incans. From here you can drive, or go on a trek or hike, travel by horseback, or take a side trip of whitewater rafting. Whatever you choose, you will sense the spiritualism of these places and the level of sophistication that the Incans had with their extensive roadways and structures and monuments to everyday life. At least two or three days are needed fully experience what this area has to offer.

Machu Picchu. The name alone conjures up images of adventure and mystery, and the place delivers on all fronts. Built at the height of the Incan Empire, around 1450, it sits nearly 8,000 feet (2,438 meters) up on a mountain ridge above the Urubamba Valley, around fifty miles (eighty kilometers) from Cusco. Rediscovered under overgrown jungle by the American Hiram Bingham in 1911, there has been much speculation as to what Machu Picchu was created for, and now it's believed that this Lost City of the Incans was built for the great leader Pachacuti, and that it has religious significance as it was built within an area that was revered by the Incans. Named after the "Old Peak" that towers above the site, it is still venerated by the local population.

We traveled there on the charming train that took us to the base of the mountain before we transferred to a small van, but the more exciting way to get there, and the way that I'll do it when I go back, is the two- to four-day hike that takes you on the Incan trail from Cusco to this UNESCO World Heritage site. The three-hour train ride makes several zigzag switches as it heads up the mountain through the lush Peruvian countryside. An hour and a half into our journey, the train came to a sudden stop and word went through the train that a landslide had occurred ahead of us. Aha, I thought, another trick by Indiana to prevent someone from getting to the top. Hm-mmm, there must be some type of treasure there that none of us knows about; I looked at my fellow passengers to figure out which of them was in pursuit. A group of us decided to walk along the tracks, passing small rural settlements and farms, until we arrived at the landslide, pitching in to clear the tracks, and ultimately heading up the hill again. No mysterious travelers here, although someone must have been incognito, I'm sure.

Regardless of how you get there, you'll have a spiritual experience due to the sheer beauty of its location. Plopped on the top of the mountain are more than 140 structures or features that range from temples to sanctuaries, parks, old residences, one hundred flights of stone steps, along with the three primary buildings: Intihuatana, the Temple of the Sun, and the Room of the Three Windows. Just stand there for a moment before you begin to explore—you'll blink your eyes at what you're seeing and be grateful that in your life you've been able to see this wonder.

Fortunately, unlike other places in the world, Peru has kept the sanctity of this place. There is virtually no commercialism near or around Machu Picchu, unlike at Angkor Wat in Cambodia, which has become a three-ring circus of tourism. At the top of Machu Picchu you'll sense history and nature in its purest form before you begin your journey back to Cusco. As we began to assemble, I have to admit that I looked around to see if anyone had quietly escaped into the surrounding area in search for the Incan Holy Grail.

Unfortunately, I couldn't do much serious investigating, as the next morning we were heading to the train station to make the ten-hour journey to Lake Titicaca. The six-car train has two classes: first class, which is usually reserved for tourists, and second class, filled with Indians heading south to a number of the villages served on the route. Across the platform as we prepare to leave the city are women and children selling playing cards, water, chewing gum and fruit.

Along the way, we moved into lush countryside overgrown with flowers, vegetation, and eucalyptus trees imported from Australia. We passed through towns of mud huts with thatched roofs named Urcos, Tanta, and Sicuani. Four hours into our journey we were served a simple lunch of chicken, eggs, tomatoes, and potatoes, along with a beverage of choice (including Inca Cola), just as the scenery began to change dramatically. The lush green valleys turn into stark mountains, and in the distance we witnessed herds of alpacas and llamas being raised at these high altitudes. Hundreds of them run in the wild, learning about life and survival.

When we arrived at La Raya at 14,172 feet (4,320 meters), the highest point between Cusco and Puno, we felt like we were on the top of the world, on a windswept plateau where for miles and miles lies uncharted territory. As we began again, we passed through micro weather systems, entering Chuquibambilla and Ayaviri, stark towns high in the altiplano. Throughout the trip we experienced the haunting beauty of this rough terrain, and as dusk began to settle and we wound our way into Juliaca, the chief trading town of the Titicaca region, and ultimately arrived in Puno.

I experienced a moment there that remains one of the great memories of my travel life. Retiring after an early dinner at our hotel in Puno, I awoke as the sun was beginning to rise, and as I drew back the curtains, there was Lake Titicaca, sleek and beautiful with two Indians in their handmade canoes, heading out for their morning catch. The simple poetry of these two lone figures, the quiet time in the morning, and the twinkling sun on what is the sacred lake of the Incans was a calming moment that I still think about when I'm trying to fall asleep or just relax.

The highest lake in the world and the largest lake in South America, Lake Titicaca is 12,500 feet (3,810 meters) above sea level, high in the altiplano of the Andes. The origin of the name is unknown, but we all like saying it, don't we? The kids in my family always thought it was a made-up word, until one day I showed it to them on the map and they couldn't believe that a place really existed.

This magical lake has a bustling life with different tribes, among them the Uru. The Uros live on the Uros Islands, forty-four manmade islands of floating reeds that can be moved to other parts of the lake at will. As you board your small boat or hydrofoil to take you across the lake to the Bolivian side, you'll stop at Copacabana to see The Black Virgin. You may pass the island of Amantani, where eight hundred families live in six villages and no machinery of any kind is allowed, or you may go to Taquile, a famous spot for textile weaving.

But everyone goes to Isla del Sol, the Island of the Sun. According to legend, the Incan Empire was founded on this island, when Manco Capac and Mama Ocllo descended to the earth sent by the Gods. The island has a high terrace of "Inca Steps" with a complex waterfall system and a shrine to the Incan Gods. It's here that I realized that I have to write to Spielberg to tell him that I just found the spot for the next adventure of Indiana Jones.

Here's the plot. The bad guys are heading to Isla del Sol to steal the life source of the Incan Empire, which unbeknownst to us is housed in an important ancient stone. Not only does it protect Titicaca, it keeps the ecological balance of the whole South American continent and in fact keeps the whole world in place. Needless to say, the bad guys want it to create ice storms in the South Pacific and drought in the major cities of the U.S. and Europe. Enter Indiana Jones. I have cast myself in a small part and I'm sure that the Incan gods would approve because at the shrine on the Isla del Sol, I paid my respects, made a donation, and honored those who maintain it.

Standing on the small hilltop with views of Titicaca for as far as the eye can see, it's hard to believe that this is where one of the greatest civilizations of all time began. The Incans, who had their own culture of laws and organization and farming techniques and public service requirements. The Incans, who had their own language, Quechua, who worshipped the Sun God, and who believed in reincarnation.

So many civilizations have come and gone in the history of the world that it begs the question of what will happen to our own culture someday. The Greeks once ruled the world, as did the Romans, the Dutch, and the British. We have to wonder if, centuries from now, some globetrotters will visit Earth from their home on another planet, in search of the great empires of the twentieth century. Some space traveler may stand somewhere and have the same experience that we just had in Peru. It could happen. Why not?

By then Indiana Jones will take on mythical proportion. People may think that he really existed and that he saved the world multiple times over. Well, that probably won't happen, but then again, the Incans probably thought that they were the center of the universe too and would last forever. What we know is that cultures come and cultures go. Civilizations rise and they fall. Those of us lucky enough to see the locations firsthand learn lessons from history. And as Asia rises on the global scene, we may have the experience of watching the world in transition yet again.

Atacama, Chile

MERRY CHRISTMAS FROM THE ATACAMA

Feliz Navidad from the Atacama Desert in Northern Chile, where it's 85 degrees, sunny and, well, it doesn't look a lot like Christmas.

For the uninitiated, Chile is one of the most beautiful places that you will ever visit. It's filled with spectacular scenery and if you love the out-doors, this place is for you. It's also a photographer's dream—I'm shooting like mad!

We flew from Santiago, the cosmopolitan capital, to Calama (about two hours north), and then drove another hour or so to San Pedro de Atacama. Chile has become an adventurer's paradise and this part of the country is filled with people from all over the world who've come here to enjoy the sights. And since the Pinochet years are far behind us and democracy has been restored for more than twenty years, the country is safe and friendly. The population is largely mestizo, people of Indian blood mixed with Spanish, German, or Croatian, which are the main groups that immigrated here.

Our home base for four days was the Tierra Atacama (tierraatacama. com). It has creature comforts, great guides, and the food is excellent. Our first day included a hike in the Valley of the Moon, followed by a drive out to the salt flats, the third largest in the world—over 15,000 square miles (38,385 square kilometers)—where we walked past wild flamingoes to set ourselves up for a magnificent sunset that hit the Andes. Imagine watching colors of orange and purple bounce off of the mountains.

There's a lot to do in the Atacama. The next day, our first full day, we left the hotel at 5:15 a.m. and drove north to the El Tatio Geysers, which sit at 14,190 feet (4,325 meters) above sea level. We arrived at sunrise to see more than fifty geysers explode into the morning sky as the heat of the sun activated them. We walked through the area of gurgling ponds of hot water with rising vapors, with the sun reflecting off all of it. Amazing.

From there we drove to the Indian town of Machuca to see the tradi-tional way of life, which included a visit to a huge llama farm right outside of town. Speaking of llamas—they were domesticated around 1500 BC, so have become very friendly. You could actually have one in your own back yard! Alpacas are domesticated too. But as we drove through the altiplano, there were wild vicuñas and huanacos in our path—no domestication for them!

The scenery is hauntingly spectacular here. Imagine vast, open views framed by the Andes with multiple volcanoes mixed in. As much as we wanted to reach the top of Cerro Toco at 18,645 feet (5,683 meters), one needs more time to acclimate to the altitude before attempting such an endeavor. But we did get some volcano hikes in. Chile has hundreds of volcanoes, and many in this area. In fact, we watched an active one smoke and sputter right before us. We passed on hiking that one.

Four days is not enough time to do everything here, but one must-do is to drive east for about two hours to see the incredibly unique geological rock formations. After our stay, we headed down to Zapallar on the coast for a couple of days of beach, and then it was off to Mendoza, Argentina for New Year's. We visited the Cavas Wine Lodge, and enjoyed Argentinian Malbecs with a very hip crowd. Cecilia and Martin throw a great party!

This is my sixth trip to Chile/Argentina. If I've peaked your interest, I'm happy to play travel agent; here are my recommendations.

There is the Torres des Paines in Chilean Patagonia, and then there is Calafate and the Perito Moreno Glacier in Argentina. I'd recommend Bariloche too. This part of the world is awe-inspiring and majestic. All of these spots offer great hiking, horseback riding, and glacier climbs. And you'll be surprised by the chic restaurants, clubs, and hotels in Buenos Aires and Santiago. And don't forget, Antarctica is only an icebreaking-boat ride away—I'd recommend that too!

Galapagos Island Iguana

THE LAND OF THE EQUATOR

For an otherworldly experience, put Ecuador, the land of the equator, at the top of your list. While it is one of the smallest countries in the world (about the size of Nevada), it has one of the most diverse geographies. Here, you can experience the Amazon basin, the Andes, the Pacific Coastline, and, of course, the incredible Galapagos Islands.

Sandwiched between Colombia and Peru, this tiny South American nation became independent in 1830, having started forming as the Kingdom of Quito around 1000 AD. It ultimately became a part of the Incan Empire and was conquered by Pizarro in the mid 1500s, along with most of South America. With fourteen million people, mostly mestizo, it is a country that has a mostly agricultural economy (it is the leading exporter of bananas), as well as rich oil reserves. And all of this is less than four hours from Miami.

What took me there was a curiosity about the Galapagos Islands, but what I discovered was the charming city of Quito and the Indian market of Otavalo, both must-sees on a trip there. And while I'd like to see Cuenca, a Spanish style colonial city that has been named a World Heritage site by UNESCO, I was happy to only spend a day in Guayaquil, a big bustling port town, but primarily the jump off point to the Galapagos. Quito, like many South American cities, has both a colonial section and a modern section, but unlike many cities, Quito has one of the largest active volcanoes in the world, Cotopaxi, on the western side of the city, although the last time it erupted was in the seventeenth century. The city itself is magnificently situated on a plateau, surrounded by the Andes Mountains and deep valleys that split off from the plateau. The area around the city is lush and green, befitting a country that in its 2008 Constitution established ecosystem rights to protect the environment.

The two-hour drive from Quito to Otavalo is one of the loveliest in the regions, past eucalyptus trees, aloe plants, Opuntia cactus, and avocado trees. Whole pigs are being smoked along the road, with banana and coffee farms in the background. Along the way, you can also stop at the Equator monument, where you can put one foot on either side of the equator, experiencing both hemispheres at the same time. In Otavalo, the Indian markets run by the Otavaleños, the largest Indian ethnic group in the country, there are wonderful ponchos, sweaters, Indian rugs, and native mats to buy from the local merchants. But I have to admit that while I was enjoying the unexpected delights of Quito and Otavalo, I was really thinking about the Galapagos, as I'd been told that it was one of the greatest travel experiences.

Getting there is easy, a one-and-a-half-hour flight due west into the Pacific Ocean. And while it is a national park and protected from too much tourism, the Ecuadorian Government has come under a lot of criticism for allowing too many tourists to descend on these fragile islands. The natural habitat has no fear of humans, but my fear is that we'll ruin this place that feels like the end of the world with its natural beauty and its natural indigenous wildlife. The moment we arrived, it was clear that we were in for a dramatic experience.

For visitors to the islands, the accommodations are on a boat of your choice and that includes sailboats, motorboats, or, in our case, an old vessel called the MV Buccaneer. It was the perfect clunky old boat on which to spend the next five days cruising around the islands, experiencing what they had to offer.

In the islands there are two kinds of landings: wet ones and dry ones. Our first stop, Bartolome, was a wet one. What we didn't expect, however, was a greeting party of sea lions, baby penguins, and sea crabs waiting for us onshore as we stepped into what felt like a lush paradise. A hike across the island took us across volcanic rock to a long, winding, and steep path, at the end of which we were rewarded with a view of Pinnacle Rock, Sullivan Bay, and natural masses formed by earlier volcanic eruptions. And for each day there, we gazed on natural wonders that you wouldn't believe unless you saw them with your own eyes.

On the island of Española, we made a dry landing, but it was clear that we were in the way of sea lions that were sunning on the dock, barking at us for waking them up, yet not budging an inch. Around us were marine iguanas and the famous blue-footed boobies, the legendary Galapagos birds. There were hundreds of them, many doing their famous mating dance, put ting their heads up in the air, spreading their wings and sky pointing, all **215** while letting out a loud shrill. But this was only part of the spectacle—to our left we saw the masked boobies and to our right, the frigates. As we hiked into the island, we came across a marine iguana nesting ground, where the female iguanas fight over territory, and soon afterwards we came across an albatross nesting ground, one of a handful in the world. Phew! All this in one morning's hike. It made us feel as if we were living in a National Geographic special.

When cruising between islands we ate lunch and read up on the area. On one particular day we cruised for three hours before arriving at Floreana, where we did a wet landing onto the white beach to prepare for a two-hour hike to visit the precious sea turtle nesting grounds. Along the way we saw finches, mockingbirds, and doves that seemed to fly around us as if we were in a Disney movie. We walked up a small hill and got a bird's-eye view of a lagoon filled with hundreds of flamingoes, gracefully walking across the water. This and a view of sea turtle nesting grounds, all in one afternoon—unreal.

Each night at dinner, our small group of sixteen people from the U.S., Tasmania, and Brazil shared our thoughts on what we had seen that day, wondering how such a special place could be protected for years to come.

On Santa Cruz, at Puerto Ayora, we visited the home of the Darwin Research Station and the Grand Tortoises. Here is one of the places that helped Darwin to develop his theory of evolution. And here is a special breeding area, where baby tortoises are hatched and held for five years, when they are then let out on their own, where they can live for another sixty years. It was while we were walking in the area that Tom, who is a veterinarian, and the local guide spotted a marine iguana that was a few feet long and had a string tied around its neck. They carefully surrounded the iguana and held him down; Tom snipped the cord, and he slithered off to freedom. That night, both of them were awarded a citation from the captain of the ship for saving the life of a marine iguana. To this day, that certificate hangs in Tom's veterinary office, The Country Vet.

And on the subject of marine iguanas, imagine hundreds and hundreds of them, three and four feet (0.9 and 1.2 meters) long, all jockeying for position on rocks and sand dunes to bask in the sun, mate, and find food for their young. It really is a spectacle to behold.

216   But wait, there's more. On the island of South Plaza there were what seemed to be thousands of sea lions, nursing, playing, barking, and jumping into the water to find fish. Here we joined them in the water, snorkeling among them as they swam around and under us and even had a playful game of tag with us.

Our days were filled with wonders, and as each hour passed we were in awe of what nature was giving us on this trip. It's almost as if we didn't care to eat or sleep; we just wanted more of what these islands in the middle of nowhere can show us.

If the wonders of nature excite you, then a trip to the Galapagos and Ecuador is for you. And you can have the experience in a week or ten days. So the next time you talk about going to the shore for a week or visiting your in-laws on the west coast, scrap that plan and head south to the Land of the Equator. It will be a trip of a lifetime and one that you may not be able to take in the not-too-distant future. Hurry, the blue-footed boobies await you!

Cavas Wine Lodge, Mendoza, Argentina

SOLVING THE NEW YEAR'S EVE DILEMMA

Talk to most people about New Year's Eve and you'll usually hear a big sigh. It's one of those nights that are fraught with high anxiety. There's some grand expectation that if you're not doing something fabulous then you are, well, a bit of a loser. Put me in that category.

I've tried it all. Fancy dinner parties, low-key get-togethers with friends, a midnight run in Central Park, dinner and a late movie. I've even gone to bed before midnight, though I rarely admit that to anyone. When I was a kid, we'd stand on the front porch of our house and bang pots. The whole neighborhood did it as we yelled "Happy New Year" into the cold, winter night.

Some years ago I discovered my answer to the New Year's Eve conundrum, and that is to build a great trip around that night. If you were in some exotic location, then the question "What did you do on New Year's Eve?" would handle itself. I'd be able to answer the question by saying, "Well, I was in El Calafate, Argentina. We did some ice-climbing on the Perito Moreno glacier, then we went back to our estancia and had a big communal dinner with everyone there."

Sounds good, doesn't it? What I didn't mention is that at 12:15 a.m., we were all in bed, lights out, as we had a long hike the next morning. But, you get my point. Now I can boast many memorable New Year's Eve celebrations without feeling like someone had a better time than me. I've managed to cover the seven continents with my global tour of New Year's Eve celebrations. Here are a few samples of what you might want to put on your list for future year-turning events.

AFRICA While I experienced the millennium in Cape Town, at a spectacular private party complete with fireworks and a native dance presentation, my real suggestion is to be out in the bush, sitting around a campfire with a bunch of friends after spending the day watching the local wildlife. Put a safari on your list to ring in the New Year.

220   **ASIA** I once brought in the New Year on a Japan Airlines flight en route from Bangkok to Tokyo, sipping champagne and eating sushi. We were proud of the fact that it was the anti-New Year's Eve, but there have been other more notable experiences. Being in India at one of the Oberoi hotels is a great way to toast in the New Year, or being on the top of a mountain in Bhutan can be a spiritual way to celebrate.

SOUTH AMERICA For me, it's all about Mendoza, particularly at the Cavas Wine Lodge. Here you'll have an intimate evening of fine food, great Argentine wines, some fireworks, and a great party that will turn into dancing under the moonlit summer night.

ANTARCTICA Ring in the New Year on a Russian icebreaker somewhere off of the Antarctic Peninsula. You'll have midnight sun and when you look up into the huge, clear sky, you'll believe that everything that you want for the New Year will come to pass. There's also something very special about sipping champagne that's been chilled in a bucket filled with iceberg shavings.

AUSTRALIA You want to be right in Sydney Harbor amidst the chaos. Since this is one of the first cities in the world to ring in the New Year, you'll feel like you're way ahead of your friends, as you'll have done it first.

NORTH AMERICA I vote for Santa Fe, New Mexico. Assemble a group of family and friends and sit around a fire pit, sipping margaritas and eating some of your favorite Tex Mex food. Go to sleep just after midnight and head to the ski slopes the next morning.

EUROPE It's all about Paris. The Champs Elysees is one big festive party and what better way to be in a good mood than to walk the streets of this spectacular city as the clock strikes midnight? Bring the Veuve Clicquot with you and take it all in!

Okay, I admit it. Maybe I'm not a loser after all. I've mastered how New Year's Eve works best for me. That's not to say that if sitting at home watching the ball drop in Times Square via TV and having a beer is what makes you happy that you shouldn't do that. Whatever works for you. I just know that as long as I can, I'll be globetrotting somewhere to celebrate New Year's Eve.

And someday, when I'm old and gray and I may not be able to do that any longer, I already have my plan. I'll get the best pots out of the cabinet, head to the front porch, and bang away.

Fiji Islands

THERE ARE THOSE PLACES THAT WE LOVE, AND THEN THERE ARE THOSE...

It's true that I'm usually pretty excited about visiting a new place. Yet often times I do get the question, "What place didn't you like?" My friends make fun of me that I like it everywhere and my response is always, "What's not to love about traveling the world?" Everyplace has something interesting about it.

But I have to admit that there are places that I have visited that have left me a little, ho hum, those places that I just didn't connect with for some reason or another. Florida. Japan. Germany. Rio. St. Barts. There, I said it. And I can already hear the moans and groans from my friends and probably from you too.

Now I have nothing against the people or cultures or cities or countries listed above. It's just that I don't quite get all of the excitement about these places. Maybe it's because I'm from the Northeast that Florida has always been a part of my experience, from the days that I spent a summer there with an aunt and uncle who lived in North Miami Beach. And like most Northeasterners, I've been there countless times for family reasons (Disney World), conferences (Palm Beach), business trips (Tampa), or winter week-end getaways (Miami).

Okay, I do like Miami. But, I liked it pre-South Beach. It's always been an interesting city, especially with its South American influence. In the South Beach era, it became a bit insane, a place where people just tried to hard to prove that they were the hippest and the coolest. Okay, not everyone, but at times it could be exhausting. But what makes me the most crazy is the weather. New Yorkers race to Miami from early December to April, and maybe it's my lousy luck, but most of the times that I've been there during that period it's been cold or windy or both. There's no guarantee that you'll have hot weather. I say, fly a little farther to Puerto Rico or somewhere in the Caribbean and you'll get the heat that you crave.

I do want to like Florida. It would be so convenient as a getaway destination, but it just isn't for me. My interests continue to take me West. And if I want a two-day getaway, I'm more apt to go to New Orleans or Charleston. So, for all of my friends who live in or have second homes in Florida, forgive me. But keep inviting me, I'm always happy to change my mind.

Rio is spectacularly beautiful. From above. There are few cities that have such an incredible setting. Sydney, Cape Town, and San Francisco would fill that bill, for sure. But I find the city itself a bit limiting. If you're not a devoted sunbather or party animal, then it may be a bit hard to completely embrace Rio. It's true that I only spent ten days there as a sun worshipper. And it's true that I was mugged in broad daylight by a transvestite, but that didn't really bother me. In fact, it's been a great story to tell. But for me, there wasn't enough to see or do beyond the obvious. I should go back again and also go to other parts of Brazil, like Buzios and Bahia and the Amazon and São Paulo. Something tells me that I'd love Brazil. On my visit list is a broader experience in Brazil.

Then there's St. Barts. People love it. They adore it. I know people who have gone there every year for twenty-five years. They are insane for it. In fact, everyone I know loves it. Not one person has ever been blasé about St. Barts. Until me, of course. I have to admit that I love landing at the airport. It's one of the coolest approaches in the world. But maybe it was because I knew half of the people on the plane that made me a little anxious. There were clients and work colleagues and neighbors and well, wasn't I going on vacation to get away from all of those people? In fact, throughout the week, I ran into people everywhere, and it was like I never left home. Too many New Yorkers for me. It's a tough place for a run, as the roads are narrow and a bit treacherous. And yes it is pricey, but then again I live in New York, so I'm used to that. But it's true that even a coffee and croissant are exorbitant. So I just didn't get it, and I know that will make me wildly unpopular with my friends.

So, what would be my beach places of choice? Southampton. It's true that there are lots of New Yorkers there too and it is expensive (or can be), but there are many things to do. I also love the small town of Sayulita, on the west coast of Mexico, where I have been going for twenty years. It's a funky little surf town where wearing shoes is dressing up. But I love the vibe there, and most of the gringos come from the Northwest or British Columbia. And it's hard to spend more than twenty dollars for an amazing meal of fish caught in the local waters. Hawaii. Fiji. The Greek Islands. I'd go back to all of those places.

Japan. Let me start by saying that I'm in love with Southeast Asia. So that is my point of reference. Thailand, Cambodia, Vietnam, Indonesia, Malaysia; they all appeal to me. Maybe it's the sensibility, or the food, or the tropical nature of these places. But it's the opposite of Japan. Tokyo is a fascinating city, as is Kyoto. The history and the culture are among the most unique on earth. I had the great pleasure of experiencing it at the highest levels through business. A private geisha dinner with some of the most exotic foods I've ever eaten. A stay at one of the best-known *ryokans*. It was all very special, but I didn't connect with it. Send me to Bangkok and my senses go crazy. Same with Siem Reap and Ho Chi Minh and even Djakarta.

What appeals to me about Germany is how it's so organized and efficient. It appeals to my own sense of wanting order and focus and discipline. But though I've roamed the country, I've yet to find a true connection to it. The language is hard for me, as is the food, as I don't eat meat and that's a big part of the German food scene. Munich is a city that I've been to a dozen times for business, and I do love being in the Englischer Garten and having dinner in Schwabing, but that's about it. And I did love visiting Berlin, especially being there just after the wall came down. It was electrifying.

But when I'm thinking about a European place to spend time, it's usually Italy at the top of the list, or France, or farther south like Croatia or Greece.

When we travel, we have natural connections to places. There are places that we go to with no preconceived notion and they end up being one of our best travel experiences. This happened to me on a trip to Turkey. I went with very little appreciation for what I was about to see and do. After a one-week trip on a gulat boat that hugged the coast from Fethiye to Bodrum, followed by a visit to Ephesus, Izmir and Istanbul, I was blown away by the richness of this country and all that it has to offer. Had I not been open to going there at the suggestion of my friend Cap who was putting together a group on the boat, I would have missed what was one of my biggest travel discoveries, and I'd go back there again and again.

What is it that makes us connect to one place and not another? A part of it is our travel sensibility. Some of us (like me) are naturally attracted to southern cultures, like the Mediterranean or Southeast Asia. We know when a place hits home. It's like anything in our lives. We're attracted to certain kinds of people, we enjoy certain types of food, and we prefer one type of music over another. So, it's not that I'll never go back to Florida or Rio or St. Barts or Japan or Germany. I probably will. And I'll look for the things that will make me happy there. And who knows, I may even become a fan of these places someday.

But with only so much time in life, I'll probably focus more on my favorite places first. Give me Argentina and Italy and South Africa and New Mexico and Paris over and over again. These places have already captured my soul, so I'm committed to them first.

Oh, and one other thing. I do know that there are some places that I'll never go to because I just know that they wouldn't be right for me, my Turkey story notwithstanding.

Bulgaria. Kyrgyzstan. Mauritania.

There I said it.

Madrid, New Mexico

GO WEST, MY FRIENDS

The American West is where my love of America resides. And when I say the West, I mean New Mexico, Utah, Idaho, Arizona, and a little Colorado and Wyoming thrown in. This is where the majesty of my country unfolds and where you should plan an old-fashioned road trip.

I could give you lots of itineraries to follow. Jackson Hole to Sun Valley. Phoenix to Sedona to the Four Corners then on to Moab. How about Santa Fe to Vail? Or Albuquerque to the Grand Canyon? The list goes on. Whatever your route, you'll be dazzled by Mother Nature's splendor as she welcomes you with many surprises along the way.

The National Parks System across the U.S. has some of the most amazing places to spend a few days or a week. And whenever I've been fortunate enough to discover a new one, I see more of the magnificent scenery we have in America. In many ways, it's better than anywhere else in the world. Combine the Great American Road Trip with National Parks and you'll discover magic.

After traveling all over the West, I recommend a ten-day trip (which could easily be stretched to two weeks or longer) that captures everything that is unique about this part of the world. I've sent my family, friends, and colleagues on this particular trip and every one of them has been a satisfied customer. So I'm passing it on to you. It will be a trip that you will remember forever, and if you have children, they'll talk about it forever.

The core itinerary is to fly to Phoenix to pick up your car or 4WD. Head right to Sedona. You'll drive through Winslow (to see the meteor crater), then to the Petrified Forest, through Canyonlands to the Four Corners, then to Canyon de Chelly, Monument Valley, and ultimately the Grand Canyon before heading back to Phoenix. But you could easily extend your trip to Bryce Canyon or Zion, or Lake Powell or St. George. It all depends on your schedule and your capacity for beauty!

Sedona, a former ranching community in the high desert that has become a main attraction in the state of Arizona and throughout the Southwest,

230 is a two-hour drive from Phoenix. En route you'll discover Tonto Natural Bridge and the Montezuma Castle National Monument, nestled in classic Southwestern scenery. Sedona is the first stop for decompression. Take in the clear, clean air, take some great hikes, indulge yourself with some great spa treatments, or get in touch with your spiritual self. It's all there for you to access on your own or with help from many of the people who live and work there. Two nights in Sedona will introduce you to the area and you can get some great tips from fellow travelers on local restaurants or cafes.

Most people who visit this area head north to Flagstaff and then to the Grand Canyon. My suggestion is to make a right turn and head east. First you'll visit Meteor Crater, a massive indentation in the earth that was created fifty thousand years ago, when a meteor hit the earth. The crater is 1 mile (1.6 kilometers) across, 2.4 miles (3.8 kilometers) in circumference, and 550 feet (168 meters) deep. It was an awesome act of nature. Keep heading east into Navajo and Apache country, where you'll visit the Petrified Forest, an appetizer before a deeper trip into the more than thirteen thousand square miles (33,670 square kilometers) of Navajo Tribal Land Trust.

This part of Northeastern Arizona is one of the hidden jewels of our country's geography and was immortalized for many of us with the Edward Curtis photograph that captured a group of Indian tribe members riding deep into Canyon de Chelly. A visit here is best started with a night at the Thunderbird Motel, where people from all over the world assemble the night before a half-day excursion into the canyon that is led by an Indian guide. Since this is a very popular destination, it's always smart to book both the motel and the guide before you arrive.

Early in the morning, you'll be met by your guide, who will take you out into the canyon in an open-air 4WD. You'll see amazing geography, Indian dwellings built into the rocks, and drawings and symbols that reflect cultures from centuries ago. Your guide will regale you with stories of ancient Indian life as you meander across the gorgeous scenery, complete with a drive right under a waterfall. This has to be one of the more awe-inspiring places that you'll ever visit in the West. Inhabitants first lived here nearly eight thousand years ago, and it's a sobering reminder of how the great Indian tribes of America once ruled these parts as part of their own empire. There are still Americans of Indian descent who live here, though it is a whisper of what it once was. Still, the history is rich and fulfilling.

One of the most fun stops on this itinerary, whether you're nine or ninety, is a visit to Four Corners, where the state boundaries of Arizona, New Mexico, Colorado, and Utah meet. Here you can lie on the ground and have each of your four limbs in a different state. Watching people laugh and children giggle is one of the great byproducts of a visit to this only spot in the country where four states meet at one place. Have your camera ready!

From the Four Corners, head north into Utah, towards Canyonlands National Park for a visit to the Mesa Arch, the Island in the Sky, Monument Basin, and Upheaval Dome, before heading on to the town of Moab.

Moab is an active person's nirvana. If you don't like hiking, mountain biking, ATV riding, ballooning, or any other outdoor activity, then don't bother coming here. One of my favorite experiences here was biking the 9.6-mile (15.4-kilometer) slick rock bike trail that crisscrosses the sandstone rocks high above the town. You can do it on your own or with a guide, and it is one of the most fun and challenging bike rides that you'll ever take. You can hike or ride on any of the trails that spell out M-O-A-B: There's the 7.9-mile (12.7-kilometer) Bar-"M" Trail, the 2.9-mile (4.7-kilometer) Circle-"O" Trail, the 1.6-mile (2.6 kilometer) Rockin "A" Trail, and the 2.2-mile (3.5 kilometer) Bar-"B" trail. Pick one or two or all four during your visit here—you can't go wrong with any of them.

But, the real reason that this is my favorite spot is Arches National Park. About five miles outside of Moab, this is to me the most spectacular National Park in the whole country. The Park is over seventy-six thousand acres (30,756 hectares) of land with more than two thousand different kinds of arch configurations that run the gamut from sandstone fins to balanced rocks to pinnacles. One way to see these whimsical and breathtaking rock configurations is on the eighteen-mile (twenty-nine-kilometer) scenic highway, but it's best to get out among them, up close and personal. Go to Delicate Arch, the Courthouse Towers, Balanced Rock, Double Arch, The Three Gossips, and Fiery Furnace. Those are only a few of the magnificent spots that you can visit. When you're at the Visitors Center, make sure that you get the photographer's guide naming which spots are best to photograph in the morning versus in the late afternoon sun. It's almost as if Mother Nature placed the configurations in the perfect spots to capture the light in just the right way.

Throughout your visit to Arches, you'll be in awe, texting your friends, taking pictures with your smartphone, posting them to Facebook, and then pulling out your good camera to get serious about what you're seeing. It's a feast for the eyes and one of the most unique places that you'll ever visit, so get ready to have your mouth open during the entire day!

We spent three days in the Moab area, but I could have easily spent three more, there is that much to do there. But our caravan moved on, and we headed south towards Monument Valley. I would be remiss if I didn't talk about Southwestern Utah. And while I have yet to go there, all of my friends talk about how you can easily spend a week meandering through Bryce Canyon, Zion National Park, St. George, and the Escalante Desert. This trip is on my bucket list, as is a visit to Lake Powell. In this part of the world, you can stay at the luxurious, world class Amangiri resort, a stunning piece of architecture nestled into the Utah/Arizona border, or you can rent a houseboat and live on Lake Powell, the second largest man-made lake in the country after Lake Mead. Day trips at both places include hiking and visits to nature that I hear will be as inspiring as one can experience. This is one of my road trips of the future, as I continue to see the American West.

As we drove south, we arrived at Monument Valley and it was as if we were in a movie, as there have been hundreds of films, television shows, and commercials shot in this part of the world. You'll feel an instant familiarity with the place, as you have seen it so many times before. But this is really another appetizer to the granddaddy of them all, Grand Canyon National Park.

Ask just about anyone in the world about the Grand Canyon and they'll be able to tell you about it. As one of the Great Wonders of the World, it ranks up there with the Pyramids and the Taj Mahal as an instantly recognizable destination, although this one is not manmade. The Park is over a million acres (405,000 hectares) and the gorge of the Colorado River is nearly one mile (1.6 kilometers) deep. The two rims of the Canyon are connected by the city of Las Vegas and the Hoover Dam, and for the visitor there's a plethora of activities to partake in. And since there are over five million visitors a year to the park, it's also a pretty busy place.

I've been to the Grand Canyon two or three times, but have yet had the opportunity to be "in the Park." Here are just a few things that you can do there. For those who want Grand Canyon "lite," you can make a day visit, entering the South Rim and driving east. Here you'll see the great vistas and be able to time the perfect sunset, depending on the time of year. The more intrepid can take the twenty-one mile (thirty-four kilometer) "Rim to Rim" hike that descends into the canyon, followed by the one-mile (1.6 kilometer) climb up. This usually entails an overnight stay at the bottom of the canyon. You can take the famous mule trip, staying at Phantom Ranch at the bottom of the canyon (you need to book this a year in advance due to its huge popularity). There are many options for whitewater rafting and camping trips that can be days or weeks, or you can just do a one-day white-water-rafting trip. You can have the canyon your way. A three- to five-day trip here seems ideal and it is now one of several places on my list for my continuing experience in the American West.

From the Grand Canyon you have easy access to either Las Vegas or Phoenix to get home. As always, I'm planning my activities for my next trip to this part of the world. I do want to see southwestern Utah, and I do want a few days in The Grand Canyon. I've yet to be in southern New Mexico to visit White Sands and the Gila Cliff Dwellings and Carlsbad. I still need to see Mesa Verde in Colorado, and while I've been to Yellowstone and the Grand Tetons, I've never made it to Glacier National Park in Montana, or retraced the steps of Lewis and Clark.

Sometimes when I'm delayed in an airport, I'll open up my laptop and start creating American West road trip itineraries for the future. There are at least ten of them because I've now spilled into the Dakotas and eastern Washington.

There's something exciting for those of us with globetrotter tendencies when we realize that there are lots of undiscovered places in a part of the world that we love. There is no question that I love roaming the globe. Hopping on a plane for eighteen hours is easy for me. But there's something very appealing about the idea that just three or four hours away from my home in New York is a long list of destinations that will keep me fulfilled for years to come.

When people ask me about my favorite places in the world, I always carve out the American West as one of those areas. At times, it almost doesn't feel like you're in America when you go there. But then again, perhaps this is the true America, wide-open spaces, majestic views, and the idea that anything is possible. See you on the trails.

Old Church in Santa Fe, New Mexico

THE SANTA FE CONNECTION

There is something about Santa Fe in August. The sun seems richer. The Mexican sunflowers are in bloom and the piñons have a particular aroma that seems crisper than other times of the year. But then again, I'm biased about Santa Fe in August. And in October and May and, well, just about every month of the year.

Let's start with a little history. Humans have roamed this fertile area for over twelve thousand years, surrounded by the Sangre de Cristo Mountains to the east, and the Jemez mountains to the west, but they didn't start settling here until around 5,500 BC. Flash forward to 900 AD and that was the beginning of the great Indian cultures and pueblos that ultimately blended with Spanish and Anglo cultures and still thrive in New Mexico today.

Now flash forward to 1610 and think about this: Before the Mayflower landed on Plymouth Rock, Santa Fe was a thriving town. There you can still see the oldest church in the United States, San Miguel, visit the oldest house in America, and also walk through the Palace of the Governors, the oldest continually inhabited public building in the U.S. I could go on, but you get the message. And I still haven't talked about the thousands of pueblo ruins in the area, as well as the many pueblos that continue to be lived in, including the Taos Pueblo, home to over one thousand people, descendants of those who established it around 1450 AD.

So, if you want history, ya' got history.

I took my first trip to Santa Fe was when I was in my twenties, when I came to visit my friend Polly, a writer who still lives here, and her then husband, David, who is a film editor. I was out for a run outside of town, and I had the epiphany. I felt the intoxication of Santa Fe that makes people pull up stakes and move here. It's true. The town is filled with stories of New Yorkers who came and never left, or Argentines who moved in, or my friend Joan, who after twenty years of living in Paris, headed to Santa Fe. After visiting more than 120 countries, I put Santa Fe in my top five places of all times. I keep coming back over and over. Now I own a house here, and okay, you're wondering what's the big deal?

236 Did I mention the light? It's transformative, soothing, mesmerizing. It's what ultimately put Santa Fe on the modern map, as painters and writers and photographers descended on this high desert town to create their work. Of course the grand lady of them all is Georgia O'Keefe, probably the most famous woman painter of all times (think about it). Here you can visit a museum dedicated to her, as well as her homes in Abiquiu and Ghost Ranch.

Think culture. This town is the second largest art market in America, has fifteen museums, a world-renowned opera, the famous Hispanic market, an Indian market, and now Railyard District, home to modern art and sculpture. A walk up Canyon Road, home of hundreds of galleries, may overwhelm you, but the locals say just let the art bring you along. Let your eyes take you into what appeals to you.

Ya' want culture? There's a heavy dose of it here.

I do have to admit that what draws me is the outdoors. Let's start with the light. I told you about it, right? But let's then talk about the hiking and the skiing and the horseback riding. There is a three-hundred-page book called *Day Hikes in the Santa Fe Area*. You can take an hour-long hike into Aspen Vista where the views are sweeping, and in October when the leaves are a shimmering yellow and gold, I promise you that you'll be weak-kneed. Or you can hike to the top of Atalaya, a two- to three-hour trek that will reward you with views as far away as Colorado. Or you can well pick any trail from the book.

Don't like hiking? Well, how about some amazing day trips to funky hippie towns like Madrid, or to Los Alamos, or to one of my favorites, Bandolier National Park, where you can walk (not hike) into the ancient ruins and the cliff dwellings that you can climb into to see how the Indian tribes here used to live. Or you can go to Ten Thousand Waves for all sorts of spa treatments, or if you're more intrepid, head up to Ojo Caliente, a mineral springs spa with different hot waters for whatever ails you. Or you can visit Tent Rocks or, how about I make you a list?

Ya' want the outdoors? Yup, it's here. But I have to tell you about the light.

Okay, so now you're filled with history and culture and outdoor activity and what you really want is a badass margarita, right? Well, you name your tequila and it's here. But be careful, after one drink at 7,000 feet (2,134 meters), you're going to think you've lost your touch. But fear not, after a day or two of acclimatizing, you'll be swigging them down at one of the two hundred restaurants in town, or at the bar of La Fonda, or at the pool hall, Catamount, or some local cowboy bar. And before you know it, you'll be buying turquoise belts and rings and jewelry for everyone you know. And you'll be in the cowboy boot store and the cowboy hat store. I promise you that you'll do this, and you may even change your name to Buffalo. Or, just cash it all in and move here. It happens to people when they come to Santa Fe.

You'll notice that I haven't talked about places to stay. We ain't got no big fancy resorts—go to Aspen if you want that. But there are some great low-scale inns and small hotels that are befitting such a special place. And it won't matter much because after a few margaritas and some great quesadillas at Pasquale's or a delicious meal at Santa Café or Geronimo's you'll be happy to just have a pillow.

What you do need to know about Santa Fe is that it is not easy to get here. From New York, you have to go to Albuquerque via Dallas or Denver or some other city. Personally, I've always liked the nonstop from Washington to Albuquerque and the hour-long drive up to Santa Fe. However, for the cognoscenti, there is now Embraer jet service right into Santa Fe airport from Dallas and Los Angeles. You can walk off the plane, get your bags, and have a rental car all within twenty minutes. (But keep the secret.) And if you have a friend with a net jet card, or better yet, a private plane, you could probably get it down to ten minutes.

Much is said about the spiritual side of Santa Fe and yup, it's all here. Dharma Centers, Zen Centers, Buddhist retreats, and more. But ultimately, you'll find your own spirit here. Because in Santa Fe, you'll become more of yourself. You'll discover more about who you are and how you want to live your life. You'll meet artists and writers, organic farmers with PhDs and former New York chefs who run diners just to be here. You'll learn to breathe in a different way and you'll experience the light and you'll be rejuvenated. And you'll notice the sky and the stars and what is in bloom. And if that ain't a spiritual place to be, then I don't know what is.

So come to Santa Fe and focus on the possibility of rediscovering you. And when you do, I have a great real estate agent for you. So, call me.

Russian Dolls

WHAT TO DO IF YOU LEAVE SOMETHING ON A PLANE

So, there I was at LAX, just off a flight from JFK. It was a perfect, balmy southern California night as I set out from the airport to my hotel. But my sixth sense told me that something was wrong. And after a quick assessment, I realized that I had left my iPad on the plane. My favorite new toy, my latest tech obsession, my emails, apps, and connection to the world; all gone. I made a fast decision to try and reclaim it, and this is a story about what to do and not to do when you realize that you've left something on a plane.

As I sprinted back to the terminal, I thought, "Right, in today's world with airport security, the turnaround of aircraft, and the likelihood that some other passenger didn't see it and grab it, well, it's a lost cause." My point of entry was baggage claim. I asked a porter what someone does if they've left something on a plane and he directed me to a customer service desk. There was actually someone there, and I told her my story. She asked me for my boarding pass and after verifying my identity, she printed out a "security checkpoint pass" that read, "Michael Clinton is authorized for access to the concourse/gates. Valid ID has been verified. Not valid for travel." "Go right to the security lines and you'll get back to the plane," she said. "It can't be this easy," I thought, but one step at a time. So off to the security line I went, where there were at least a hundred people in line. I needed a plan, fast!

Walking up and down the line was a security guard and she looked kind of friendly; I told her my story and that the plane was going to leave and that… She took my hand (literally) and walked me over to the front of the line where they were checking IDs (this was about fifth person in), and I showed my pass and ID, and asked if I could go to the head of the line, and the TSA agent said no. And when I told her that I'd left something on the plane she said, "Well, I have too" and moved me along. No one ever said that security equals passion, but in the corner of my eye I saw my friendly security guard and she came up to me and said, "Keep moving to the head

240

of the line," and basically escorted me from afar, past all of the people in line (who weren't happy, I might add). There were lots of "excuse me," "thank you," *"permiso,"* and *"excusez-mois"* coming out of my mouth! And the moral of the story here is that politeness rules!

There I was at the front of the line and, in Spanish, my guardian angel tells the agent at the x-ray machine to let me in. How do you thank such a guardian angel? Profusely! She just smiled and gave me the okay sign and I yelled, "I'm sending you a huge hug." And I was in—twelve minutes from entering baggage to this point, a world record for sure. United Gate 72 wasn't that far away, but when I got there, the gate was empty and there was no agent. There was a plane and it looked like my 757, but all the doors were locked. And there was no one at the neighboring gates either.

Okay, now what?

And then I saw a sign for an international first class lounge and I bolted up those stairs. I entered to find a sign on the desk that said "Back in ten minutes." A dead end. Back down to the concourse and back to gate 72, but still no one.

And then I saw a gleaming sign that read "Customer Service."

Well, that's what I needed, so off I went to a line of maybe five weary travelers. I decided to be a pushy New Yorker to get to the front of the line. I asked the woman in charge if it was possible for me to go next because I left something on the plane, blah, blah, blah; she gave me a pass and within seconds I was babbling my story to her. She was one of those rare efficient types who started asking questions and making phone calls. She asked me to step aside for a moment until someone called her back.

Two minutes passed and she said, "Sir, is your iPad in a brown case?" Yes! Could it really be? "The cleaning people found it and they have it, but I have to escort you to the gate." And she left the desk and walked me to the gate (yes, telling the others she'd be right back). And at that point, I completely avoided eye contact with all of them.

When we got to the gate, the cleaning man was standing there with it, and now I am happily typing this story on my reclaimed iPad.

Lessons learned?

● Obviously, pay attention. My own dumb fault for leaving it in the first place.

● Second, go for it. I could have written it off, but hey, nothing ventured, nothing gained.

● Politeness rules at all times, and harried airport and airline people appreciate it. At the end of the day, they want to help.

● Pray for good karma! I just had it with me every step of the full twenty-five minutes that it took. No cash was exchanged and no promises were made. It was good old-fashioned ingenuity and luck that won the day.

Happy flying.

Southampton, New York Backyard

HAMPTONS SIMPLE

My summers begin with the first blush of the peonies. The forsythia and tulips have come and gone and the daylilies have yet to show themselves to the world. It's in early June that Eastern Long Island begins to show its summer stripes, and the peonies lead the way.

It's not like that in New York City, one hundred miles (160 kilometers) east, where summer is usually already in full force by early June. But once it arrives on the East End, as the locals call it, the summer months are simply breathtaking in their beauty.

To most people, Eastern Long Island is synonymous with the famed Hamptons, and its mention conjures up images of helicopters ferrying investment bankers to their multi-million dollar waterfront mansions or celebrities parading through fund-raisers at swanky dinner parties featuring private entertainment from major musicians. All of that exists here and yes, I've attended many of these events over the year. "Nice to meet you John Bon Jovi." But for many New Yorkers like me, Eastern Long Island is really a refuge from the intensity of city life, business travel, and other commitments. I go there year round, but it's the Hamptons summer that holds the magic.

Before I embellish on this idea, let me first establish the fact that this part of the country has had a rich role in American history. Hamptons, an English word that means "home settlement," was founded in 1640, when English Puritans from Massachusetts landed on Conscience Point in Southampton to establish what is the oldest settlement in New York. At the time, the Shinnecock Indians were in the area, and it was a friendly relationship that led to the English learning about growing corn and potatoes and the digging for clams and scallops. Named Southampton after the British Earl of Southampton, the moniker later influenced the naming of Westhampton, Easthampton, and all of the hamlets that became a part of those towns.

As the area grew, new places like Sagaponack (a Shinnecock word that means "land of the big ground nuts," which actually refers to potatoes) were

244   created, along with Water Mill, Amagansett, Wainscott, and Sag Harbor, all borrowing English or Indian names. In 1644, England bequeathed forty acres (sixteen hectares) to Edward Howell, who built a mill for settlers to grind grain into meal. Water Mill, the hamlet where I live, still proudly displays the original water mill and a big windmill in the center of town.

Mostly a farming and fishing area, it wasn't until the 1800s that parts of the East End, like Sag Harbor, became bustling spots in their own right. In the mid 1800s, Sag Harbor boasted sixty whaling ships in the port along with a thriving fishing industry. And once the railroad was created from New York to the East End in the 1870s, wealthy New Yorkers began to make the trip east to the pristine beaches and bucolic land.

The East End is divided into two parts, the North Fork and the South Fork, which are divided by Noyac Bay. It is the South Fork that has seen the most development and enjoyed the most notoriety over the years. When talking about the Hamptons, the light inevitably comes up. Perhaps because of the flat terrain surrounded by the sea and the physical location, the light here is of a special variety that is unique to the East Coast. This in combination with unspoiled and non-commercialized beaches can take your breath away. Which is why beaches in the Hamptons always show up on lists of the best beaches in the U.S. You can walk onto Cooper's Beach in Southampton, always one of the best beaches, and stroll for an hour seeing very few people. So if your idea of a perfect day is to sit on a quiet beach with few crowds and read a book or to talk with friends, this is the place for you.

The light and the beaches and farmlands that dot the East End have long been inspiration for artists and photographers who have lived and continue to live in the area. It may have all started with Jackson Pollack, who in turn inspired Willem de Kooning, Mark Rothko, and Robert Motherwell. Then came Andy Warhol, and Peter Beard. It also made way for fashion designers, media moguls, filmmakers, and fashion editors; they have all come here in search of their own paradise. And while some of them live the same frenetic lives that they have in the city, many of them try to decompress. At a local farm stand you might have seen John Irving when he was writing *A Widow For One Year,* or find Jeremy Irons and his son playing a game of tennis at a local court in Water Mill.

Admittedly, the Hamptons are home to almost parallel universes. You can roam through the Morton Bird Sanctuary, kayak on Georgica or Mecox Ponds, or ride at any of the established horse farms. Then you can shop the chic boutiques, attend flashy and lavish backyard dinner parties, and visit multi-million dollar yachts that float where whaling vessels were once docked. But as we like to say, you can have whatever you want in the Hamptons, it's your choice. Pick your flavor. Pick your style. Dolce & Gabbana or Quicksilver. Or both. I've experienced all of it, but give me Hamptons Simple any day. To me, the ideal weekend involves a long run through the potato fields (yes, the famous Long Island potatoes), or getting together with family and friends to have a relaxed dinner, sometimes around an open fire pit on the beach.

I also like to take a spin in a Cessna. It is in the Hamptons that I learned to fly and to appreciate how beautiful the geography of the area is from the air. From Westhampton to Montauk, there is the long stretch of beachfront. And despite complaints about development that I've heard for more than twenty years (and people heard for twenty years before that), there is still a remarkable amount of untouched land and many working farms there. In fact, thanks to the local and county governments, along with a number of groups like the Peconic Land Trust, there has been a great effort to protect farmlands and to create reserves that will always keep the area a bit rural. From the sky you can see this at work and most of us are big supporters of the initiatives. I'm fortunate to experience this myself with a house that sits on the edge of a working farm that has been in the same family for over two hundred years.

From above the Hamptons one can see north to the North Fork and Shelter and Gardiners Islands, with Connecticut and Rhode Island in the distance. To the east lies Montauk, and every time I take someone on a sightseeing flight, we head there for a swing around the famous Montauk lighthouse. Off in the distance is Block Island and Fisher's Island, and further off in the distance is Nantucket and Martha's Vineyard. At 3,500 feet (1,067 meters) on a clear day, you can see it all and be seduced by it's sheer beauty. With the lone whir of the single-engine propeller, I look out at the splendor before me and appreciate how lucky I am to live there. If you are fortunate enough to visit this part of the world, go to the local airport in Easthampton to arrange your own sightseeing flight; you won't be disappointed.

While you're out there, you'll probably find yourself on Highway 27, the two-lane road that snakes through the Hamptons and goes through the charming towns and hamlet of the East End. But I say, bust out. Take the back roads. Drive Deerfield, Scuttlehole, Mecox and Three Mile Harbor Roads. Get lost north or south of the highway. The tranquility will inspire you and the miles of farms will surprise you. I suggest that you do this in a convertible during the summer when the sky is big—at night, when you can look up at the stars, you could feel like you're somewhere in Nebraska.

Stop at the local farm stands and go to the local fish markets. You can find the "in" crowd at the chic restaurants of the moment, or you can try a lobster shack on the way to Montauk, or the Candy Kitchen, or the Sip 'n Soda, or Estia's; these are all family establishments with a small town feel. Just don't be surprised if you see Julianne Moore or Jerry Seinfeld and their families sitting next to you.

One of my favorite summer activities is to take the car ferry from North Haven to Shelter Island. When you disembark, it is like entering another era. Just a drive around the island will decompress you. The Shelter Island 10k race on the Fourth of July weekend is my idea of the best way to see the island; you'll go off the beaten path and into local neighborhoods, where families wave you on with the American flag. The course runs through Dering Harbor, one of the most charming spots on the whole East End. And while one of the coolest and hippest beach bars in the Hamptons is on Shelter Island (I can't even name it because it's so hip), I say pack a picnic lunch and sit on one of the many isolated beaches on the island. Such an afternoon will replenish you.

Go surfing at Ditch Plains near Montauk, ride horses on the beach in Amagansett, and rent a bike to ride the back roads. You may be tempted to shop in some of the plentiful designer boutiques and high-end antique shops, but don't forget to look for the smaller stores that sell unique products, like those on Main Street in Sag Harbor. Visit the local independent bookstores where you can still touch books and find out from the knowledgeable clerks what the "must-reads" are for the summer. What I'm saying is go native. Go local. And go slow. There's a secondhand bookstore in the garage of the Bridgehampton firehouse and there's an author's lecture every Friday afternoon at the local library. One of the local nurseries sets up an outside movie on Friday nights at dusk, where you can take dinner and watch a classic movie under the stars. You can take windsurfing lessons, go wine tasting at the local vineyards, and pick your own strawberries and peaches. Or, just let the sand run through your toes.

If you've been avoiding the Hamptons because you can't afford to buy or rent a fabulous house with a pool and a tennis court, or you haven't gotten an invite to the party of the season, or you haven't been able to find the right designer clothes, I say that you aren't thinking about my Hamptons. It may cost you some sand in your car and a sunburn if you don't lather up with a high SPF lotion, but there is a Hamptons experience in your future that can be magical.

There was a great t-shirt circulating around the area a few years ago and it read, "Summer People. Summer Not." For those of us who go there year round, the sentiment is perfect. We love the summer and we love the other seasons too. But in all honesty, we do try to avoid the summer people who drive their Porsches to the local farm stand, decked out in spandex and high heels. From June through August you'll find the year-rounders on our decks sipping a local wine, watching the potatoes grow, and reading one of our favorite (hardcover) books. We'll be plotting out how to avoid the major roads and to see how simple we can make our weekend. Well, at least until we have to get ready for the amazing party that our friends are throwing at their newly built house on the ocean. It's a political fundraiser for a presidential candidate and, well, we have to go. By that time of summer the peonies are gone. But I'll head to the garden to cut some blue hydrangeas. Let someone else bring the Dom Pérignon.

Above New York City

OF COURSE YOU SHOULD COME TO NEW YORK

Since I've seen so much of the world, people often ask me where is the perfect place to retire. My answer is always the same. New York City. I usually get looks of surprise and comments like, "Not Hawaii, or Fiji, or some island in the Caribbean?" Nope. New York City.

What other place in the world offers so much at your fingertips? You live in an apartment, so there are lots of people to talk to, including the doormen and superintendent, who keep an eye out for you. Neighborhoods in New York are like small towns. You get to know your local restaurant owners and dry cleaners and shopkeepers. Walking in the city lets you exercise regularly and it's an easy way to get around. We have great public transportation, great parks, great museums, theater, and entertainment. There's always something to do here, so you never get bored. And you get to do it with New Yorkers, the most interesting, energetic, and fun people anywhere.

Yeah, it gets crowded and the weather is lousy in the winter and it can be expensive (but doesn't have to be), but I say, so what? This is the kind of city that you love or hate. There is no gray here. If you are gray about it, the city will eat you up. If you love it, like me, then you take all of the pitfalls in stride, and the city will make your life rich and happy.

I didn't lay my eyes on New York until I was ten years old, even though my father was a native of the Upper West Side. He had one brother who lived in New York, but for some reason he would always come to visit us in Pennsylvania. So when the family piled into the Rambler station wagon to drive to the big city one summer, I couldn't wait to see where my father was born and lived as a boy.

There is a view of the city skyline when you approach it via the Lincoln Tunnel—there's a long, curving highway that takes you down into the entrance, and there is the city across the water. I can remember the precise moment when I saw it. And I remember in my ten-year-old mind when I said that this is where I would be someday. It seemed as natural as breathing. New York is where I really belonged and that was that. It was just a question of when.

During that trip, I did see my father's boyhood neighborhood and I saw all of the sights, from the Empire State Building to the United Nations. Driving along the FDR gave me a rush of excitement, as I watched the city unfold on one side and the bridges and river life on the other side. The week there sealed the deal in my mind. New York was in my future.

Throughout high school, I went to New York to visit my relatives and during college I spent every summer working there. I learned how the city worked and I came to realize that I was right all along. This is where I belonged.

During my years in New York City, I've watched it become more and more vibrant, more cosmopolitan, and more international. It is the ultimate melting pot with citizens from all over the globe. In the New York City Public Schools alone, there are students from more than one hundred countries. And that's where it all begins, with the people. Of course I'm biased, but to me New Yorkers are the most fascinating people anywhere. Many of us come to the island of Manhattan to find freedom from the small towns and cities that would have constricted us. We come for the energy, the possibility of success, even fame. But make no mistake: New Yorkers come here to participate in life. And anything can happen here. As the song goes, if you can make it here, you can make it anywhere.

On any given day, fifth generation WASPS are interacting with immigrants from Bangladesh, Muslims are working next to Jews, and Salvadoran neighborhoods intersect with those of Nicaraguans. And it all works. During my day, I say hello to my doorman from Malta, my superintendent from Ireland, and my colleagues from Mongolia and Italy. And on any given day, I can learn about the customs of these people, or taste their foods, or learn a few phrases of their language. This is not the kind of day that you have in a homogeneous suburb out there in Middle America.

Within two blocks of my apartment I can eat Turkish food, or Vietnamese, or Thai, or Italian, or French, or Argentinian. And in a taxicab on the way to work I can get into a conversation with the driver who is from the Ivory Coast, and discuss what is happening in West Africa. This is only one reason why I love New York City. Talk to its people and you'll discover a treasure trove of stories. You'll be awed by how they got here and what progress they've made since getting here.

What other place on earth opens its arms to so many? It has always been the legacy of New York and of Lady Liberty, now 125 years old, who continues to welcome so many to our city.

New Yorkers are a bit snobby about their own geography. Someone who chooses to live in Tribeca or Soho or FiDi would never think of living uptown, or vice versa. But then again, I've seen diehard Tribecans pick up and move to the Upper East Side to be near the greenery of Central Park and the overall order and cleanliness of Uptown. And I have a seventy-year-old friend who, after raising her family and finding herself widowed, sold her uptown townhouse and moved into a loft downtown. So underneath it all, New Yorkers kind of go with the flow of their lives and pick their neighborhoods accordingly. The hippest suddenly become bourgeois and vice versa.

I choose to live near Central Park, since running is my antidote for urban stress. And with regards to geography, I believe that the park is the center of the New York Universe. The first landscaped public park in the United States, Central Park was established in 1853 to emulate the great parks of Europe. Designed by Frederic Lane Olmstead, this 843-acre (341-hectare) wonder in the middle of the city can transport you to places far away from the density, the noise, and the crowds that the city can sometime create.

Here you can watch New Yorkers at play in lots of different forms: families at the carousel built in 1871, kids marveling at the animals in the Central Park Zoo, lovers snuggling in the horse-drawn carriage rides, and birders being lead through the Park's wooded areas to spot the peregrine falcons.

Central Park is my favorite place in New York. For me, it's all about running a six-mile (9.6-kilometer) loop, or a four mile (6.4 kilometer) loop or a couple of trips around the reservoir. But I have also bicycled there and played tennis and gone ice-skating at Wollman Rink with the city twinkling in the background. I've gone rowing on the lake and played baseball on its open fields. But mostly I run there, watching the people and the dog walkers and the food vendors and the sunbathers. And it is there that I feel like a true New Yorker.

The Park also has lots for you if you're not an athlete. If you're lucky, you'll be there to catch a wonderful concert on the Great Lawn, or you'll experience The Met in the open air of a balmy summer night. You can watch the fireworks on the Fourth of July at the Sheep Meadow. Stroll the pedestrian walkways to the Bethesda Fountain, one of the most beautiful anywhere, or visit the Obelisk, the seventy-one-foot (twenty-two-meter) sculpture created in 1500 BC and given to New York as a gift from Egypt. Visit Belvedere Castle and the Turtle Pond and stand on the top of Summit Rock, the highest point in the Park, for a great view of the city. Pack a lunch and sit near Strawberry Fields or one of the many open spaces to take it all in.

I'm always discovering new parts of the Park, like the time my friend Steve and I were out for a run and he turned me on to the Conservatory Garden at 105th Street and 5th Avenue, an exquisite six-acre (two-hectare) retreat with a French garden as well as Italian- and English-inspired ones. It took a Canadian national to show me one of the splendors of my own city.

Somehow the Park is always with me. I see it from my office window, watching the four seasons unfold. And I often stop in on a hectic day just to take it all in, never taking it for granted. In so many ways the Park is my refuge. A run or a walk there gives me the peace in which to make an important decision. I was there later in the day on 9/11 to try and make sense of what had happened. It's a great place after a big snowstorm to hang out with friends and find your inner ten-year-old with a good old-fashioned snowball fight. And there's nothing like being there in the first days of spring, when the daffodils and the crocus start to sprout their heads.

Try it in the early morning hours, during the day, or at dusk when the sun bounces off of the water near the Loeb Boathouse. I guess what I'm saying is to go there anytime. If you live in or visit New York, there is an embarrassment of riches to partake in. Museum exhibits from Picasso to de Kooning. Theater that will suit any taste, from Shakespeare to American Musicals to experimental workshops. We have the Yankees and the Mets (I'm a Yankees fan), and the Knicks and the Giants and Islanders. You can see world-class photography, dance, jazz, ballet, or your cultural pursuit of choice. You can be as fancy as you want or as laid back. We have it all. You can shop in secondhand clothes stores in the East Village, or at the most prestigious luxury stores on Fifty-Seventh and Fifth. Or you can eat at the Second Avenue Deli or Per Se. Whatever your budget or tastes, we have something for you. Which is why I say that you don't have to be wealthy to visit or even live here. There are ways to create your own New York.

Yes, you can hire a car and driver and stay at the best hotel and shop the finest stores and eat at the best restaurants, and that is one way to experience New York. But here are a few tips that will give you a different experience and get you closer to us.

WALK AS MUCH AS YOU CAN. Unlike Los Angeles or Dallas or Miami, this is a city that you can walk in from top to bottom. Walk from Central Park to the tip of the island. And if that is too long a walk for you, do it in sections, taking the subway to fill in the other sections. The New York subway is safe and one of the most interesting places to see New Yorkers. It will underscore the point about our multiculti city. And you'll see street fashion and what people are reading and talking about. It's the only way to get around town.

MAKE A PLAN. Don't show up and expect to get tickets to the hottest play. There are many sources that list what's happening in New York. Decide what you want to do and plan accordingly. You can save money on museum fees by going on the nights that it's free. The Saturday farmer's market at Union Square is a great place for a casual and affordable breakfast as you walk among the food stalls. Tickets to Letterman take months to reserve. So make your plan.

GET OUT OF MIDTOWN and head to a local neighborhood, especially for dinner. Every neighborhood has great and affordable restaurants. Plus, you'll get to see how everyday New Yorkers live. Mingle with the natives. Fantasize about what neighborhood you would live or retire in.

GO ONE STEP FURTHER. Try Williamsburg in Brooklyn, or a great Greek restaurant in Astoria. Take the Staten Island Ferry. Go to the Bronx Botanical Gardens or the Bronx Zoo and stop at The Cloisters on the way home. You'll feel even more like a local.

254 **CHECK OUT THE NON-TOURISTY SPOTS** for some of the best experiences you'll ever have. What's happening at the 92nd Street Y? You may get to hear Spielberg being interviewed. Check out the New York Times Talks for great lectures and interviews, and see what's showing at the auction houses. Here you'll get to see some great art or photography that will inspire you.

If you do all of these things, you'll begin to feel more like a New Yorker. You'll start moving faster and talking faster, and you'll begin to realize that this is the greatest place on earth. And you'll start to think about whether you should rent or buy when you move here. You'll figure out your best timing to start a new career, jumpstart a current one, or just downsize now that the kids are gone and the financials are in pretty decent shape.

I had some friends who sold everything and moved to New York for six months. They're still here six years later, working in different industries, loving the city, and loving their lives.

But remember, you have to love the pace, the noise, the crowds, and the intensity. All of that becomes background noise for me. New York is my kind of town, and when it gets a little intense, you'll find me out running in the Park to regroup. You'll find your antidote too. We're here waiting for you with open arms.

Vilnius, Lithuania Airport

EPILOG TO THE GLOBETROTTER DIARIES

My life as a globetrotter led me to write this book. I wrote on airplanes, in the hills above Santa Fe, while overlooking rice paddies in Southeast Asia, and in the mountains of Argentina. The goal has been to share some of the things that I've learned along the way and to tell some stories of the places that I've been enough lucky to visit. One of the tough decisions was to determine which places would make the book versus those that wouldn't. For the U.S. part, I wanted to tell a tale or two about Charleston and New Orleans. Then there was Miami and Chicago. And how about Sonoma County? I never got to write about Barcelona and Budapest, or about the trip to Croatia. Then there was all of Northern Africa, from Morocco to Tunisia to Egypt. They all deserve to be written about, as does Madagascar and the United Arab Emirates! All of these spots have their own unique memories for me, filled with potential tips for the intrepid traveler.

Exploring the souks of Marrakech, cruising up the Nile to Karnak, crossing the river from Buda to Pest, and searching for lemurs in Madagascar all have their special places in my travel life.

Here's a tip should you go to Madagascar. Your guide will take you on a jungle walk in search of lemurs in their natural habitat. Remind him that you shouldn't be left alone for an hour while he's off searching There we were, a group of five; stupidly, none of us had brought compasses or enough water or food. That was the longest hour. We didn't know if the guide was coming back for us, but we did know that we couldn't leave the spot in the thick jungle. Make sure you have a clear understanding with your guide before he leaves you alone anywhere.

Here's another tip. If you go hiking in the Himalayas, take plenty of moleskin and a couple of bottles of aspirin. The moleskin will be for your blisters and the aspirin will be for the locals, who will ask you along the way if you have any for their everyday pains. It's a great way to show a little of kindness in a remote part of the world.

258 We learn these little tips along the way and should pass them on to everyone we know, especially when they're traveling to out-of-the-way places. I'll soon be heading into more remote places; Mongolia, Papua New Guinea, Borneo, Mali, Ethiopia, and Samoa and Tonga are all on the list. These are all spots with challenges for any globetrotter, so I'm open to tips and advice.

My whole life has been an insatiable quest to see as much as I possibly can. As I write this, I'm in Northern Thailand, getting ready to cross into Laos, the 122nd country that I will visit in my life. Our group is headed to Luang Prabang and I'm as excited about going there as I was going to my first foreign country at the age of twelve.

Some of us are lucky enough to discover our passions early in life and, some of us are even luckier in that we can pursue them. Never give up on your dreams. You become more of yourself as you pursue them. In my case, I became the globetrotter that I'd dreamed about becoming. Ultimately, it's how I define myself. And I hope to spend the rest of my life fulfilling that destiny.

My fellow globetrotters understand. See you on the road.

Rome, Italy

INDEX

262

ACKNOWLEDGMENTS

A special thank-you goes to Marta Hallett, who is always encouraging me to develop the next book project; her enthusiasm and support are creative inspiration. Thanks also to Sarah Karp, our design director, to editor Judith Durant, and to Jessica Guerrero and Fran Crane who are always there to help make it all happen.

During the development of these stories, a group of women were indispensable with their feedback, encouragement, and sharp editing eyes. For that I'd like to thank Joanna Coles, Colleen Daly, Pamela Fiori, Martha McCully, Nancy Novogrod, Deb Shriver and Kate White. I am a very lucky man.

For their consistent support in my photography and writing endeavors, thank you to Tom Arnott, Frank Bennack, Judith Bookbinder, David Carey, Andy Carter, Todd Davis, Tom DeVincentis, Emily Henry, Haideh Hirmand, Jessica Kleiman, Ellen Levine, Ken Lewis, Jay and Penny Lieberman, Chris Richter, Mary Rolland, Chuck Santoro, Steve Sharp, Chris Shirley, Cap Sparling, Steve Swartz and Frank Valentini.

And finally to the Clinton brood, especially Mom and Dad, Janet Clinton and my Globetrotting sister, Peg Pardini, who is crazy enough to join me on our quest to run seven marathons on seven continents!

To all of the Globetrotters out there, I say feed your passion and thank the gods that you have the ability to travel.